MW01241123

Library and Archives Canada Cataloguing in Publication

Jefferies, Kathryn, author.
Awake: education for enlightenment / Kathryn Jefferies

www.educationforenlightenment.com
www.kathrynjefferies.com

Issued in print and electronic formats.

– 2nd edition.
ISBN 978-0-9939633-2-2
1. Kathryn Jefferies 2. Education 3. Consciousness tranformation—mind—intellect, limits of.
I. Title.

Front and back cover designs: Kristyn Reid kristynreiddesign@gmail.com
Content design, typesetting and layout: Joanne Haskins thinkcom.ca
Cover photo: istockphoto.com
Author photo: Darrin Davis darrindavis.ca

1st edition, February 2015
2nd edition, April 2016

Published by Mariposa Press

AWAKE

Education for Enlightenment

Redefining Intelligence in the Age of the New Consciousness

By

Kathryn Jefferies, PhD

To my parents,
For always being there.

And to Bella,
For being.

I shall continue to hold a vision of the kind of education
I know is possible in this world
and continue to do my best to be part of bringing it about,
that it may support you in realizing the greatest creative visions
you have for your beautiful life.
Even still, always remember the only teacher you ever need is inside you.

The human mind is not capable of grasping the Universe.

Albert Einstein

Awake, my dear.
Be kind to your sleeping heart.
Take it out into the vast fields of Light
and let it breathe.

Hafiz

Table of Contents

Foreword

I first heard Kathryn Jefferies' name when it landed in my inbox on January 1, 2013. I had spent the last few months promoting my book, *The Curiosity of School*, and Kathryn wanted to know if I would make an appearance at Lakehead University, Orillia campus, where she was teaching B.Ed. students out of a series of low-ceilinged basement rooms. She had built an entire course around my book and wanted me to visit toward the end of the semester, when her students would be finished studying it.

My first thought was to say no. Kathryn seemed nice enough—I wasn't turned off by the tone of her email or the thought of driving to Orillia. My negative reaction came from my longstanding fear of public speaking. An introverted person, the idea of getting up in front of people and talking about something—even if I'd spent the last three years researching the subject—was so terrifying as to warrant immediate dismissal. There's no way I can do that, I thought. Sorry, but no.

My book had come out on a Tuesday in August. By the following Friday, I got a call from my publicist saying *Curiosity* had made the national bestseller list, and that a well-known radio personality wanted to conduct an interview. Soon after that, I got a call from this woman's producer, who walked me through the hypothetical conversation. He gave me all the questions I would be asked and assured me the session would be taped and not conducted live on the air. I could even bring some notes into the studio—a major boon considering all the facts and information my book contains, and the difficulty in remembering it all. These little conceits helped assuage my concerns, and after some hemming and hawing, I agreed.

On the day of the interview, I had sweat through my suit jacket before

I even arrived at the sound studio in Toronto. By the time I sat down in the chair, I was so nervous that my short-term memory was completely shot. Luckily I had my notes with me, and remembered to pull them out as the interview began. I did pretty well for the first few minutes, but shortly thereafter my host seemed to get annoyed by how concise my answers were. She began deviating from the script, and would follow each of my responses with a few seconds of silence, a tactic designed to unnerve me and make me second-guess my answers. It worked, and when I corrected an earlier comment, she pounced.

"But you just said that scholastic test companies are privately held in Canada as well as the United States…"

"Well, I may have said that, but that's not what I meant."

She seemed to actually delight in destroying my credibility. When the interview was over, she didn't shake my hand or even thank me for coming in. As I let myself out of the studio, her only comment was that she'd come from a long line of teachers. From this I gathered that she thought my book was an attack on the teaching profession, hence her aggression, and in that moment I realized she hadn't even read the book we'd spent the last half-hour discussing. (Radio hosts rarely read the books of the people they interview. Producers read them, then brief the hosts shortly before they go on air.)

It was an exhausting experience, but it wasn't over yet. Two days later, we heard that the interview had been pulled from its Monday morning, prime-time spot. The producers felt they didn't have "enough material" to put the segment together. To have gone through all that work and stress to do something that ended up getting canceled was disappointing, and for weeks after I wrestled with a mix of emotions. There was the guilt of having let my publishing team down, the embarrassment over my own performance, and most of all the frustration at having to defend my work to someone who hadn't even read it. I was caught between not wanting to do any more public performances and knowing I had to in order to support my career.

That was why I had a "no" reaction to Kathryn's email. On one hand, I knew I should speak to her class; on the other, I had no desire to go through that process all over again. After a series of halting exchanges, mediated by my publicist, I tentatively agreed to speak with Kathryn over the phone to get a better sense of what she expected me to do. A month passed. Then, without warning, I called Kathryn at 5:00 one night. It was the end of February, and she was making dinner for her daughter. What first struck me was the timbre of Kathryn's voice: it sounded like smoke being blown across a beach of stones. There was something instantly comforting and almost familiar about it, as if she could see through my awkwardness and introversion and accept me just the same.

In that first conversation, Kathryn said she understood my concerns— she was an introvert as well—and that if I decided to come to her class, she would make things easier for me by turning down the lights, arranging the desks in a circle, and having a "conversation" format rather than getting me to monologue.

That was how I finally agreed to do it: because Kathryn, in that empathetic, understanding way of hers, had made me feel comfortable. By the end of our conversation, I surprised myself by saying that I was looking forward to the visit.

It was March by the time I arrived at Lakehead University. I discovered that Kathryn was just as easygoing and down-to-earth in person as she'd been over the phone, and as we sat together in front of perhaps 70 students, discussing the book they'd spent the last nine weeks reading, I found myself actually enjoying the experience of speaking in public. When it came time for the audience to participate, a young student raised her hand. "I have two questions. The first one is, do you want to have children?" Taken aback by her frankness, I said the first thing that came to my head. "With you?" In the roar of laughter, we somehow never got to her second question.

In the many months since that day, I have had the pleasure of becoming Kathryn's friend as well as her occasional colleague. When she asked me to write this introduction, I said yes, this time without hesitation. I knew that whatever Kathryn had written in these pages would be smart, compassionate, and of extreme relevance.

We live in an age where schooling is abundant and the new low-water mark of credentialism is the Master's degree. At the same time, a mixture of scholarship and ordinary observation tells us our world is advanced but not necessarily educated—progressive, but not wise.

What follows is Kathryn's attempt to correct that. It is her dissertation—what she wrote to become a Doctor of Philosophy. It's that substantial and important a book. Kathryn asked me to edit it as well as write this foreword, and after a great deal of consideration, I decided to leave it more or less the way it was. While all writers benefit from a little refinement, I wanted Kathryn's voice to remain intact. It was that voice, after all, that led me out of my own fear and into a place of greater comfort and understanding, and it's that voice that continues to move through these pages, doing much the same thing.

Zander Sherman
September 2014

Preface

This is a book about finding another way to live as much as it's about finding another way to educate our children and ourselves.

When I first read a snippet from Byron Katie that read *Ultimately, the only thing I can know is myself*, I thought to myself, "Well, there's my entire PhD dissertation summed up in one sentence." It can also be summed up with the following story. You may have heard it . . .

One morning in a subway station, a man in a baseball cap took his instrument out of its case and began to play. He was standing next to a garbage can. It was the height of rush hour, and throngs of people rushed past him, not hearing, not listening, not caring—it's uncertain. We only know they didn't stop. There were some people who did stop, however. These people all had one thing in common: they were little. We call them children. They tugged on their parents' and caregivers' hands, pulled by the beauty of the music. For they knew intuitively that this was genius in action, though of course they wouldn't have described it like that. They would have just told you that they liked it very, very much, that there was something about it.

The next day, or maybe the day after that, many of those same adults would have heard on the radio or read in the newspaper that *The Washington Post* had performed an experiment wherein they asked virtuoso violinist Joshua Bell to take his three million dollar Stradivarius to a subway station and perform, to see what would happen. Would people recognize brilliance when they heard it (both his and Bach's)? Would the same people who pay in excess of a hundred dollars to attend the symphony take advantage of a free concert?

The newspaper got its answer and the children got yet another moment of presence and beauty in the stream of moments of presence and beauty arising in their experience. Intelligence, operating through them, as them. . .

Introduction

The greatest achievement of humanity is not its works of art, science, or technology, but the recognition of its own dysfunction.

Eckhart Tolle

Our current dominant education paradigm[1] presupposes many things; yet, since education has been built on these assumptions (operating under them as it has for so long) they are hidden from view and taken for granted. Our first task as educational researchers, then, is to make visible the assumptions we are making about children, human nature, and learning.

For instance, the dominant paradigm presumes that children are not self-motivated—or at the very least, not self-motivated *enough*. Hand-in-hand with this is the idea that children are not capable of being able to decide or know what is important to learn; that is considered the domain of experienced and knowing adults. Furthermore, it's assumed that they need to know certain truths or facts about our world in order to orient themselves in it and become valuable people in our society. (Not to mention that often these 'truths' and 'facts' are at worse actually *theories* presented as fact and at best, as second-hand truths that are meaningless unless and until students come upon them themselves.) The paradigm also operates from the assumption that children learn at the same rate as one another—that they *should*. This education paradigm believes that very little is inherent—

---

[1] I acknowledge that there are other paradigms of education; these fall under the holistic education umbrella. See Rathnam (2013) for a brief outline of these paradigms.

and inherently good—in children, and what is inherent is on the level of personality (rather than knowledge or wisdom, for example) and therefore deemed either good or bad but unchangeable.

In short, the dominant paradigm of education as we know it is unremittingly limiting, not to mention prejudiced and oppressive, in its view of children.

Discovering, exploring, and making visible the ways in which it is most significantly and generally limiting, and undervaluing and underestimating of children is part of the purpose of this book. We need to be able to see the whole clearly before we can begin to change it.

The other part is what to do about it.

~

I explore "the domain of ultimate concern" which is how theologian Paul Tillich (in Vaughn, 2002, p.30) defines spirituality. I like this definition of spirituality because it is inclusive, since we all have ultimate concerns.

This, too, is how I see spirituality and is why I contextualize the research in holistic education, as one of its distinguishing characteristics is its acknowledging and attending to one's spirit, however that is defined. I don't, however, talk about spirituality per se in the book, as I find—like the terms *God* and *love*—that there seems to be a fixed idea of what this term represents for most people; my goal is to start and end with as much openness as possible.

Scholar and transpersonal psychologist Frances Vaughn (2011) outlines the various possibilities for the content of *ultimate concerns*. One of these, "connection to the transcendental ground of being" is what I'm in search of here, ultimately. It comes, in a way, out of an ultimate concern of "the highest levels of any of the developmental lines, for example, cognitive, moral, emotional and interpersonal." In other words, getting to the base level—*the ground*—of what it is to be human, for without answering this, we cannot possibly begin to be able to talk about what education should and can be for.

The phrase "domain of ultimate concern" reminds me of *the ground of being*—a phrase that I considered for the title of this book. To me this means, *Where can I rest?* which is the same thing as *What's it all about?* or *Who or what is God?* even though these questions might seem very different. The questions feel simple enough: it all amounts to giving space in education to inquire into the human condition, which means inquiring into life itself. It has just never made sense to me to talk about how schools are doing a good job or bad job when we haven't secured a vision of the big picture.

Part of Vaughn's research exploration[2] is aimed at understanding "how spirituality can *contribute* to the good life, defined in humanistic terms as living authentically the full possibilities of being human [italics mine" (Vaughn, 2011). I would alter this slightly to say that spirituality (for what could be more important than the domain of *ultimate* concern?) *is* "living authentically the full possibilities of being human" in my definition of the term.

So, to me, the exploration needs to be framed in the broadest sense by: *how can education contribute to living authentically the full possibilities of being human?*

It is from this place that I begin my research that is now what you're holding in your hands.

~

In my estimation, Jiddu Krishnamurti was one person who went deeply into this question by starting where one needs to: by asking what it is to be human, for then we can know for what purpose we are educating children. He came at it through asking questions like, *What is mind?* And then finding out for himself through direct experience. For this reason, his work figures prominently in these pages.

I also look particularly at three contemporary so-called spiritual teachers, Byron Katie, Eckhart Tolle, and Esther Veltheim, whose lives and words demonstrate the *awakened consciousness* of which they speak, but who do

---

[2] I do not go much farther into Vaughn's or Tillich's work. However, I find both their definitions and language quite useful as yet another way to talk about (and in this case introduce) what I am exploring in this book.

not necessarily speak about the applications to education; their insights and accounts serve to support Krishnamurti's claims into the nature of consciousness and its transformation, as well as my own.

Finally, I draw on experiences of my own consciousness and its transformation by way of experiencing and studying from within a first-person account of the transformation of consciousness.

In the first edition of this book (2015), I put the more academic section as Part 1, followed by my personal experiences in Part 2. I received feedback from several people — especially those that don't consider themselves particularly academic but are deeply interested in awakening — that my personal story was what drew them in and allowed them to connect to the academic material even more. (In fact, this is the order that I put them in in my PhD dissertation.) For this reason, I have switched the order for this edition. Of course, read them in whatever order interests you.

Also included in this edition is a whole new section (Chapter 3) detailing the lasting awakening experiences of Krishnamurti, Tolle, Katie, and Veltheim, largely in their words. In the research methodology of narrative, people generally try to present the material in the subjects' own words rather than interpret them in their own voices. I have done that here as I did not see the need to interpret and felt their words best left as their words — doing otherwise would've taken something away. So you will see mostly quotations here. My job was to distill the four subjects' words and correlate them with one another in hopes of painting a picture of the awakened consciousness.

~

The main ideas here are not conceived as a putting forth of an argument for the reader to decide whether I am right or wrong (although this is an inevitable outcome of both writing a book and determining its merit).

Rather, it is an attempt to convey lived experience, which in my estimation does not really fall into a right or wrong dichotomy, as it just simply is. So an undertaking of reading this book is a challenge to the reader to seek to understand rather than to analyze; this objective, or paradigm, of reading to understand rather than reading to judge mirrors the journey I have been on and continue to be on in my attempt to move from intellectual understanding of a transformation of consciousness to its lived reality. (*What does it matter if I 'understand' if it hasn't changed anything for me internally?*)

It's also the definition of an open mind. In my experience, when I am approaching anything in life from an orientation of seeking to determine validity through analysis, I am caught solely in my mind and the trouble with this is that the mind cannot truly 'understand' (which is to say, know); it can only analyze and judge.

It is my view that if we reorient education as a seeking to know ourselves rather than setting educators and children up as inhabiting roles of judge and jury by educating for the intellect, we will open up a whole new avenue of creativity whereby solutions to problems heretofore unfound will become apparent. In my experience, the judge and jury roles come naturally as a byproduct of training only the intellect-mind[3], for its role in decoding and experiencing our lives *is* to play judge and jury, as I will explain in more detail in coming chapters.

In the preface to her book *Beyond Concepts*, Esther Veltheim says: "Clearly, books are collections of concepts and to entitle one *Beyond Concepts* is an obvious paradox. What this book is about is exactly that—paradox" (2000, p.3). And so it is with an openness to paradox that I am suggesting that you approach this book as well, since I, too, am using language (which is conceptual) to address the problem of concepts—a clear paradox. Thus, one reading without an openness or curiosity of the validity of paradox will not ultimately be able to 'hear' or 'see' what I am saying, for it lies *beyond* words.

---

[3] I like this term (which I made up) to signify the thinking portion of the mind. Mind is bigger than intellect. 'Mind' is a pointer to intelligence, as opposed to just the intellect. Mind can exist in the heart, as we'll see towards the end of the book.

What I have described above is well-illustrated by David Skitt (2003) in his introduction to Krishnamurti's book, *Can Humanity Change? J. Krishnamurti in Dialogue with Buddhists.* I quote him at length below, as he nicely describes the different orientations of what I'll call *intellectualizing* and *experiencing*, and both the attempt and difficulty that Krishnamurti has in getting this across to (in this case) Dr. Walpola Rahula, "the eminent Buddhist scholar." (p.vii). Krishnamurti attempts to direct Dr. Rahula to *speak from his own experience* rather than to intellectualize:

> On each occasion, however, instead of discussing whether Dr. Rahula's argument is right or wrong, Krishnamurti moves the debate into quite a different direction. Why, he asks, compare? What is the value of such comparison? Why bring the Buddha into the discussion between the two of them? Courteously, and with a lightness of tone, Krishnamurti challenges Walpola Rahula to say whether he is taking part in the conversation as a Buddhist or as a human being, whether he considers that humanity is in any sense progressing psychologically, what he understands by the word "love."
>
> Dr. Rahula continues, however, in most of these conversations to draw parallels between what the Buddha has said and what Krishnamurti is saying, so that a reader interested in that inquiry will find much of interest. But at another level there is something quite different going on. Time and time again after describing, say, the role of thought in creating the self, Krishnamurti will ask Dr. Rahula and the other participants: Do you *see* that? The word *see* is rightly emphasized, because the seeing in question is clearly meant to be seeing with such depth and clarity that consciousness and simultaneously action are radically transformed. It is also notable that Krishnamurti unfolds his argument by a series of questions, some of which he wants his listeners to allow to sink in rather than to answer—a distinction they do not always find it easy to make.
>
> This moves the debate into an area which all of us are familiar

with, to some extent at least—understanding verbally, rather than understanding so deeply that we change our behavior.

… So what brings about a fundamental change in a human being? And one that brings about an endless, unfolding awareness? This is a question that runs like a silken thread throughout these conversations. Repeatedly Walpola Rahula says all the right words, and Krishnamurti does not deny that his Buddhist questioner may well see the truth to which these words refer. But Krishnamurti urges him to go further and to explain how such seeing comes about, and to discuss the nature and quality of the mind that has such clarity. This is really the kernel of the encounter.

In the context of Krishnamurti's urging above, then, this book seeks "to explain how such seeing comes about, and to discuss the nature and quality of the mind that has such clarity" as well as to determine the implications of such a transformation for education.

Implied and included in the above are the following: *What is mind?* Another way I see of stating this, is: *What is the relationship of thought to one's whole self? What assumptions do we make about mind and one's 'self' in the current education paradigm and what are the effects and implications? What is the result of moving beyond identification with mind? What is required in education in order to move beyond identification with mind?*

The above questions inform the three driving questions of the book: Is there something beyond conceptual understanding? What is the nature of mind and of consciousness? What are the implications (of the above) for education?

In a sense, this book could be said to be about what we call "enlightenment." Despite using it in the subtitle of this book, I don't really find this word helpful, as, like I mention above, people who are familiar with this term can have a certainty or concept about what this term refers to, and this can hinder the investigation. Therefore, I do not use it to frame the investigation, although I do use the term awakening at various points. As

Veltheim explains,

> The meaning of the word *enlightened* is "free of prejudice." Unfortunately to many the word enlightenment has connotations of human specialness and is really misunderstood....*When enlightenment "happens" there is total conviction that there is no such thing as enlightenment.* (2000, p.191, italics original)

In other words, in an attempt to move into a lived reality as opposed to an intellectual one, it seems helpful to either avoid commonly used terms of the phenomenon or expand how we write about the phenomenon to include all terms used to describe it.

Note to readers:

1) Krishnamurti, writing and speaking in the mid-20th century, employed the masculine pronouns to refer to both males and females. It is a good and revealing thing that reading them now is jarring for me (and likely for many of us). I began placing "[sic]" after every male reference but, given the sheer number of instances, it cluttered the quotations significantly. So, I have kept them as is and have used only the feminine pronouns occasionally in my own writing by way of balancing it out.

2) I sometimes employ italics to highlight words that I might have put single quotation marks around. This is to both call into question their commonly associated meanings and to demonstrate that I am aware of a possible plurality in meaning.

3) In some cases, on the advice of my editor, I have excluded internet citations that would've been long and cumbersome in-text. Curious readers who want the original source for these references can find them through my PhD dissertation published online and available through academic databases as *Ontological Intelligence: Consciousness, Mind, and Inquiry in Education.*

PART 1
ANATOMY OF AWAKENING

*Instead of indulging in mere speculation, devote yourself here and now
to the Truth that is ever within you.*

Ramana Maharshi

Chapter 1

You become the wise teacher as you become a student of yourself.
It stops mattering if anyone else hears you, because you're listening.
You are the wisdom you can offer us....

Byron Katie

~

During a meeting about a draft of my PhD dissertation, one of my committee members urged me to go more deeply into my autoethnography. She posed questions, including: "Where does the hunger for a higher consciousness come from? Because not many people get there," she said. "Where did this inner sense come from? What's authentic in your lived experience? What is the connection between consciousness and spirit for you?" She suggested that I should be writing from my heart, that I must pull out more of an authorial voice.

The irony and perhaps paradox of this occurs to me now as I attempt to do what she asks—in fact it is the very fact of the subtle but incessant authorial voice inside me that has drawn me to this path of investigation of higher consciousness. This voice is both the higher consciousness and the one who calls for 'me' to recognize it. It is a knowing that has permeated all of my living, even when I attempt to convince myself otherwise (i.e. that I do not know, that I am lost, that there is no way out to the inner peace I seek, that there isn't a knowing inside me). It has been this ever-present sense of myself that lurks behind the 'I' that has propelled me forward, the sense that what I knew (cognitively) about myself and the world was limited, that it was also somehow all a lie, really. It is the sense that has never left me that there is a reality that exists behind what I am perceiving, where the world makes absolute, unmistakable sense. I find it difficult to describe and find myself wanting to say that it is merely self-evident.

For example, I imagine speaking about this to someone else and instead of laying out any evidence for this reality's existence, I only say, "You feel it too, don't you? Look there, inside you." In other words, it's a reality that can't really be spoken about accurately. As the Tao Te Ching says, that which can be named is not it. This is very frustrating to the mind in my experience, but elicits a sigh of relief from this other self, this reality behind the mind. It's the end of knowing. It's the stopping of trying to play a game that can't be won. Even my mind is relieved, ultimately. It can rest. It no longer has to throw up questions and thoughts, nor attach to thoughts by believing them.

Yet I return to my committee member's questions above, for my sense is that for the purposes of the autoethnography that is at the core of this dissertation, I need to explain how I came to arrive at this place—this place of even being able to look back and have some perspective on my life, a position that I inhabit because of some sort of an expanded awareness that a higher consciousness even exists in the first place.

The short, sweeping answer is that it has always been there, this inner, valid sense of authentic self that encountered many more or less obvious contradictions, or counters, to it. That is, looking back, I see moments of recognition of 'not I, not I, not I' that showed up as discordant to my being, though my mind could not make sense of any of this at the time. Not then, as now looking back, did I see any adults (as teachers, or parents) explaining or modeling to me how to live in the world from my authentic self rather than from rational thought. So it was a bewildering sense of living at odds with the world, a feeling that there was some force within me that ran counter to another force within me and to the way I saw people living and interacting. I felt a natural compulsion to find alignment within me, given that the discord was so uncomfortable.

This is still the case now as I write this; I am aware of this desire that would be impossible to override, that seeks to in accord with all that is, to be at peace, to cease the inner argument. Another way to say this is a desire to be fully myself. And I've noticed that I can't pretend myself into this state, nor argue to gain it, intellectualize for it, cajole or mimic it. For me, it's a simple recognition that I am at war with what is. And it's like a pebble in my shoe or the pea in the stack of mattresses in the fable *The Princess and the Pea*: if I'm even the slightest bit in disagreement, it feels terrible inside me. There's no rest. My mind begins a fruitless attempt to get rid of the uneasiness by controlling my outside circumstances. Katie describes this as attempting to fix the projection instead of working with mind, the projector. In my life (and also, of course, in reference to education), I've been trying to sort out what is true from what I've been *taught* is true. Turning my attention toward the projector is to turn my attention inward, to my own experience. My feelings of confinement and pervasive confusion come, I believe, from a war within me: at ground, it is a war between the truth that I am and the many concepts I have adopted through living that are at odds with that. Many of these concepts are there as a direct result of my formal schooling—in other words, because I was a good student and learned well what I was taught.

And so it was with great relief when I first picked up a book by J. Krishnamurti and finally, here was someone calling a spade a spade, pointing out the elephant in the room—someone saying that the mind is constantly seeking psychological security and exists in a state of fear. And that there is an intelligence *that is who we are* that is not of the mind. *"Yes,"* I thought, *"this is what I've always known to be true. And now I have words to put to it."* Evidently, I felt I needed this outside corroboration, that I needed permission to feel what I was feeling in order to allow it to be valid. (This points to another concept entrenched in me: that I could not rely on my own authority; that by definition, authority was a voice from without, that there is no innate, internal, individual authority. I will speak about this further in chapters 5 and 6.)

To be specific, the fear and discord showed up within me when I felt that others had power over me, when I was urged to move away from my inner knowing inside me to what someone else wanted me to think and believe or was convinced was true. It showed up when I perceived that others, especially adults who could physically hurt me or withdraw their love and approval and thereby emotionally hurt me, could get angry and very angry when I disagreed with them, when I challenged their point of view, especially when it pertained to their description of me—for instance, when it seemed they wished me to feel badly, to feel ashamed even, for something I had done or failed to do, something I didn't even understand. Yet, in their certainty about it and in the face of my lack of certainty, I thought that they must know something I didn't about me and so I agreed with them. It felt like a matter of psychological (if not physical) survival.

It felt that there was no safe place in the world, that my apparent job was to get others to approve of me, and yet this approval was always tenuous and so fragile and could turn to anger and disapproval at any moment. (I think it's important to point out here that I would describe my childhood as good and not what we would call physically or emotionally abusive whatsoever. The point is that some cruelties are subtle, accepted as they are by the dominant paradigm of how we perceive and treat children.) My own evaluation of myself, where I felt certain (though not consciously aware) that I was a pure being, was left behind; I abandoned myself in the seeking of approval from others. My life seemed perpetually doomed to failure, in my eyes. At a less than conscious level, I knew I was in a game that couldn't be won but it certainly didn't seem like I could remove myself from this game or that there was any other game. *Trust us. Do as we say and you will be fine*, was the implied message.

This resulted in the locus of control—of the ability to discern truth from untruth—being moved from inside to outside of me, to others. The foremost implicit lessons I learned in school in addition to an absence of inner authority was 1) *to rely on the mind, the intellect and* 2) *that the education I received in school would prepare me for life.*

Yet, throughout my life, some part of me has never been able to accept this framing of reality as correct; it just didn't ring true. What I felt was more true was that I *did* have an innate knowing—call it wisdom that is not acquired but that we are all born with—and that this was the most valuable part of me. In addition, when I felt even moments of peace and contentment, this felt like myself. This is what I mean when I use the word authentic: it feels like me, like who I am behind/underneath the 'I.' These moments showed up during laughter, during witnessing acts of kindness, during connection with someone that felt like meta-verbal and meta-cognizant, during a noticing of sunlight sparkling across a tree's green leaves, when I was dancing. *Yes*, I felt, *this is what is true*. And yet.

This state, this knowing brought forth into my conscious awareness, was fleeting and elusive. I couldn't will it back. It was a state of grace. It came or it didn't, and mostly it didn't. The image that comes to mind now is of me swimming but being pulled under the surface of the water such that I have only brief moments to grab a breath (the moments I was in alignment with my true self) and am back under again. In this metaphor then, my life has been lived mostly under water. At least, that is how I experienced it, how it looks to me now. I can't say this definitively because of this knowing behind the self I describe above—it was always there too, it's just whether or not I recognized it. That is, in moments *now* of a state of grace, I would say that below the water was also above, that there was nothing that was not a state of grace. As one friend said of her awakening to the reality of her lived life as she looked back on it, *"What a beautiful life."* It is indeed possible to live life in retrospect, to see a different life than the one I thought I was living.

But at the time I didn't see that. I wasn't aware of it. I was only aware of the discord within me that, untalked about as it was—left unexternalized—was internalized. Always it was turned inward to the self, the 'I:' *it must be me who isn't perceiving accurately, who doesn't understand, who must be unwilling and defiant and mixed up about it all, who is just never good enough, who can't get it right.* In short, the discord was both my fault and my responsibility to figure out. And so always there was suffering. And always the hope for non-suffering, for a day when I would feel free and loved and accepted. I did not feel *in* myself, but fractured. (Krishnamurti often uses the term *fragmented* and I believe this is what he was referring to.) I did not have a sense of fullness of myself, but always always something missing. There has always been *the search* from as far back as my memory goes. This makes sense in light of Katie saying that our first memory exists in relation to our wanting something—in this moment the 'I' was born, the me who wants something and doesn't have it. The seeker is born. I identified myself, literally. The one who doesn't have this thing. The one who wants.

For me this memory is when my mom brought my little sister home from the hospital when I was four years old. I remember holding her. I was sitting on the couch. What it seems I wanted was my mom's attention; I didn't want this new person siphoning energy and focus away from me. The game of me identifying as "Kathryn" began. Before that, I do not remember identifying as anything. Without memory, I can only speculate that there was only being. Memory seems to come into effect only as the mind identifies as something. Looking back, it seems the rest of my life was and is the creating and attempting to break free of lie after lie, whether perceived positive like, *I am athletic, I am musical* or negative: *I am stupid, I am ugly*. It's been a journey borne along by the persistent inward knowing that I am meant to be at peace, that there must be a way.

The most persistent of these lies has been the belief that 'I' could figure it out, that 'it' must. And this was the domain of the intellect, this 'figuring out' entity. So I thought and I reflected and I studied and I looked and I asked and I read. Deeper, stronger, with what seems now like unwavering determination. All the while I felt I must be getting closer to the truth of life, to solving this feeling of discord that felt like emptiness within me. *For what was life for, if not to solve this?* it seemed to me, to find a way to be at peace in each moment.

It is this that I wonder if Krishnamurti was referring to when he said, "The whole movement of life is learning." That life itself—the living of it as we do—is set up perfectly for us. To learn about it. And ourselves. To have us mirrored back to ourselves so we can ultimately see that which we are.

Yet as my suffering deepened the older I got—the more life I lived and the more complexities were added—I had to concede that somehow my intellect wasn't doing the job. Despite recognition of my intellect from academic institutions (and therefore others, in acknowledgment of my success), the reality of my lived life was that I did not feel any closer to a life lived in peace and truth—a definition of success that seemed apparent to me. I was confused about what decisions to make, about who I was and how to best live life. My schooling, as it turned out, completely neglected something crucial in my education of life and the world: me. I have felt wholly unequipped to make my way in life.

There was no shortage of people professing how to find happiness and how to make life work for oneself. (A whole genre of books called "self-help" is devoted to this endeavor and seems to have grown exponentially in the past few years.) Yet it internally didn't feel like enough for me to follow their ideas. Following other people's ideas felt like what got me into the mess in the first place. Something inside me wanted me to know for me. 'I' wanted—needed—me to follow my own voice.

It's something I have told my university students is a "truth meter" that I know must exist inside each of us, not just in me; it's a desire to know the truth for ourselves and we can't rest until we do.

It is this that I believe the spiritual masters refer to when they say that no one can do this—take this journey—for us, that *truth is a pathless land*, that ultimately words can only point to the truth and we must jump off those words into the world of our own experience. "It is up to each of you to work out your own liberation," said Siddhārtha Gautama. And in this lies the only true knowing; it is here where the truth is unmistakable. Gone are the theories, suppositions, and speculations.

My committee member who I refer to above, asked me also to identify early experiences in childhood that created this desire in me to understand the nature of consciousness. Really, it can perhaps all be summed up by saying that there was no tending to my inner life by anyone outside me in an explicit way; there was not even acknowledgement of its existence, in this emotional inner space that is a world unto itself[4]. And so, despite it being the only thing that felt real and tangible to me, it simultaneously was as if it didn't exist. At the very least, I believed an implied message: *this is yours to take care of, yours to handle. You are responsible for this inner world.* That this inner world of my emotions, thoughts, and beliefs where wounds and fears and questions reside wasn't acknowledged, that I wasn't shown how to take care of it, never felt okay inside me.

And this feeling has only deepened with my becoming a mother, when I look at my daughter and ask myself what I think she needs. More than anything, I think she needs to have tools to tend to her inner life. I want this for all children (and like Katie says, all of us are children in that we have never learned to do this, to take care of—and responsibility for—ourselves). I want her to have tools to take care of her difficult emotions, ways that she can access and make sense of who she is and what this means about life, beyond limiting concepts.

Put up against what she is learning in school (math, science, social studies, etc.), it *dwarfs* these things. This subject matter can't hold a candle to what is really important to learn: the nature of self and life. To me, it seems so simple and obvious, that it's hidden, in a way, in plain sight. We can't do anything with this subject matter of information that we currently call education unless we know first who we are and what the nature of life is. And to the query of whether or not this can be known, I would say that surely this must be the first inquiry. In other words, we can at least try to find out.

In my inner life, too, there's a feeling of contraction, almost of suffocation. It's related to the feeling of fragmentation/fracturing, like something is missing from myself. I feel as though I am trying to fit myself into a smaller being than what is true for me, that this bodymind with all of its concepts and accumulation of knowledge is too small for me. What feels true is that

---

[4] I refer to this with my B.Ed. students as "the elephant in the room" of education, this inner reality that is the most immediate, most real to all of us and yet is not addressed.

a feeling of pure freedom is my birthright and any feeling that runs counter to that feels like a lie within me.

So it is that these feelings I've described above have existed like clues within me that I'm meant to follow to find a Self that is true beyond everything I have been taught, every concept I've acquired. I would describe it as my search for meaning except that this phrase feels like it's personalized and therefore leaves room for individual interpretation as in *What gives her meaning*, when that is not what feels accurate for me (thought it may be included within this wider sweep). Personal meaning is one thing but I am talking about something else, about what is true. Personal meaning still leaves isolation rather than connection; it still feels incomplete in me. Instead, I am aware of an intuitive sense of something uniting me with everything and everyone else and that connection is what I'm looking for. So I continue to follow this 'voice' in me that is not really a voice at all but a silent guide; it's me unmediated, unknowable.

Ground of Being

I asked my undergraduate education students how they thought Krishnamurti came upon his insights, his information. They responded that he must have studied them. I wasn't really surprised to hear this answer, despite having introduced my students to the idea that it's possible to know the truth for oneself, by oneself. Yet, I was struck again with how absolute is the idea of the intellect, of the pervasiveness and dominance of the intellect, that the intellect is all there is. It doesn't seem to occur to anyone that anything new—real creation/creativity—must have been come upon directly, not by studying other's words/experience. So I tell them about Einstein, hoping his lauded name will give them a portal in to seeing intelligence in a different way. "None of my inventions ever came from rational thought," he said.

To me, there seems there must be a ground of being, as it were, something that allows all other things to exist. And it seems intuitive to me that if I can conceive of it, I must be able to experience it directly, it must be *encounterable* by me (by anyone). And the drive I feel to experience this ground is the drive to experience truth, to stand squarely and firmly in the centre of life and then from there be able to know how to proceed given that I can now see life in its totality.

I realize that the experiencing the meaning of life may come only through its living, that I am engaged in a chicken and egg dance that may be yet another illusion of mind. Yet what I am trying to convey is the existence of this undeniable impulse within me to know the ground of being. To me, there's nothing more obvious than the need to find out what life is (and by extension who I am) and without it nothing else makes sense. I may as well be inert matter, not able to set my course.

Autobiographical Narrative #1: Learning and Teaching

"*This dissertation is part of an ongoing exploration of who I am and what it means to be alive*" (Kull, 2005, p.3). Just as Bob Kull's dissertation (where he uses himself as the research subject in a yearlong experiment of living alone in a remote wilderness area) "is not an abstract discussion of solitude, but a personal narrative . . . locate[d] in a broader cultural context," I situate my autobiographical narrative in a broader context of self-inquiry, including inquiry into the nature of experience, thought, and consciousness.

My sense is that Bob Kull, like, most famously, Henry David Thoreau went into solitude in part to try to isolate himself in order to study himself, a way to sort of highlight his "I-ness" by putting it against a back-drop where there were no others like him (i.e. no other humans). I can understand this impulse, having done it myself for a brief period, and Thoreau's writings from solitude have yielded tremendous insights into its nature that can benefit us all. However, it's my feeling that one need not isolate oneself from the rest of humanity like that in order to study oneself—indeed, that creates an abnormal human experience that most, if not all, of us will ever experience and those of us who do will experience for only brief periods of time. Humans are social creatures and as far as we know, have always been so. We live amongst each other. While studying oneself as a sort of pure (in the sense of singular) 'being' in the absence of other human beings I'm sure offers its own insights (for example, I can imagine that one feels less inhibited in expressing one's 'true self' in various ways), it can be likened to taking children out of their classrooms and putting them into a lab setting in order to try to better see how they interact with one another. Of course, there has been some recognition that studying those in their natural or habitual environment seems to naturally yield more accurate and reliable data, giving rise to the research methodology of ethnography. In this light, and in light of the fact that I am looking at an education paradigm (Krishnamurti's) that expressly states that one not only can, but must, examine oneself as an ongoing inquiry into the nature of self and life, a major part of this dissertation is in the realm of self-examination.

I divide this chapter into two parts: the first is my remembered experience as a student in the formal education system; the second is likewise my remembered experience, as a formal teacher in various systems of education in various countries.

I share my perception of my teaching and learning influences and experience because 1) I want to show my breadth of experience in various teaching situations, as well as 2) show my length and depth of contemplation over educational questions, and finally 3) use examples to help elucidate my educational orientation as a researcher. In short, I am establishing authority. Or expertise. Or at the very least, experience. As Grace Feuerverger (2001, p.8) explains, "I wanted my 'psychic signature' to be evident and for my interpretations to be understood through the embodiment of my own life story." The previous and following narratives frame this study.

The Student's (Teacher's) Journey

Being a teacher is the only thing I ever remember wanting to be. Although I find it interesting that this is not exactly because I had a great educational experience myself. I did in the sense that I was often rewarded for my efforts with straight A's (elementary school) and high percentages (high school). Yet, I can remember often feeling bored and imprisoned, looking out the windows and wishing I was outside instead—feeling that a lot of the work was 'make work,' used to keep us occupied lest we become unruly and stage a rebellion or something. No school work could ever satisfy my yearning to know the bigger questions of why we are here (as in: as people, on Earth), and what life is all about, which surely we needed to answer before we could contextualize any other learning. For instance, how on earth could I begin to understand the relevance of the War of 1812 (and I know something important happened in 1776 but I can't remember what) if I don't even know what it means to be human? I would like to emphasize that I am not being glib here whatsoever—I couldn't be more serious. Likewise, I do not see this as naive at all either. Our seeming societal assumption that these questions are either irrelevant to living life or impossible to answer seems to preclude asking them. I am saying that for me, asking these questions has fuelled my life. Whether or not they can be answered has not stopped me from asking them. I suspect I am far from the only one. On the contrary, I feel that these questions fuel everyone on one level or another (which is to say, on a spectrum of being more or less aware of these questions.) On a deep level, I believe I knew that teachers—supported by the whole system of education and indeed, society—were afraid to ask these questions because they didn't know the answers, and felt that they should, and perhaps were afraid that there were no answers. Likely, I was no different, because I did not think these thoughts out loud but kept my questions to myself. Still, I wanted to be a teacher, because I wanted to give to children what I wished I had received, what I felt I was missing out on, and what I felt was not only an opportunity but an obligation of education.

High School English Class

In all of my education, I can remember one particular moment when it seemed to me I was learning something about life—when I felt I actually learned something important. I'm not saying there weren't more of these instances; there may have been. I'm saying that this is the only one that I can remember, and it had a lasting impact on me. It was an insight, and what was crucial about this, and why I call it an insight, was that I experienced the moment as a *remembering*; it literally resonated in my body, as if somewhere in my body something was saying, "Yes, this is truth. I *remember* that this is true."

The experience happened, as it seems many of these experiences do— for those who have them—in English class. It was Grade 12. We were studying *A Separate Peace* by John Knowles, and there was a passage about the Maginot Lines that made mention of "the enemy" that we persist in thinking is 'out there.' (To this day, I still do not know what event they actually refer to, which is very revealing about my approach to education: I take the essence and forget the rest.)

Here is the excerpt that struck me with such force: "All of them, all except Phineas, constructed at infinite cost to themselves these Maginot Lines against this enemy they thought they saw across the frontier, this enemy who never attacked that way—if he ever attacked at all; if he was indeed the enemy" (Knowles, p.196).

The evocative prose of the author led me to the insight that there *is* no enemy out there—it is *we* who are our own enemy. I didn't have to *think* about this to know that it was true; I *knew* somehow that this was indeed the case. It is exactly the (mistaken) belief that we need to construct defences around ourselves that *creates* the enemy, I realized. 'What, exactly, are we continuously guarding against?' was the crucial question that arose within me and opened a treasure trove of even more questions.

It really was the most astounding moment, in education, and in life in general. It felt like an incredible insight. That moment was indicative of why I majored in English literature in university; it was the only thing (that I can recall) in all of my schooling years that offered something that meant any sense to me. It seemed the beginning of my journey of seeing the possibilities of education to help us understand who we are as humans, and what we could potentially be capable of creating in life. It seemed at long last that I was getting the chance, within education, to explore those questions I had long been yearning to ask. And just maybe, we could even figure out some answers.

I came to define the study of English literature as the study of the human psyche, and therefore, the study of myself. It was only later, when I encountered the work of J. Krishnamurti for the first time that I understood why it had made sense intuitively to me to see the highest — perhaps the only— function of education as self-understanding. Krishnamurti said that "to understand life is to understand ourselves and that is both the beginning and the end of education" (1953, p.14). Education only made sense to me insofar as it helped me to better understand myself. Thus, math was my worst subject, science my second worst, and so on. These were courses where I could not see the direct connection with who I was, so I couldn't care about them. I only did as well as I did in math and science out of a drive to 'succeed' and have top marks. Failing didn't feel good. I'm not saying that math and science aren't about who we are and English is, but for me, making the connection between life and the study of English came more naturally.[5] Or, another possibility, is that without teachers making overt connections to my lived life, the connection between people's stories in literature and my own were more obvious to me.

English was one of my passions, both inside and outside of school. In fact, although this moment with *A Separate Peace* was perhaps my first educational moment of real eye-opening significance, my love-affair with reading began at a very young age. I believe it was my love of novels that set the stage for me to be able to connect with the lessons embedded in books in a profound way. For someone else, math or science has perhaps done the same thing. However, my belief in literature to guide me to a deeper, true meaning of myself only carried me so far.

---

[5] My theory is that the reason people are drawn to certain subjects over others is precisely because they can connect with them on a deeper level, in a way that integrates with how they make meaning in life.

University

When I got out into the big, wide world after graduating high school, armed with my high marks and ready to take on the world, I gradually started to become disillusioned. I went through my first year of university relatively unscathed: I was excited to be in an environment that seemed wide open with possibilities, to really inquire into the nature of life and human existence. I finished my first year amongst the top students at the university. But by second year, I started to slip. I started to not try so hard because I wasn't sure my efforts meant anything of value. I really allowed myself to finally wonder with full consciousness, *What does it all mean anyway?*

In high school I had also been an athlete. I continued that into second-year university, too, rowing on the varsity team, but gradually let it slip as well. Slowly, I was allowing the objects outside me that I had been using to build an identity for myself to erode away. (Or, perhaps, they were doing the eroding and I was just witnessing it.) I wasn't sure who I was anymore. Or perhaps more accurately, the realization was slowing dawning that I never had. I allowed myself a first glimpse into really wondering, *Who am I?* Although I didn't know it consciously then, I believe it was the beginning of allowing that who I was, was not made up of my accomplishments. I started to experientially challenge what my education implicitly told me: that if I played by the rules they laid out for me, if I did really, really well, then I would succeed in the world—and what is success, if not to breed happiness (I assumed)? I had graduated with the highest marks in my class, I was the top athlete in the school for successive years; I could not have succeeded in playing by their rules any more than I did. Yet I felt lost: I did not know what life was all about, and there was no one to guide me to find out.

Although I couldn't have articulated this at the time, I felt a deep sense of betrayal beginning in my second year of university. I felt the child in me yelling at all the adults who ever had presented themselves as knowing something I didn't: *But you pretended you had all the answers! You said you would guide me in life! You said, 'Follow me and you will not fail.' I did everything you told me to do, and now you have disappeared, your rules have nothing to do with real life, and I am left to start all over again on my own.* My friend would describe it to me in the summer after my second year of university as a "loss of innocence." I was familiar with this term as a literary theme but until then I never thought of it as something people here and now (as opposed to characters in novels) go through as a sort of rite of passage. Now, of course, I recognize this time in my life as what spiritual leaders would call the beginning of the quest, or the dark night of the soul— the journey that starts with one question: *Is this all there is?* Of course I see the benefit—even the necessity—of having gone through it but I still never lost the feeling that somehow we had it all wrong in education. We seemed to be missing the greatest opportunity for people to really inquire about life, to really inquire into themselves. All those years of sitting at desks, and to what end? If we judge based on amount of time in school, those years should have yielded something profound for everybody.

I had started out my university journey at Dalhousie in Halifax (based solely on my desire to have an adventure which I decided at the time would be best facilitated by going to either the east coast or west coast of Canada) but I transferred into the Concurrent Education program at Queen's University for the start of second year. Ostensibly, this is the event that seemed to precipitate my 'fall' into disillusionment. My decision to go to Queen's was based on my perception that it was important for me to go to what was widely reputed to be the best school in Canada. That, and that I had already gotten into teacher's college by virtue of being accepted into Concurrent Education—a difficult program to get in to—and I didn't have enough confidence in myself to get accepted based on my (yet-to-come) graduating marks. This, despite my first-year English professor reassuring me that I was among the best students at the university. So I left some of the best friends I'd ever had and went to Queen's. And the disillusionment of school—of life—began in earnest.

To say I was disappointed in my university education classes is an understatement. Surely, I thought, at the highest echelons of learning, there is some real inquiry happening into what it means to teach, to learn, to be educated; yet, if there was, I did not encounter it.

On the positive side, since I was in Concurrent Education, I did an enormous amount of practice teaching—one practicum every year for four years, and then five straight months of teaching in the final year. The beauty of this was that I got to experience many different learning environments before I became a teacher. To name a few, I was in an inner-city elementary school, a very rural high school, an outdoor education centre, and a highly academic high school, considered the best in the city. I worked with teachers with many different philosophies. However, after eighteen straight years of education—of classes and classrooms every day—I was good and ready to be finished with formal schooling.

Wilderness

Throughout my university years, I maintained the same spring and summer jobs: planting trees in northern British Columbia and being a camp counselor at a camp based in Algonquin Park. Both of these jobs were enormously physically and psychologically demanding (especially the former); I felt it important to challenge myself in these ways at that time, but mostly, I just wanted to have a job where I could spend the entire spring and summer outside. Being inside so much of the time during the school day, and especially during the warmer months, has felt wrong to me for as long as I can remember.

Through these jobs, I experienced life in remote wilderness areas that most people will never see, and I will likely not see again in my lifetime. As a counselor at a camp specializing in canoe tripping, I lead canoe trips of three to six weeks in length. These trips never actually encountered Algonquin Park; it was considered too 'tame,' far from the 'real' wilderness we were all seeking. I think of my counseling as the beginnings of my teaching career. Though we had no formal training whatsoever to be camp counselors, I was determined to be the best counselor I could be. This came in part from the fact that I had suffered greatly from homesickness as a camper at this same camp and felt I could be there compassionately for any of my campers suffering the same, showing them that even though I was a stranger, I cared about their suffering. I also felt so strongly the inquiry that was alive within me and I included my campers in this sphere of my questioning about life, through my questions and our conversations.

For the most part, my campers and I forged a close bond over our time together. Out in remote wilderness areas with no hint of civilization around, there's a real sense of needing to stick together for survival, as well as a sense of real possibility of discovery—for me, the discovery of an ontological, epistemological nature more than a physical one (i.e. of the geographical landscape) though the one seemed certainly to support the other.

It was while tree planting one day—a job where there's nothing to do for hours every day but be with one's thoughts, or without them as the case may be—that I had two deep insights about life. I can still picture the exact moment and the landscape around me (which is rather remarkable given that we were in clear cuts that essentially all looked the same), when I realized that no human being can truly know another, and that what unites us is our suffering. It came to me through a metaphor: in tree planting, you can plant alone, or with someone by your side. On this particular day, my friend whom I often planted with was relatively nearby, just across a small ravine. I could see her, but realized that in essence we might as well have been miles apart, because the closeness and connection I desired were just not possible—not with her, not with any other person. A real sadness washed over me at this realization, but at least it helped me understand the sadness that I had been previously feeling throughout my life.

It has taken me years of experience (and suffering) to realize that the connection I am looking for is of that to myself *and/or* (it seems to me it is one and the same) of that to the totality, or to what some call God. This explains the sort of background feeling I've had my whole life of isolation and aloneness, but also an intuitive knowing that it need not be this way, that there was a way to feel at one with life; otherwise, it seemed to me, I wouldn't have this sense of what oneness might feel like.

In other words, I realized I could only know something as my internal experience in relevance to some other experience. It seems to me that what has guided my whole life from as far back as I can remember, is a desire for the feeling of wholeness. I have felt a sense of something missing, and that thing feels like it's *me*. I could say that it's a part of me that's missing, but that makes it seem less consequential than it is, and it couldn't feel MORE consequential; it is the only real part of me that feels missing. It's like living through a veil or half-asleep. And I've had the sense that I would know I'd found this me because I'd feel HERE, FULLY ALIVE. That is the way I would use to describe it. I know intuitively that every other human being must share this experience—whether they are aware of their experience is another matter.

To me, this is one way to sum up the human condition: perceiving separateness and attempting unification. Separate and unified from and to what or whom, we don't seem to ask; other humans, we seem to assume, and attempt to coalesce through relationships, family, community, nations, etc. We form alliances and groups where we can identify as an 'us' and therefore create a 'them' to attempt to create this sense of belonging. (From this forming of alliances, then, it's easy to see how violence erupts, or any sort of subjugation, between individuals, groups, or nation states). That this sense of belonging is only superficial and never penetrates to the essence of ourselves, does not appear readily apparent to most people. A few years ago, I was given a book by Esther Veltheim called *Beyond Concepts: The Investigation of Who You Are Not*. In it, I found the following, which was confirmation for me that my perception has been accurate:

> The instinct to feel at one with life, consciously or unconsciously, fuels all actions. You are constantly trying to bridge the perceived gap between the world and yourself.
>
> The desire to heal the separation between self and others is merely a reflection of your split focus between your essential nature (the impersonal Self) and the person you think you should be (the personalized self). (2000, p.145)

In other words, it's a model where 'reality' as we perceive it is a projection onto the external world of our own internal reality. So, our attempt to get closer to others—often seen manifested as couplings in intimate partnerships, but also in, for example, one's search for fame or prestige or power that one imagines will bring them closer to others through attention, affection, and appreciation—are really a felt gap within ourselves. The gap is between our manufactured idea of who we are, and who we actually are.

The Teacher's (Student's) Journey

After graduating with my B.A. and B.Ed, I took a year 'off' (this is how I thought of it at the time, because it wasn't a 'real' job) to do informal teaching: downhill skiing. Having grown up ski racing, I was hopeful I could get a job at Whistler teaching skiing, which I did. Again, the drive to be able to be outside whenever I chose and not be imprisoned inside informed my job choice. I want to emphasize that this was no small thing: I felt like I was making up for years of being confined to a classroom. While I did relish waking up to the beauty of the mountains, being outside and active each and every day, and connecting to the young children in my care, it did not feel like a meaningful enough way of life for me. I longed to experience both the wider world (i.e. other countries)—and the classroom—for myself, which took me to Copan Ruinas, Honduras the following year, and the first classroom of my own. (I arrived three weeks before Hurricane Mitch—and an unknown illness—hit, which is a whole educational journey unto itself, the details of which are best saved for another time.)

Central America

Copan is a small, mountain town close to the border of Guatemala; it is on the site of an ancient Mayan city and as such is an (out-of-the-way) tourist destination. I loved it there, which is not to say that I didn't struggle very much at times. For starters, I did not speak any Spanish, and I was teaching children who did not speak a word (and I mean a *word*) of English. It would have been surprising if they did, given that they were only three and four years old. Which brings me to my second major struggle: I was certified in the intermediate/senior grades, not even junior, never mind primary or early childhood. My class was the "Nursery/Pre-kinder" class and the reason I was teaching them (instead of my certified grades), was because the school year had already started when I found out about the school, and this was the only class they didn't yet have a teacher for. I don't think this was a coincidence, as I would never have chosen this age, given a choice, but I am deeply grateful for my experience with them. I came to describe my experience there, to friends and family back in Canada, as running a birthday party for seventeen students every day—twice! (Nursery came for the first part of the day, and then the Pre-kinder kids would come for the afternoon.)

I felt supremely incompetent to say the least, but found some determination to at least do something better than what had been done before—which, from what I could gather, consisted of these little tykes sitting at their individual desks, reciting words from the chalk board over and over. Rote learning. Horror! If there was one thing I thought I knew about early childhood learning, it was that children needed to get their hands dirty. They just had to get in there and learn something for themselves. Experiential learning. Paint, play with water, get dirty, run, skip and jump, sing and laugh . . . many things, but NOT recite words over and over again like robots. So I set up learning centres in the classroom, and moved the desks so the children sat in clusters instead of rows. And then we just played. A lot of the laughing came in the form of the children laughing at my attempts to speak Spanish, and at my not understanding what they were saying. I remember one child in particular—Vilma—teaching *me*: an obvious example of the transaction or blurred roles between 'teacher' and 'learner', where there is really learning and teaching going on, on both sides. She was so patient with me, and seemed to really understand the situation (i.e. why I couldn't speak Spanish) so she employed her own form of sign language. It was really extraordinary. I wonder sometimes if she became a teacher herself, so earnestly did she take on the task of teaching me. In the absence of a shared language, communication came from somewhere deeper.

In the spring of that year, I felt I had taken these youngest of students as far as I could go with the limited amount of what I knew about early childhood learning, and when the opportunity came to take over the grade six class, I took the new post with very mixed emotions. It was so difficult to leave these kids who now felt like my own children, and yet I felt that they could be better served at this point by someone who spoke Spanish. I also felt ready for a less taxing assignment: the grade 6 students all spoke English quite well. Yet my educational struggles were born anew, as I struggled with both delivering the established curriculum and questioning its relevance to these students' lives as well as creating some new curricula (which I had the chance to do). On my lunch breaks, I would often go across the road to the cafe at the ancient Mayan city (incongruous though that may sound) and write philosophical letters to my friends (or to myself in the form of journal entries) about life, and education. Despite my struggles as a teacher, I found myself giving a speech to all of the parents, students, and distinguished guests at Graduation, Escuela Mayatan, 1999, for in Honduras, graduation from elementary school comes at the end of Grade 6 and I was the Grade 6 teacher. I felt very honoured as well as somewhat undeserving, and wish now I had my speech so that I could look back to what I said—probably mostly how much I loved my students, and teaching, and education as a chance to inquire into our deepest questions about life.

It was while I was in Copan that I started to read Krishnamurti in earnest. I saw myself in the mirror of his words. (Impossibly, I would find another book by Krishnamurti in a tiny shop in Copan Ruinas that allotted one small corner for travellers to leave their already-read books and take another.)

Although I briefly thought about staying in Copan to teach another year, I was getting paid barely enough to cover my (frugal) living expenses there, and wanted to start paying back my student loans. Also, I felt that my heart was in teaching English literature, so I wanted to try my hand at it. So it was that on Labour Day, two months after leaving Honduras, I headed to Ottawa where my two sisters were living, to get on the supply teaching list. Instead, I got a full-fledged English teaching position at one of Ottawa's most respected high schools: Glebe Collegiate Institute. The school was not semestered at that time, so I had six different classes and little time whatsoever to get ready to teach them. I found out on the Friday that I got the job, and began on the Tuesday. Yikes! Trial by fire to say the least! I will sum up my time at Glebe as I often have for people who have asked me about my experience of that year: I confirmed for myself that I loved teaching, but had far too many questions to ask about the purpose and nature of teaching and learning to stay in the classroom. Just as I had as a student, I again felt confined and confused, and could just see those same feelings of confinement, confusion, and exasperation in the students, despite my giving one hundred percent at helping them make meaningful connections to the curriculum. I felt I could not participate in education until I felt better about it, which I would do by answering some of my nagging questions for myself.

South America

So even though it was a full contract position (I could still be doing it now—a coveted position in these days of few available teaching jobs), after weeks of deliberation I made the difficult decision to resign in August after that year, and after a three-week stint marking the Grade 10 literacy tests for Education Quality and Accountability Office (EQAO) in Toronto (interesting to have a first-hand experience of these tests), headed to Guyana, South America, for more of a taste of the world. There I led a group of 18- to 25-year-olds (I was only 27 myself) in volunteer development work. Other than my informal teaching to the group, the closest we got to formal education was in helping with the construction of a schoolhouse in a remote, river-access only village. Yet, the whole experience was obviously an extremely educational one for me, including living and working at an orphanage and woman's shelter, and living and working on remote beaches protecting and monitoring sea turtle habitat.

At the end of my contract with Youth Challenge International I wanted to stay longer in Guyana as I wasn't ready to leave my rich experience there yet. I found a job at the School of the Nations private school in Georgetown, the capital city, where I taught French and English to Grades 4-6. It was fairly challenging to step into this role towards the end of their school year. (I don't recall what happened to their previous teacher.)

In addition, I had last spoken French ten years earlier when I lived in France for three months on an exchange. I didn't feel particularly competent in the language. What I did feel confident in was my ability to connect with the students, which I had long ago decided was paramount anyway.

Of course, as a foreigner, I knew I had much to learn about Guyanese culture and any particular struggles of the students. I suspect they were probably pretty curious about me, but I don't recall much in particular. Not surprisingly, the same theme seemed alive and well in the school: students who didn't seem to obviously connect with the material they were learning and so would rather be outside playing. I remember classroom management being difficult, and I was happy to be there for only two months. It was while I was in South America that I heard of my acceptance at OISE/UT into a Masters of Education. I was thrilled. I really had doubted my ability to be accepted (a common theme in my life, I came to discover).

North America

In my Masters, I finally hoped to formally delve into these questions I long had about education. Unfortunately, I didn't do that—not in the way I wanted to. I took some interesting courses, but I didn't find the mentor that I was looking for, whom I felt I could really talk to about my educational concerns—maybe even someone who was familiar with Krishnamurti's writings. I did find some hope in Dr. Jack Miller, whom I took *Teacher As Contemplative Practitioner* from, and who seemed to be the only person at OISE devoting his scholarship as a professor to holistic education.

He agreed to supervise my Major Research Paper, which I completed after a wee interruption: I became a mother (talk about an educational journey). My MRP was my initial attempt to write about myself as the subject in the context of Krishnamurti's work, though I was years away from hearing about self-reflexivity and autoethnography. (Unfortunately, I did not keep track of a copy of this paper; it would be interesting to read it now when I am attempting a similar methodology, though inquiring more deeply now and in greater detail.)

I went back to teaching while working on my Master's thesis, this time at the college level, where I taught academic reading and researching. I knew even more clearly that I loved teaching, but I needed to be able to fully engage in the educational questions I was asking, whether through teaching education classes where the students and I would be able to co-inquire, or through PhD work. I was ready to head back to OISE to finish what I had started: a full, in-depth inquiry into holistic education, particularly through Krishnamurti education and self-study (that now, thankfully, was considered a research methodology under the name of "autoethnography").

Autobiographical Narrative #2:
Arts and the Nature of Being

In a research methods course, I began exploring my beliefs about the arts, education, and myself in order to examine myself as an educational researcher who would perhaps use an arts-informed research methodology for my dissertation study. Unexpectedly, I discovered that there was a close link between what I think of the arts and the nature of being.

I feel it is important to share my findings here because of their ontological and epistemological relevance to this study. I find special importance in remembering what it's like to be a child; in many ways, my childhood experiences have driven my research interests. It seems as though I have carried my childhood experiences with me and they now inform my understanding of how children are in the world and what, then, could be helpful to attend to for them in a teacher/parent capacity.

The research I did and the paper I wrote for the arts-informed research methods course was in the context of autobiographical narrative.

Arts and Education

This methodological process mirrors the content; that is, the means is also the end in that my belief that education should be as much about valuing each student's own experience as anything else, is the aim that drives this articulation of my own voice. So, I must start with my own knowing: *What is my own experience* (as opposed to what I may think about my experience)? What does it feel like to express my own authentic voice, to reveal what I know to be true for me? How do I know that it is true for me (i.e. and not just a story I'm telling about my experience)? Is there a physical place where I locate my knowing, for example in my head, or heart? Is there tension between my head and heart? If so, why? Is there a hierarchy of knowing in my experience that is structured along a conceptual/non-conceptual continuum? How have I come to know? As arts-informed researcher Mary Beattie (personal communication) explains, I have to be able to know for myself before I can help anyone else (i.e. students) to know—I have to "connect the personal with the professional with the scholarly." This echoes Krishnamurti's assertion. So, it starts with self-examination.

Data

The data for the following narrative was collected in four ways: 1) reflective writing, where I wrote numerous notes consisting of any memories I have of engaging in the arts, and how the arts were presented to me through my parents, my teachers, and the culture at large while I was growing up; 2) a partnered presentation, where I presented to a colleague something I made as well as something that inspires me while my partner took field notes for my subsequent use. (The exercise was intended by my professor to begin to draw out ways I understand creativity.); 3) partner interviews, where this same partner asked me a series of questions beginning with my perception of my own unique educational gift and where I might have acquired this. (This session was recorded in order that I might begin to hear my own voice mirrored back to me and to continue to flesh out how I have obtained the educational views that I have); 4) a class presentation, where I summarized the major themes I found emerging after completing an initial draft of my narrative; I received feedback in the form of field notes from my classmates and an oral summative mirroring from my professor.

I analyzed the data by going through the field notes to see what words and phrases appeared again and again in my own words. In the case of the fourth method of data gathering listed above, I compared my professor's words with my own to see where I could look at creativity and education in possibly another light in order to situate myself in a larger context of creativity and education, as well as to fine tune what I thought it was I had been saying. I interpreted the data in sections of artistic endeavours, consisting of three main categories: music, dance, and reading and writing. I finish with a final section on education, weaving it with the arts to better understand the two of them, as well as myself.

Beginning

I initially balked when my professor asked me to write a paper on how I understand the role of the arts and creativity in shaping my perception of education. An all-too familiar 'voice' in my mind suggested that I am not an artistic, creative person and could not possibly know enough about arts or creativity to write this paper.

This somewhat panic-stricken voice is very familiar to me: it's the voice that always believes everyone else knows, and I alone do not, or that all wisdom and knowledge exists outside of me. I see my experiencing of this voice as reflective of a fundamental *mis-educating* for me, and one that I suspect many people experience because of a false premise presented as true in general in society and especially in our educational systems: that we are not born knowing—that is, we are not born with what we might call an intuitive intelligence, therefore we must *listen outside of ourselves if we are to discover answers or the truth.* Yet when I examine my experiences in the context of what I think of as art, I find that there is some kind of innate knowing or intelligence within me. However, to see it requires a reframing or reimagining of what intelligence means. One of the questions that arises in this dissertation is, *How would education change if we allowed that there might be an innate intelligence within us?* And then, *What is the nature/significance/purpose of that intelligence?*

Art

For me, art is a way of *being: being as art, art as being.* A way of experiencing. When I am being creative, when I am engaging in anything I think of as art, I am also aware of a physical place of experiencing in my body; I am aware of my body when I am coming from this place of Self. (I use the capital "S" on purpose here, as I have begun to think of this aware part of me—the witness, consciousness, whomever or whatever it is—as my essential, or core, self.) When I am *being art*, I have an image of a very deep—endlessly deep—dark (that is, in appearance, not emotionally) centre within me that I locate somewhere in the vicinity of my heart. It is where I go to and simultaneously where I come from when I am being only authentically myself and where my deepest wisdom seems to be stored. I would call it a place of emptiness if it wasn't so full of something.

I think of the essence of art as I do this part of me: the psychology of *don't-know mind* as Byron Katie calls it, or how I understand *beginner's mind* from Zen Buddhism: arts as permission to explore, to question, to create, rather than to know, to answer; 'being' rather than 'doing.' It is to exist in an awareness of moments, that I know are enough, I am not supposed to be other than that which I am; there is a sense of all being well as it is. The sense of mental accumulation—adding more to my sense of self as Eckhart Tolle describes it—is entirely displaced. Being in a place of creativity is, for me, to dwell in the possibility of everything; everything is before me, and I do not know what is to come; and additionally and essentially, *I do not have a sense of needing or wanting to know.* It is a being in the moment, a trusting of life and what is to follow. There is an allowing of both things as they are and as they will be; it is a radical *being* as opposed to a *doing.* (As I read this now, years after I wrote it, it occurs to me that this is what the word "surrender" means to the spiritual teachers who employ it.)

Education, in contrast, seemed to me upon reflection to be a process of answering: of coming up with the right answer, learning the right answer, being proud of the right answer, that there *is* a right answer and that the teacher knows it and you have to find out. Education did not seem to me to be an opportunity to explore, to find out for myself. There was no sense of a personal meaning; all knowledge existed outside of me. Yet I somehow always knew, could feel it there inside me, as a kernel deep in my heart, that the most important knowledge existed inside me, and 'came out' most easily, and perhaps only, when I was engaged in something artistic. In this, 'being' is poured into 'doing' spontaneously, as a logical manifestation rather than a premeditation.

Education

What I wanted to have for myself that I never got in education growing up, I want to give to others—to all students but particularly to children. What I wanted for myself as a child of the world, as a student of life, was to be seen by the adults in my world for my own unique self, so that I felt safe to bring from inside me that which I felt was my unique, special contribution to the world. I did not know what that was per se, but I knew intuitively that I had it. It was there, in me, waiting to come forth. It did not need to be taught, it needed to be allowed. It only needed permission, and there it would be. It felt like a quality that does not need to be expressed in any one particular way and, indeed, wants to express itself in many ways. I would describe it as a certain quality that I can bring to things that is effortless, that is beautiful, timeless, creative, distinct, unquantifiable, and unpremeditated.

I felt it come out most strongly in non-language environments, when I lost 'myself' in playing the piano or guitar, or singing or dancing. It was also what resonated within me when I heard music that I found moving. It was also there when I was playing sports, some intelligence that told me where to be when, but not conceptually, not through language; it bypassed that faculty as far as I can tell.

But in school, in a world that seemed the domain of adults where they knew and we did not (unless we learned from other adults or books), I did not feel this presence. Rather, up I would go into my head where sometimes I would think so hard I got a headache. Ultimately, I felt that my head could learn and memorize and figure or analyze a tremendous amount (I was always a strong student) but that it was not my place of power. The place of power seemed to me to be in my heart which I have always thought of as my essential self, and it would come out and lead in music and sports (themselves requiring a certain kind of creativity) and dance[6]. I suspect it was also there when I was a young child, in play by myself and with others, but I do not really remember this time of my life.

Music

I came to see that music (at least, music that I found beautiful) and my essential self were in cahoots: there is a direct and close relationship there. Music is truth-revealing for me, a sort of lie detector test. For example, at a point in my early adult life, it got so that I couldn't listen to music that I found moving because I felt that it would destroy me; or, at least, that something in me would be destroyed.

Looking back on that time now, it was because there were aspects of my life that were not in alignment with who I was so I was living a lie, so-to-speak. But I didn't want to face it. There were ways that I was living that did not sit well with my essential self, and music would put the lie to all of it. I did not know that consciously at the time; all I knew was that I could not bear to listen to beautiful music. So I didn't.

Clearly, I was not yet ready to let my essential self do the talking; I was afraid of what it was going to say. So this experience makes me wonder, what is the relationship between truth and the arts? Do the arts somehow

---

[6] In his book *Waking From Sleep: Why Awakening Experiences Occur and How to Make Them Permanent* (2010), Steve Taylor is particularly interested in the glimpses of awakening many people experience during everyday life, and gives a context for what I discuss above.

allow us to tap into truth[7] or into a deeper wisdom? Is this a personal or universal truth or both? For me, when I am in my artistic self, there certainly is a deep resonance there that feels like truth. Yet, I now see that this is just where my essential self or innate intelligence was *allowed* out; it in no way needs to be relegated to these activities.

Literature

It is no surprise to me that in high school, English quickly became my favourite subject. I felt elated that my personal favourite pastime could be translated into something officially productive: reading coupled with writing was a school credit! I discovered that reflecting on the character's experiences brought out even more richness; looking for evidence to support my literary claims felt less like a chore to me and more like the solving of a mystery. It was through the reading of certain novels that I remember for the first and only time in my education that I could bring something of myself to this world of learning. I could bring my personal insights, my feelings, my thoughts, my questions ... reading was already such a deeply personal experience for me that marrying it with the scholarly was a piece of cake. What I was being rewarded for were my own unique insights. It was incredible! If only all of learning was like this! It occurred to me that I could find answers inside me (as opposed to some outside authority, as in the rest of my classes) by relating my experience to those of the characters I was studying. I understood on some level that this was about me, about human nature (though I don't recall this being expressly stated by the teacher) and that there was nothing more important to learn about than myself as a human being, albeit a unique one (as we all are). I felt like I was reading secrets about life and happiness, encrypted on the page for me to decipher.

---

[7] An exploration into the nature of truth is obviously fraught with difficulty and while I go into the experiencing of it in this book, discussing it in the context of its description in the literature is largely beyond the scope of this book.

I went on to major in English literature concurrently with education at university, having known intuitively without ever being told directly that novels and poetry, while fictional, represented truth in more of a direct, accessible way than a non-fiction book of description ever could. It is only recently that I see why this could be so: art seems to bypass the conceptual faculty within our brains, to communicate a truth directly as opposed to mediated through concepts.

I thrilled at what I was reading. I could not believe that such personal, intimate feelings of mine were clearly felt by others, and even more than that, these authors were able to use a story or a word to convey the experiences so accurately. I felt understood and a little less alone in the world. Taking English courses was a study in life and myself and a chance to share myself with the world while learning about how others see it.

Yet despite doing my education degree simultaneously with my Bachelor of Arts degree, I don't remember consciously connecting the two domains. That is my task now, as I use autobiographical narrative to explore the connection between the two, which is really a connection within myself.

As Researcher

So what? What do these recollections and relationships have to do with me as a researcher? In short: everything. The research I am interested in is holistic education, which is education tending to the whole person and, in particular, how that education can help students know for themselves who they are; in my experience, it is our own experience that holds the truth— *is education helping us to listen to our experience?* In this, I see students' gateway to freedom, their gateway to choose, for it is only in understanding themselves both as a result of their conditioning, and as separate from it, that they are free to choose. So it is with me: this narrative is a process whereby I am unhooking myself from my conditioning. I am seeing that it has been 'I' all along who is enacting, and reacting to, my experiences. I am unravelling for myself that which I would like to see students being asked— being allowed—to do in education, starting with being facilitated in the story of 'self': *Where has my story of my self come from? What is the relationship between thought and emotion and experience? (As in, do my thoughts create my experience?) Where do thoughts come from? Do I choose my thoughts? What effect do thoughts have on me? Who am I without my thoughts? What is the significance of this?* In other words, I want the elephant in the room revealed: *What the heck are we all doing here? What is it all about?*

I was always perplexed over why this subject in school was either: 1) so taboo or 2) never crossed the mind of a single teacher I had in over twenty years of schooling (which I find highly unlikely). What else could possibly matter until we answer the two basic questions: *Who am I* and *What is life?* Or is it enough just to be able to ask them, to inquire into them? And who can ask and answer these for us but ourselves? This book is my attempt at 1) inquiring into these questions and 2) inquiring into what would happen when we allow students to inquire into them.

I want students to see their wholeness so that they live joyous and fulfilled lives into adulthood—because I think we can, and most people haven't been able to sustain the joy they feel naturally as children. I feel the secret lies somewhere in self-understanding, or self-knowledge, which in turn leads to knowing another, to knowing life. It is a bridge-building of communication. It is a deep connection with self, other, and life that is joy and fulfillment incarnate. It only makes sense to me that it must be this way. I know intuitively, I suppose, but it is also logical: as Byron Katie points out, in her experience what opposes truth feels bad to us and what is true feels good. Perhaps because it is too simple, this fact is overlooked. Perhaps our emotions are not something to be overcome or suppressed, but to be used as guidance that we are believing something that is not true for us. Which is why as a researcher I am also interested in studying intuition, because it seems related to, if not the same as, this innate intelligence which produces our emotions; logically, it is also likely the same thing as truth and the essential self, everything I have been talking about in this narrative that informs my sense of myself and life. Can we teach how to identify this source of intelligence, or intuition? Are students who are involved regularly with the arts more in tune with their intuition? If so, how are they served by it? And what does it have to do with our consciousness? Are they perhaps brother and sister—intuition and consciousness—separate but intimately related? Does an expanded sense of self mean an expanded consciousness and vice versa?

My research undertakings are to make me whole or, to help me to finally see that I am already whole, that I have always been. I have been aware of this personal motivation in my scholarship. I enrolled in graduate school in education precisely because I realized that everything I was interested in in life was education. *(What is it that we need to know to live glorious lives? Who are we really and why are we here and how do we find out?* Isn't education, after all, supposed to be about setting students up to succeed in the world, and to give to it, armed with the skills and knowledge they have acquired?) I was reading book after book and making notes in most of my spare time, when it occurred to me that I was probably an example of a person who undertakes a graduate degree, that I would just be getting acknowledged with a degree for what I was already doing. I have questions about my own life and education that perhaps through the asking and answering of, may serve others as well as myself.

So my personal motivation to become whole or to see my wholeness so I can enjoy myself and life fully, drives my scholarship. And this, this is what I want to give to children. In fact, I'd rather they never start thinking they aren't whole or complete. I'd rather they were celebrated in all their wholeness from the start: perfect as they are and becoming more, just as I am, but never this sense of 'not-enoughness,' never quite arriving.

Chapter 2

It is up to each of you to work out your own liberation.

Siddhārtha Gautama

~

Introduction

In the preface to her book, scholar Frances Vaughn (1979, v) explains something that I can certainly relate to and applies particularly to this section of the book. (While Vaughn is referring to just "intuition," in my case I would expand this to refer to "consciousness"):

> Writing a book about intuition is truly paradoxical. Others, wiser than I, have rejected the impossible task of translating intuitive learning into the rational, linear language of words. But despite the fact that musicians, artists, poets, and others who use nonverbal forms of expression give more direct access to intuitive ways of knowing, many of us persistently feel the urge to communicate our experience, and attempt to use words to do so.

I do think there is a place for words, despite that to ultimately 'understand' (which is not to say cognizing), we need to transcend language. I have endeavored to stay as close to my own experience as possible in order to avoid temptation to move into interpretations and therefore abstract concepts. I think this offers the best chance to the reader to grasp what I am saying by relating it to her/his own experience (which is to say, transcending language and language-mediated experience). However, in giving detailed descriptions of my experience, I also explain why something is happening, taking us into concepts, something that seems to me unavoidable.

I write the autoethnography framed with the following claims, intending to connect my experience to the broader one of the purpose and potential of education:

1. Education focuses on training the intellect (or solely the left brain), which:

   a) intensifies mind identification, and

   b) ignores the (transcendent, or 'real') Self, or larger consciousness

2. Education is lacking the clear intention of educating for creative problem-solving (which is the logical outcome of educating for giving the tools and knowledge that children need, to both succeed in the world and become positive contributing members of society)

3. Creativity does not arise out of the intellect but out of the Self, or pure consciousness.

Part 1 *The Enlightenment Intensive*: Direct Versus Conceptual Experience

It has been my experience that reading academic work with the purpose of trying to understand all of what we might call the thought systems or knowledge structures which scholars have created, named, and organized throughout recorded human history, takes me out of presence and moves me further from actual, deep, and true understanding. It seems that what is happening is that I am trying to absorb and make sense of a sort of 'false' knowledge, an arrangement of concepts that don't have any basis in reality, only in conceptual reality. This knowledge is based on assigning names to things, after all, and the names, while perhaps not arbitrary, are not real things. So this insight, then, prompts the inquiry: *What* is *true, actual, deep understanding or knowing (versus conceptual knowing)? What does this experience/insight mean for education?*

I believe I have gotten a taste of reality beyond a conceptual reality on a few different occasions (in addition, it seems that I am experiencing a gradual expansion of my consciousness over time, as I engage in contemplative practices and inquiry.) Over four days during Labour Day weekend in 2007 I participated in something the facilitator called the "Enlightenment Intensive." It is a process of deep inquiry and contemplation, whereby the participants respond to essential questions such as: *Who am I?* and *What is life?* among others. The brief, introductory description Noyes[8] gives on his website is as follows:

> The Enlightenment Intensive is a modern answer to the question, "Where can I go to directly experience the true nature of life, others and my self?" With one foot rooted in the ancient tradition of Rinzai Zen and the other in the modern dyad process of communication, the Enlightenment Intensive is a three-day retreat capable of producing deep spiritual awakenings at the core.
>
> Not a seminar, a religion or an indoctrination, the Enlightenment Intensive is a total support system for you to make your own inner journey, at your own pace, into the nature of reality.
>
> The enlightenment discussed in this book is a unique condition of direct, conscious experience that reveals in an instant of penetration of our ultimate nature. This experience goes completely beyond our personality, our body, our problems, and our ideas about ourselves. It is a transformative union of self and truth that is not an insight or even an intuition. Its nature lies outside the realm of our thinking and sensing processes. Yet it is real. And it is the condition that evolves consciousness at the core, revealing the inner splendor of the true self in ways that must be seen and experienced to be appreciated.

---

[8] Noyes studied with the originator of this contemplative process, Charles Berner.

In the introduction to the book, he explains the intensive is "a unique method for transcending the morass of the intellect and directly experiencing into the ultimate reality" (1998).

I was attracted to the process by one statement in the promotional email: something to the effect of, "You have read about the spiritual experiences of enlightened masters through the ages—now experience it directly for yourself. Instead of reading it in books, you will have your own *direct experience* of yourself and the truth."

What did that mean, a *direct experience*? At the time that I read that statement, I was long familiar (intellectually, anyway) with Krishnamurti's idea that we live through concepts; in other words, how we experience reality is mediated through conditioned thought. We never experience life directly.

So, for example, Krisnamurti explains how no two people have ever met, because our images of ourselves meet the images we have of the other and vice versa. This wouldn't be a problem (people could go on living happily ever after, deceptively) except that it always is a problem—untruth, it seems, breeds problems. Only the truth (of anyone, anything) seems to contain its own inherent order. False reality seems to breed conflict.

What I had come to realize, however, was that understanding intellectually that I live through concepts and don't experience life, or myself, or others directly, does not in itself, of course, produce the opposite experience (i.e. of experiencing life directly).

This might seem like an obvious statement, but this in fact is what the whole of our education system and indeed, societal structures depend— that knowing something intellectually, is the same thing as knowing it directly, or that we can somehow arrive at truth through intellectual understanding. Consider Tolle (1999):

> Until you practice surrender, the spiritual dimension is something you read about, talk about, get excited about, write books about, think about, believe in—or don't, as the case may be. It makes no difference. Not until you surrender does the spiritual dimension become a living

reality in your life. When you do, the energy that you emanate and
that then runs your life is of a much higher vibrational frequency
than the mind energy that still runs our world. (pp.122-123)

I went to the *Enlightenment Intensive* to find out what, if possible, it
is to directly experience something, instead of experiencing things once
removed through the intellect. Though I have since come to experience
surrender, then it was completely foreign to me.

I have been reluctant to speak about my experience at the *Enlightenment
Intensive*, never mind write about it. I felt that I had experienced something
profound but I knew that unless people have experienced something
similar, or at the very least read accounts of what I might call "spiritual
insights," they would have no context with which to understand my
experience; I knew I was likely to be dismissed for being capricious or
deluded. On the one hand, it is nice knowing that there are others who
seem to have experienced what I experienced. On the other hand, I notice
that the experience itself seems to sustain me—in other words, it is enough
for me to know what I experienced; it is self-validating and self-supporting.
In any event, I need to articulate it here because it has direct bearing on this
research. However, in my view, it is impossible to truly understand what I
will describe below unless one experiences it for oneself, in the same way
as one couldn't 'understand' bike-riding until one rode a bike oneself. The
map is not the territory.

After the first enlightenment intensive, I ended up doing two more
intensives over the next three years, as the first experience was so
profound. Although all three experiences were profound, the first one was
significantly so, given that it was the first time in my conscious memory
that I experienced myself—life—*directly*.

The inquiry process of the *Enlightenment Intensive* is a type of intense
contemplation, in that the participant contemplates a question, given in
the form of an instruction by another participant. For example, the first
question I worked on was *Who am I?* given to me by random participants

(who were paired with me at the time) over the course of the four days as: "Tell me who you are." The question I worked on for my second Enlightenment Intensive was *What is mind?* and for the third intensive I chose *What is life?* The schedule is gruelling: the participants do not know the time of day throughout the whole process (watches and clocks are removed), but find out afterwards that we engage in the "dyads" (as these paired inquiries are called) from 6am to 11pm every day, and are even instructed to contemplate our question as we are falling asleep. The format was refined over time by its originator Charles Berner through trial and error in order to facilitate the greatest chance of awakening to the truth. The arduous process is designed, in my experience, to have people confront in full consciousness who or what they *think* they are and open them to the possibility that this may not be true—in other words, that they have been 'asleep,' living out a *story* of their lives rather than living out the truth of their being.

The participants are given specific instructions as to what to do both when they are the receiver or "speaking partner" of the instruction and when they are the giver of the instruction, or "the listening partner." These instructions are essential but can be difficult to grasp and most participants need to be guided with reminders before they truly grasp what it is they are supposed to do and not do. Besides the initial instructions and demonstration of "the techniques" the facilitator gives a talk every afternoon to guide the participant to a proper understanding of the technique.

The technique itself is relatively simple: partners are to remain in eye contact the whole time, except when the contemplating partner closes his or her eyes to contemplate the question. Even then, the listening partner keeps her or his full attention on her or his partner. Both partners are to avoid any facial expression or nodding or shaking of the head, etc. which can subtly influence and distract the speaking partner. The partner who is receiving the question closes her eyes upon hearing the question and notices what occurs—it could be an image, body sensation, or something else—and then *intends* to directly experience what that *is*.

For example, if an image of a spider occurs (as it did for me), the person in contemplation would simply intend to experience what that image of the spider is. (Of course, this is where the challenge lies, because this is a brand-new 'idea,' never mind experience, for most of us, and the only way to find out what to do is by doing it.) And then once more, notice what occurs.

Once the contemplator has been in contemplation for a short time—usually less than two minutes—she opens her eyes and does her best to get across what she experienced/is experiencing; her goal is to get the listening partner to fully understand what it was she experienced in contemplation. For the listening partner's part, he had to try his best to fully understand and when he felt he had, he would say, "Thank you," nothing more, and the partners would change roles.

Participants would remain in silence throughout the four days, whenever they were not speaking in the dyad; this was to keep the focus on contemplation and not in any way on socializing. In most cases, by the end of the four days we did not know each other's names, but we came to know the most painful and intimate details of each other's lives and had been moved to tears and laughter (to say the least) together many, many times.

The pairs of people are seated in two rows facing one another. They are only about two feet apart across, and the neighbouring chair is only one foot beside each partner. As a result, everyone can hear what everyone else is saying in the room.

At first this was very distracting, but I could eventually see its purpose: often people will have an experience (ex. perhaps a painful emotion came up that they had to communicate to their partner, which they do through sobbing or even screaming, on the far end of the scale) that will trigger someone else's fear or pain in the group and this in turn will be brought up and out to communicate to their partner. It seems to me to be an effective tool for expediting a process of someone confronting all of what is within them that they are afraid to face.

Peter Ralston's instructions below of seeking truth (Winter 2012 Cheng Hsin newsletter; he is not referring to the *Enlightenment Intensive*, although he did participate in at least one himself several years ago at the beginning of his own awakening journey) is a helpful context:

> Questioning serves to lead us to the truth. It is always appropriate. The truth is what is. Directly experiencing this, no question needs to be asked. If there is a question then something is still unknown, isn't it? And there is always something still unknown. The goal is to be conscious of what's true; the goal isn't to be certain about some conclusion or other. (p.16)
>
> Remember, it's not useful to believe anything I've said. It is only useful to experientially understand it. These matters are very challenging to understand because you can only experience them directly. It can't be figured out through logic or found within any knowledge. (p.23)
>
> Don't extrapolate. If you think something is true, then go there and experience the truth for yourself. Otherwise, it is merely an intellectual exercise and doesn't count. Don't imagine what's true, experience what's true. (p.25)

Who Am I?

You are what exists before all stories.
You are what remains when the story is understood.

Byron Katie

At one point—perhaps the second day in—what started to become obvious to me was that many participants were telling the 'story of themselves' in response to the question "Who am I?" (Tell me who you are). It was a retelling of their personal history—all the drama and pain. Hearing their past started to make less and less sense in relation to the question of who they are that it became almost comical to me as an observer, except that in most cases it was the story of their painful past that they were caught in which produced both fear and compassion in me.

Despite seeing that people were just telling stories and that this couldn't possibly be who they are, I was apparently no exception. When receiving the question, most often a body sensation or image would take me into the painful parts of my past and despite a great reluctance on my part, I followed the instructions given to me and got this pain across to my partner, which usually included a recounting of the original pain-causing event. The process was tremendously difficult psychologically, emotionally, and physically and had I known what I was getting into, I probably would not have done the Enlightenment Intensive. (Not surprisingly, all of the participants I spoke to afterwards felt this way). Thankfully, I didn't know and so didn't stop myself from going resulting in a profound, 'mystical' experience.

Of course, the process is intended for people to experience truth, not just— or necessarily—pain, but by the end of the four days (the dyad process itself is three full days, followed by an integration day) I could see that it seemed necessary for people to clear the pain in order to access the truth. Once it was up and out—or perhaps it was just that participants were ready to move out of their stories—they began to have what I would call mystical experiences.

The way it happened for me, was I was actually in the midst of great pain, from what felt like tremendous fear and anxiety that I had carried around my whole life. I can recall crying, in great distress, when an image of a small white daisy appeared to me and as I was trying to get across—through tears of awe—the absolute pure beauty and perfection of this flower to my partner, one of the staff monitors who was crouched by my chair asked me, *"What is that flower?"* to which it became immediately obvious that that flower was *me*. I could see that the attributes I ascribed to this thing we call "daisy" were my own—beauty, sacredness, simplicity, etc. And not just this, but in fact that I *was* the daisy. I didn't understand this cognitively but the need for cognitive understanding at that point was gone. It was really just self-evident that I was looking at myself in the mirror of the daisy.

I was filled with such awe and amazement. The best words I can find to describe it is that I merged with myself—I was no longer in some sort of 'outside' looking 'in' but was rooted right behind my eyes. Veltheim (2000) encapsulates the experience precisely for me: "...there is no longer the experience of parallel worlds. It can almost seem as if something has been lost. This is because the sense of a witness, or parallel worlds has stopped" (p. 201).

Furthermore, I was aware that this is where I had been the whole time—my whole life—that I somehow had separated myself from this 'looking' apparatus ages ago and then experienced life and myself once removed. (I tried being my mind, is what it was.) But in that moment—and it continued for that night and the next day before it gradually began to diminish—I was not separate, I was fully integrated, whole. In this state, I knew I was perceiving accurately; there was a deep sense of peace as if I had finally, after all this time and all this separation and searching, found my home and could rest there. It was like heaving a great sigh and knowing all was really well with me and the world.

It was such a simple and obvious truth in those moments, that I was amazed I could ever separate from myself as I do. The monitor asked my partner to again give me the instruction: "*Tell me who you are*," she said. "*I am me,*" I responded, "*Kathryn.*" There was no mistaking it. There was nothing else to say, no elaboration necessary. I was what we call a "*Kathryn*" and it was perfect in its obviousness and simplicity.* I had no need to be different from that which I was—there was none of that present. It would have been inconceivable because—despite the inherent perfection—it was so obviously not even possible. The monitor laughed. I laughed. "*Are you sure,*" she asked, playfully. "*Yes,*" I responded. The truth, apparently, is hidden in plain sight.

This fact is captured by spiritual teacher Adyashanti when he writes: "The plot twist changes. But underlying that, something is the same,

---

* I would, a few days later, describe myself as "a unique manifestation of all that is."

and as far back as you can remember....You think that enlightenment is something other than what is happening right now. This is your primary mistake." Veltheim (2000, p. 181) describes it in the following way:

> The only constant you know, that no-one has ever had to prove to you, or teach you, is the knowing "I am."
>
> *The sense "I am" is the only constant, unchanging experience you have ever known. Just because you have added labels to it ("I am in pain." "I am lonely"), you think the experience of Being changes. All that has been changing are the labels you have added. In order to experience these labels, the sense of being is necessary.* (italics hers)

Tolle, on his website, gives a description while speaking to an audience that captures the insight that I came upon through contemplating the question *Who Am I?*

> Who are you really, beyond the story of your life, beyond your personal history. Who am I really? There's no conceptual answer—would be just another thought—but direct realization. And suddenly there's the space of open, spacious awareness in which you don't seem to know anything anymore. You can look at the world in absolute innocence and see its beauty and aliveness and miraculousness without calling it even beauty and aliveness. You merge with whatever you perceive because the . . . Considering yourself to be a separate entity, this delusion was created by compulsive, unconscious, continuous mental interpretations and labellings and judgements—so-called knowledge, opinions. ...Spacious awareness replaces, so-to-speak, compulsive thinking. And that's enormous liberation, to realize that dimension in yourself. You're liberated from the person, the thinker, the me, the troublemaker, the problem maker, the one who dwells in almost continuous discontentment, non-fulfillment and anxiety and fear.

Tolle also explains how much courage it takes to be willing to let go of what we think we know: this, it turns out, is the 'death' that we are all afraid of rather than the death of the body (which we think is one and the same as the person). In fact, our real fear is the death of our identity with all our stories/concepts, which is the paradox in that it never existed in the first place. It is the death of who we think we are, and what we think we know.

I certainly felt fear on a level as if I was dying. It really is to jump out of an airplane without a parachute: by definition, leaving the known *means* the mind has no anchor anymore, no ground. The mind is no longer the centre and it experiences this as its death. The new cannot come in until dis-identification has happened; yet, the mind would like it otherwise—it would like there to be a replacement before it feels safe enough to disembark. However, the thing is, *it* cannot *do* the disembarking; it is the 'one' that needs disembarking *from*.

> But you have to have the courage...to go to that place of—what looks like from an external, habitual, mental viewpoint—where you don't know anything anymore because the compulsive interpretations have dissolved. ...continuous conceptualization of reality, compulsive conceptualization of reality, a deadening habit.
>
> To know that you are, to know it *directly*, is joyful. So to know your being, is joyful—just the fact of being.

So, for a period of time (a day or so) following this awakening experience, I experienced what Tolle describes above. What felt as remarkable as what I was experiencing is what I was not experiencing, what was gone from my experience.

I felt extremely light; I wasn't dragging along with me any thoughts about the past or future, trying to analyze or make sense of anything. And in this altered state, I was able to see how compulsively I do this. Normally, this is hidden from my view. For Tolle (2004, p.xii), his experience of this remained, so complete was his transformation of consciousness.

I understood that the intense pressure of suffering that night must have forced my consciousness to withdraw from its identification with the unhappy and deeply fearful self, which is ultimately a fiction of the mind....What was left then was my true nature as the ever-present *I am*; consciousness in its pure state prior to identification with form.

Later on, during the remaining time in the workshop-retreat—a day or so—my awareness of myself seemed to deepen. I particularly remember walking in the woods in the sunshine and being absolutely amazed I had use of this body. It was completely obvious to me that I was not my body but I was overjoyed I got to *use* it. Again, a passage of Tolle's describes my experience well:

The key is here...Another word for presence is the alertness. And so you become alert also within. You feel the aliveness of your inner body. Rather than having a mental concept of who you are, you feel the entire energy field, that which animates the physical form, and you are in touch with that.

My hands were of immense fascination and I turned them this way and that, noticing how 'I' could make them move! This 'I' is what I might describe as an energy field larger than my body (but I don't know beyond that). It seemed a miracle. In addition, the duality consciousness that I had always unknowingly experienced as my perceived reality disappeared, as Tolle also descriptively relates below:

...For the first time, I could walk, I could Be, without having a relationship with myself. And that—there is something so precious in that I or presence, so...it's beyond words, it's like a diamond—very, very precious. ....but this is not comparative....It knows itself to be that in a non-dualistic way without needing to compare itself to others—it has nothing to do with a form or any mind-form. ...So then suddenly you don't love yourself anymore nor do you hate yourself because there's no self to love; there's simply the state of this, which is love. It emanates.

Also, a few years later, I found a passage in neuroscientist Jill Bolte Taylor's book (2006, p.171) that echoed my experience perfectly. (Note: "right mind" refers to the right hemisphere of her brain vs. her left. I will explain this particular context further on.)

> If I had to choose one word to describe the feeling I feel at the core of my right mind, I would have to say *joy*. My right mind is thrilled to be alive! I experience a feeling of awe when I consider that I am simultaneously capable of being at *one* with the universe, while having an individual identity whereby I move into the world and manifest positive change.

I, too, felt both at one with all that is, but also somehow a unique being—me. This is a paradox to the mind, but it was certainly experience-able, for both me and Bolte Taylor. In retrospect, I realize it was/is the perfect set-up: I got to still be 'me'—i.e. a unique entity and therefore able to encounter other unique beings but at the same time I was unified with all that is—so, both a feeling of individuality and unity. I felt such graciousness at being able to experience both in the same moment—all at once. It seemed my heart had craved this sense of homecoming all my life, this exact coinciding of experiences. It occurs to me that it's ironic that the mind fears this dissolution of identity when in fact it gets to have a sense of identity after all, but one that is so much more than the story we concoct about ourselves.

In the remaining dyads, I was joyful and full of laughter. In the process, images would come to me like a tree, and a frog, and as I intended to fully experience them and then get them across to my partners, it became apparent that I was all of these things too. I was the tremendous strength of that tall, perfectly straight and persevering pine tree. I seemed to be able to 'inhabit,' to be, any being that came into my mind as well as the inherent qualities they possessed. The information about what these images represented—what they are capable of symbolizing in the human consciousness, things like strength and playfulness and most of all beingness—came out as I was speaking to my partner, *despite my not knowing that I knew this information or even knew I was going to say it before saying it*. I knew for the first time what it meant to be using words that were not from thought, not from memory. I can't emphasize enough how extraordinary this realization was. The talking seemed to come first, and then the knowing. There was no premeditation; I did not experience the concepts 'in my head' (i.e. stored in memory) from which I then spoke. It was more like I was watching myself knowing, after I heard myself speak the words. Again, this is tremendously difficult to describe. So, this, then was knowing without knowing how or that I knew—or, knowing without concepts.

By way of a post-mortem of what I would call an 'awakening experience,' I would say that my central dilemma and impediment to experiencing pure Being in advance of, and during, this workshop-retreat was this idea that I had to get rid of something in order to experience it. And as hard as I tried, 'I' couldn't seem to accomplish it. Veltheim (2000, p.185) addresses this in the subsequent way:

> Don't fixate on the idea that the "me" must fall away before you can Know who you are. Rather, understand that it is unreal—an appearance only. Then ask, "Who is having this understanding?" This changes your entire focus because you are not trying to rid yourself of something that isn't there.
>
> When the "me" identity is exposed as false, your natural personality traits are expressed minus censorship.

And

> The "me" is the false self—an illusion—un-real. This faulty perception cannot be recognized by the "me." That's because it *is* the faulty perception. The cat you think you are in a dream has to disappear before you remember who you are. The cat doesn't realize it isn't you.
>
> The trouble is, this pseudo-identity wants to—and thinks it can—awaken.

Veltheim continues: "The Knowing of your true nature is already there, but like some deeply buried treasure, you need first to uncover it. Your beliefs and accumulation of knowledge obscure the treasure of who You are. The question to ask is, "Who is experiencing this delusion?" (2000, p.186). When I ask this of myself (which is to say my intellect because it is the default answering mechanism) now as I write this in 2011, I literally feel as though my brain is bending back on itself trying to look at itself—as if it's seeking to step outside itself to get an objective view—in order to answer the question. I *feel* its inability to do this—it feels like feeling limited, trapped. The question forces 'me' out of the perceiver, which is this mind. It can't answer these types of questions, for it can't seem to *see* outside itself—outside, to the 'who.' On the other hand, when I ask the question "Who is having this understanding?" or "Who is experiencing this delusion?" and just watch—that is, just let the question float there and not try to answer it—what seems to happen is the 'who' falls away and there is only 'understanding' left. That is, there is no separation between the 'understanding" and the 'understood' because there isn't a perceiver anymore—no perceiving vehicle. Just perceiving—raw, just the act of seeing. I believe this is what Krishnamurti meant when he said,

> You must ask questions, not only of the speaker but of yourself, which is far more important….Question that and find out the answer; and you cannot find out the answer by asking another. You see, you have to stand alone, completely alone, which doesn't mean you become isolated. Because you are alone then you will know what it means to live purely. Therefore you must endlessly ask questions. And the more you ask of yourself, do not try to find an answer but ask and look. Ask and look and when you ask there must be care, there must be affection, there must be love in your asking of yourself, not beating yourself with questions. (p.109)

So, asking and allowing rather than asking and thinking brings about a whole new depth of awareness that the intellect alone can never touch.

The 'looking' is a noticing of what's true—this is the "intelligence" of which Eckhart and Krishnamurti speak. To me, the "love" Krishnamurti talks about is really an absence of attachment, noticing that any attachment to a concept hurts. It's freedom from this that is love. The "aloneness" is being free from anyone's influence, which is to say concepts, including one's own.

What is Mind?

My left mind thinks of me as a fragile individual capable of losing my life. My right mind realizes that the essence of my being has eternal life.

Jill Bolte Taylor

During my second *Enlightenment Intensive*, instead of intending to directly experience *Who I Am*, I instead inquired into "*What is mind.*" It was my intention to directly experience that which we call "mind" for myself. Three insights in particular seemed quite profound both at the time and since, and they have stayed with me in my awareness. The first was when an image arose in my mind's eye (in response to my partner's instruction, "Tell me what mind is") of what I saw as a "file clerk." She was a very well-intentioned, very determined-to-please assistant to me who was ready, at the drop of a hat, to respond to any situation I met in life (and every moment is a situation) by pulling on one or more of her files. The files stretched to eternity as far as I could tell. Immediately I knew that what she was doing was preparing me to meet any new situation with old information: whatever I encountered, she would pull the file on the closest things (i.e. that resembled this new situation) that I had previously encountered in order to protect me from any possible danger resulting from not being prepared or accustomed to what I was facing. She was very endearing, this file clerk, working so hard as she does to perform well and please. She seemed tireless, strictly existing to serve. So it was clear to me in that moment that a part of the mind's function (at least, according to itself) is to try to keep us psychologically and physically safe by storing information (and this could be the collective (un)conscious(ness) that both Krishnamurti and Jung refer to, and not just our personal life history/experiences) and then using that information to meet or mediate life however it arises for us. In this, I encountered directly for myself what Krishnamurti means when he says that the mind can never meet life anew for its very nature—its very make-up—*is* the old (or the catalogued).

Bolte Taylor confirms my, and K's[9], insight. In her experience, the cataloguer is found in—or is—the left hemisphere of the brain.

> Along with thinking in language, our left hemisphere thinks in patterned responses to incoming stimulation. It establishes neurological circuits that run relatively automatically to sensory information.
>
> ….Because our left brain is filled with these ingrained programs of pattern recognition, it is superb at predicting what we will think, how we will act, or what we will feel in the future—based upon our past experience" (pp.31-33).

This precisely describes what I experienced and somehow knew as revealed through the file clerk image. The question is where this image came from; the wonder is that it appeared at all.

The second image that arose was very similar in its feeling to that of the file clerk: I 'watched' (i.e. internally) as I handed a sweet, young schoolboy, wearing a cute, little school uniform, the equation "$E=mc^2$" and he, too, so eager to please, immediately took the sheet of paper and sat down at his desk to go to work on solving it. Again I immediately saw the absurdity of asking such a young mind to answer such a complex problem. The meaning of the metaphor became clear at once: I was asking my mind to

---

[9] Krishnamurti was regularly referred to as "K," and I use it sometimes out of sheer laziness to write out his whole name.

do things it was never intended for, things like seeing clearly and finding the meaning of life. It would try its hardest in a desire to serve to its utmost capacity, but it could never succeed at such monumental tasks. I was overcome with such love and tenderness and compassion for this wee little aspect of myself that was so willing to work very hard on my behalf at something far beyond its capability, that I was moved to tears after laughing in amazement at this direct experience of mind. Even more, I had come to vilify in some respects my mind—this thing that I saw as preventing me from attaining a realization of my true nature, that kept me stuck in the same ways of thinking and attending to life such that I was unable to mold life, and especially my reactions to it, in the ways that I wanted to. For example, my tendency to be fearful in life and carry around a daily tension that something awful was in store for me I saw as the result of thoughts I kept thinking that I could not untangle myself from. While I was right about this, what I did not see was that this was happening because I was giving my mind the task of freeing me from this fear and did not see, until this moment in the dyad process, that this was something it could never do. In other words, the mind has done its job perfectly to the fullest of its ability and is *neither* the villain we have made it out to be (which could be summed up by the disdainfulness that the word "ego"—which is attributed to Freud but has enjoyed particular attention in popular culture in recent years—has come to be associated with), nor the hero we have made it out to be in education and beyond, believing that it is *thought* that will save us from our most dire problems. I think this is an extremely important point.

Throughout my explanation to my partner of what I was experiencing, I found myself gesturing up at the left side of my head—it seemed as though this aspect had something to do with that area of my brain. Given that my hand was up unpremeditatedly points to my knowing somehow that indeed these aspects of my mind were actually physically expressing through the left hemisphere of my brain corroborating Bolte Taylor's claim.

The third profound insight-as-experience that arose in me—again in response to the instruction, "Tell me what mind is"—was words. I don't recall now if they came as an image of the words or an actual hearing of them, a feeling or simply a knowing. (In the literature, these are skills known as *clairvoyance, clairaudience, and clairsentience* and *claircognizance* respectfully.) It was of someone whom I took to be the most benevolent, most loving father[10] I could ever fathom. It immediately occurred to me that what I was experiencing was what some people have in mind when they say "God." It loved me so much, in fact, that I noticed (in my internal vision) that it was just an essence, a presence—a sort of 'allowing factor' that made experience possible—that nodded its head, "yes," "yes," "yes" to everything and anything I asked to experience—even experiences we would call negative or painful. It was precisely *because* it was so pure in its love, that it did not constrict me whatsoever; it was as if my wish was its command.

I found this incredibly profound—here, indeed, was pure love: that life became all up to me, that I was the total and complete controller of my life experience, even if that meant choosing events that would ultimately cause severe anguish. I saw it as the essence of freedom and what might be called "free will" that is debated in philosophical and religious contexts. I later discovered Veltheim's work and a passage in alignment with my own experience:

> When it is said that "God Is Love," the word love signifies neutrality. It has nothing to do with the opposite of hate. God is just another word for neutrality, and neutrality denotes "not helping or supporting either of two opposing sides." God recognizes no "other"—only "you" continue to think in terms of me, God, and others.

I experienced the neutrality as "yes, yes, yes" in the *Enlightenment Intensive*. Also a few years after this *Enlightenment Intensive*, I discovered Byron Katie's books and came across a passage that reads: "It becomes a

---

[10] I'm not sure why this 'essence' came to me as male in some way, yet that is my recollection. Even still, I refer to it as 'it' rather than 'he.'

thing that's timeless, because when you're opening to that, there's no time and space in it. It's just a "Yes. Yes. Yes." That's why I say boundaries are an act of selfishness. I don't have any" (2007b, p.186). I was amazed to discover that Katie describes it *exactly* as I'd experienced it. Katie has also described God as "reality" "because it rules" (personal communication, March 2013). In other words, reality is as it is—it doesn't wait for anyone's permission or acceptance. Krishnamurti also uses the words God and reality interchangeably (1953, p.109). He also uses God interchangeably with "creation" and "truth" (1953, p.113) which is something I now understand for myself.

I found—during my attempt to get my experience across to my partner—that my hand involuntarily was gesturing up around the right side of my head. And I found myself saying that this was where this essence resides—on the right side of the brain. Again, some years later, I came across Jill Bolte Taylor's book, *My Stroke of Insight*, where she incredibly describes her personal experience of being in the process of a stroke that occurred in the left hemisphere of her brain, ostensibly shutting down that half, leaving only the right brain functioning. Hence, she was able to have a direct experience of the role and capability of the right hemisphere of her brain. She became the science experiment by experiencing herself through the lens of only the right hemisphere, and through this, she was also able to realize what it is that both hemispheres do. She describes herself being in pure bliss, pure love, where she was quite literally not separate from anything she was perceiving; she was just energy as were those objects around her. Like me, she experienced the miracle of herself by being able to move her fingers around—simply that:

> Instead of finding answers and information, I met a growing sense of peace. In place of that constant chatter that had attached me to the details of my life, I felt enfolded by a blanket of tranquil euphoria....As the language centres in my left hemisphere grew increasingly silent and I became detached from the memories of my

life, I was comforted by an expanding sense of grace. In this void of higher cognition and details pertaining to my normal life, my consciousness soared into an all-knowingness, a "being at *one*" with the universe, if you will.

...I found it odd that I was aware that I could no longer clearly discern the physical boundaries of where I began and where I ended. I sensed the composition of my being as that of a fluid rather than that of a solid. I no longer perceived myself as a whole object separate from everything. Instead, I now blended in with the space and flow around me.

...As I held my hands up in front of my face and wiggled my fingers, I was simultaneously perplexed and intrigued. *Wow, what a strange and amazing thing I am. What a bizarre living being I am. Life! I am life!....Here, in this form, I am a conscious mind and this body is the vehicle through which I am ALIVE! I am trillions of cells sharing a common mind. I am here, now, thriving as life. Wow! What an unfathomable concept!* (pp.30-31, italics hers)

Knowing nothing about the right and left brains previously (beyond that the left is considered logical, and the right creative), I was astounded to see that Taylor's descriptions of the right and left brains from her own personal experience, exactly matched mine. I would sum up Taylor's book as primarily a firsthand account of the power and purpose of the right hemisphere of our brain, which seems to be the perceiving mechanism and therefore connects us to the whole in any situation. Aligning with, or allowing, the right hemisphere's awareness shifts our focus away from "the churning loops of our left cognitive mind" (p.169). In other words, her book is about leading us out of immersion in the world of thought, into the world of experience and intuition which has been left out in our society's (and therefore education's) obsession with the conceptual, analytical world of form.

Self-described spiritual researcher and writer Melody Beattie (1998, p.36) describes an identical experience of heightened perception to that of Taylor's that revealed the energetic essence of our world and its seamlessness: "... [W]hat once appeared as solid...all began to weave together into one vibrating energy field....I saw the energy grid of all that is. It was a living, vibrating energy....It even permeated the space between objects....Life and I were really one." This is something, then, that can be experienced in normal waking consciousness.

Of course, in all three instances listed above in my personal experience, there is no empirical 'proof' that what I experienced were the two aspects of mind just because they seemed to arise in response to the instruction, "Tell me what mind is." The only 'proof' I can offer is my own experience of where these images came from or how they occurred: and that is, that I was not *thinking* about them. I was not purposely putting forth any willed effort towards a response, and I had not had any of these previous images ever occur to me consciously before, nor have I ever heard or read anyone refer to mind in these ways. What I was doing when the images/information arose was just noticing any event in my body or awareness; it was the opposite of trying to generate any response. I was not a calculating filter of my experience but a *noticer* of it. And like many previous moments in this dyad process, I did not know what I was going to say before I said it. It was not premeditated (except in the case of describing the images, where I had just seen them in my mind's eye; yet, the information related to them—that is, what they represented to me—was not known until I heard myself saying it). In other words, I really felt going into this inquiry (i.e. *"Tell me what mind is"*) that I did not *know* what 'mind' was, and the further I progressed into it, the more this was so. So again, the knowing came *afterwards*, after I heard myself speaking. Where did this information come from?

Bolte Taylor offers an explanation for my experience, by way of using layers or levels of cognition or knowing that she calls *insightful awareness*: "Finally, when someone contrasts what he or she *feels* intuitively about something (often expressed as a "gut feeling") to what they think about it, this insightful awareness is a *higher cognition* [italics mine] that is grounded in the right hemisphere of the cerebral cortex" (p.20). In other words, the knowing that is more closely described as feeling versus a thinking about, is a more valid knowing. It is superior to what the mind-as-intellect can accomplish.

Finally, Bolte Taylor posits a consciousness of the heart that links directly to the consciousness of the right hemisphere of the brain: "Just realize that deep inside your right mind (deep within your heart's consciousness) rests eternal peace" (p.173), and, "…my right hemisphere's heart consciousness" (p.174). So it would seem that our body gives us clues—in my case, portals even—to the direct cognition: the "gut" seems to know something, as does the "heart," whereas the mind can only 'know' secondarily, or abstractly. In other words, the 'I' known by me as my identity did not know I knew this information about the hemispheres of my mind but nevertheless the knowing was there, as something we are or have access to. In addition, Taylor links the right hemisphere directly to heart.[11]

My experiences at these Enlightenment Intensives has been part of driving the research in this book through my attempts to place them in the wider context of the literature on awakening experiences and on how this informs my understanding of the purpose and possibility of formal education.

Part 2: Experiencing *The Work of Byron Katie**
now also called Inquiry Based Stress Reduction (IBSR)

Experiencing What Can and Can't Be Known

On two separate occasions in the year I was writing this (2013), I had the chance to participate in Byron Katie's intensive workshops. I attended her Nine-Day School for The Work[12] as a participant and her inaugural Forgiveness Intensive as staff, both in Ojai, California. I had previously attended a weekend workshop with Katie in Toronto in 2008 and was amazed at how effective and simple her tool—which she calls "The Work"—

---

[11] An institute, Heartmath, is leading research into the intelligence of the heart.
[12] Since writing this, I have also staffed her School for The Work, in March 2014.

was in puncturing the veil of illusion created by the conceptual mind. It was clear to me after watching Katie facilitate others that anyone could do this, supporting Katie's claim that no one is wiser than anyone else. It really only takes courage to uncover the truth, nothing else, no matter what it is nor how painful it might be to get there.

It was quite a profound experience doing the School, and I offer a contextualization of it here by relating it to the Enlightenment Intensive. I experienced the School as a less dramatic, less intense and equally penetrating process of arriving at the truth. Given that I still use The Work often (in fact, it's really rather an automatic process of questioning I do when I realize I'm wedded to a thought) speaks to its utility and practicality. I encountered the similar phenomenon as in the Enlightenment Intensive of self-revealing something I had known, but not known I'd known. In addition, I encountered the ability to step into my natural self as it were: in examining who I would be without my stressful thoughts, there was always a clear experience of inner peace and calm, often (if not always) accompanied by compassion and love. Any action that would be optimal to take was revealed to me. I saw all of this clearly, internally, after working through the first three questions.

The reason Katie's process is so powerful is because it externalizes—makes apparent—the internal process going on all the time in the mind. For most of us, it was considered normal to be told as children by the adults in our lives to suppress our thoughts, usually because they weren't nice, because *we* weren't being nice to even think them. The adults believed, and therefore influenced children towards the belief, of course, that people are responsible for their thoughts. Thus we are those grown children who are now adults waging an internal battle: feeling tremendous guilt over having these thoughts that in fact, by their very nature, plague everyone. We do not create thinking; this is the great myth. We take credit for agency when in fact we can't say for sure that we generate them.

The parents among us in turn feel it our duty to teach our children that they are bad (or are *"behaving* badly," considered the more enlightened descriptor) for having certain thoughts and they must not think them. Thoughts like, I hate her; he is mean; life is unfair, etc., etc.

What's missing is instruction for children that they have the choice of whether or not they *believe* their thoughts. Without this knowledge, we are at the mercy of our thoughts. It also sets up an immensely hypocritical situation where the adults pretend (and indeed have convinced themselves) that they have learned to be kind (for example), when they have done no such thing. What they have really learned to do is to mask their true feelings. So, it is enough to *appear* kind. An immense importance is placed on how one *appears* as opposed to how one really *is*.

Thus begins the chronic but unconscious approval-seeking behaviour and manipulation that runs one's life, just out of reach of one's daily, conscious awareness. The underlying belief is that the best we can hope for is to *act* kind because there is not innate kindness within us, or alternately, it is not as strong as the cruel tendencies within us. In fact, the truth is the opposite (in this example, it is kindness, not cruelty, that is our true nature) and encountering that truth directly is not only possible but quite simple. Truth is what's there when the concepts are removed. Furthermore, the living of this untruth causes suffering in anyone precisely because it counters the *reality* that is alive within them. In order to make sense of this, I offer the following example from my experience at the School.

On the seventh day of the School, we were bussed somewhere just outside of Los Angeles, where we were set adrift without food, water, or personal identification (of the hardware—not conceptual—type) and with the "invitation" to be completely silent and not to spend any time with another participant. In other words, we had no safety net; we didn't even have the tool of communication. We did not know where we were going nor even if we were expected to stay out overnight somewhere. So the main point is that there was no *psychological* safety net in addition to no apparent physical one[13].

---

[13] I desire to keep the curriculum of the School confidential, and I also wish to set the context for what I am about to describe.

At one point, I found myself on the pier wandering amongst the throngs of people there. I became aware that I was surprisingly at peace, which is remarkable in itself, given that I tend to avoid crowds and in addition I was in an unfamiliar place. I was able to question any stressful thought that came to mind but surprisingly few did after a week spent in almost non-stop questioning of my conceptual world. Later on, I remembered watching a man on the pier, who appeared to be homeless, eat food as he retrieved it from the garbage. It occurred to me only afterwards that I experienced that act of observation without any stressful story, whereas witnessing something like this in the past has always caused me severe distress. In the moments I stood watching him, I had no thought that this was sad and unjust, that he shouldn't have to be doing this, that it was disgusting, etc.; instead, I saw beauty. I just saw him the same as I saw everyone else on the pier that day: people with free will experiencing life. I want to be clear that I realize that my comments above could be taken as insensitive and unenlightened, and I wish to explain that I am not commenting on homelessness, I am commenting on my inner state. So I am not saying that one shouldn't take action from a place of compassion to ease human suffering. I am saying that in the absence of a war against reality, I felt internally clear and peaceful and from this place I can see that action springs purely and clearly. Logic and argument is unnecessary and can only lessen the impact through lessening the energy of action. I think this is an extremely important point in its implications for education, in light of citizenship education, participatory democracy, activism, etc. where the idea is we need to be *taught* to be compassionate and to take action. Indeed, every aspect of life from one's relationship to oneself, to others, and between nations is affected by this insight. Krishnamurti referred to this clear action stemming from absence of concepts as "right action."

Something I was prompted to do through attending the School was to examine the concept of control, and its relationship to fear especially as it pertains to schooling. Schools of the dominant paradigm for the most part are places that teach control, mostly by virtue of example but also by way of intimidation (ex. teachers controlling student behaviour through threat of punishment or more subtly, through grades, or bestowing kindness and attention, etc.) The idea of control really is wanting things to be other than they are, and this is really the message of ideals again.

As teachers, we give the message to children that we need to control their environment in school, that something would be better than what they're experiencing, creating the belief in them that it's not okay where they are, that they can't handle it, that they're not in control of their own internal environment. They don't have the benefit of knowing that they are in control of whether or not they believe their thoughts. This, above all I believe, needs to be the message to children: YOU and no one else is the creator of your experience insofar as you are ultimately in control of whether or not you believe the thoughts that appear in your mind, and in the absence of stressful thoughts, the truth—which is kind—is obvious. It's there for everyone and it is our freedom.

Like what I experienced in the Enlightenment Intensive, doing *The Work* allows for a non-conceptual intelligence to come through/to me. I am asked four simple questions by someone (I can also ask them of myself, though in my experience it's easier to be held in the inquiry if someone is sitting in front of me rather than me trying to hold myself in it) and I go inside myself and await—and then notice—the answers. It's really that simple. The answers—the insights, the information—are there. It's what we knew all along but didn't know we knew. The unknown unknowns (as opposed to the known unknowns). It happens in the mirror of life, particularly in the mirror of relationship. We judge others on paper by writing down these thoughts we have of them and see how these are really judgments we have of ourselves, and that this is what's causing such pain and our desire to attack others. Furthermore, it's the believing of something

---

* The Work consists of four questions: 1) Is it true? 2) Can you absolutely know it's true? 3) How do you react, what happens, when you believe that thought? 4) Who would you be without that thought? The "turnarounds" consist of turning the original statement around to its opposite.

that is not in fact true for us that causes the discord within us. So logic tells us, then, that truth *is* there within us; it's in us *as* us. It's the same on the micro/personal scale as on the macro/global scale: people in conflict, nations at war. Not knowing what to do with the pain, not knowing what causes it in the first place, we *assume* it is caused by the behaviour we are observing in others that we just can't accept (worshiping the wrong God, taking our land, killing children with chemicals, etc.). It becomes inevitable that, believing this, people are attacked. Other action is not possible. Katie points out that we are all innocent because we can't *help* but act in accord with the thoughts we are believing. So again, it is back to the thoughts we are thinking that we must put our attention on, or, as Krishnamurti puts it, if you want to transform the world, you must transform yourself first.

The amazing thing—and what I find so important about Katie's work—is that she and the process make clear that it is *through* questioning one's thoughts that the intelligence comes, *not* in subduing them as is a common belief in spiritual seekers/the enlightenment community. Yes, they are transcended, but it is through welcoming them and seeing what it is they are showing you. It is for this reason that Katie speaks of her thoughts as "the beloved" saying "they turned out to be my freedom" (personal communication, October 7, 2013). This fact calls to mind my experience in the Enlightenment Intensive of finding my 'ego' so endearing, so hardworking and supportive. It did, indeed, feel like the beloved to me. Then, in addition through doing *The Work*, I have experienced questioning a thought that seems like a clear enemy because it causes such pain (a thought like, "He is controlling my life"), and found that it holds within it some profound truth(s) that I discover through meeting this thought instead of trying to suppress it or destroy it. Indeed, my thoughts do seem like children who are scared, that are looking for a home to rest in (an analogy Katie uses). After engaging in *The Work*, I find myself feeling more love that *begins* as self-love. And in my experience, love for others and self-love are one and the same: if I feel self-love, it can't help but project to all others as them and in the same vein, if I don't feel self-love, no amount of effort will create love of other. It's not possible. Yet, again, we admonish children to "love others" etc. as if such a thing were possible just by adopting a concept.

Of course, what Katie's *The Work* does is allows—indeed, forces—one into an experience of their own answers *precisely because she is asking questions.* In my experience, my mind has only ever been able to rest (the byproducts of which are peace, love, joy, compassion, energy) when it/I give myself its/my own answers. The veiled/obscured but felt truth within me all my life that others' (particularly teachers and other adults) answers would never be enough for me turned out to be true and through doing *The Work* was brought into my full conscious awareness. It is this fact that has the most profound implications for how we are educating, I believe. *Where is it, how is it, that we can provide a space/paradigm for children/teens to discover their own innate wisdom within the context of education? Where we can explode the erroneous concept of the supremacy and omnipotence of the intellect (or left-brain seat of logic) and open the way for the awareness of self-reliance and self-response-ability?*

Part 3: Bringing Awareness to my Daily Life

When I first read Krishnamurti I began examining my conditioning of fear; in retrospect, it acted like a planting of a seed over fifteen years ago and during all these years my intention has been to experience/see for myself what Krishnamurti—and, since, other spiritual teachers—are talking about.

However, what I have come to see is that also, all these years, I've been trying to add 'not-knowing' to my knowledge bank, to my list of attributes that make up this 'self' I conceptualize as 'Kathryn Jefferies.' It has been so very subtle that even though I knew of this liability, 'I' thought I could escape it. The difficulty is the 'I' *is* the knowledge bank, or the repository of constructed experiences. I've noticed that trying to grasp—to understand, to move towards, apprehend—the truth of myself outside my mind doesn't work because I have created the idea of me as separate from the truth.

Hence, Tolle's, Veltheim's and Krishnamurti's negation approach: instead of trying to grasp "consciousness" (who one is outside of concepts of oneself), remove the obstacles instead. It is a placing of attention on who or what is and noticing that reality. We can only find out who we are not, and then who we are becomes apparent. This is Katie's process too in her Question #4: *Who would you be without this thought?* (after asking Q.3: *How do you react, what happens, when you believe this thought?*) Katra and Targ point this out below—including a quote from the spiritual teacher Gangaji—using suffering as the *what is*:

> ....the experience of a state of awareness that cannot be reached—only *recognized* as our true nature, which is infinite and unbounded consciousness. According to spiritual teacher Gangaji:
>
> We have tried everything to get rid of suffering. We have gone everywhere to get rid of suffering. We have bought everything to get rid of it. We have ingested everything to get rid of it.
>
> Finally, when one has tried enough, there arises the possibility of spiritual maturity with the willingness to stop the futile attempt *to get rid of*, and instead, to actually experience suffering. In that momentous instant, there is the realization of that which is beyond suffering, of that which is untouched by suffering. There is the realization of who one truly is. (Katra, 1999, p.11)

This, really, sums up my experiences of *The Work* as well as the Enlightenment Intensives. I sat with my suffering and walked through it to the other side.

So it would seem that there's an aspect of me that believes it can and must accomplish things, the highest of which is what I think of as 'enlightenment.' And yet it became apparent to me that reaching in this way through efforting (which really means, conceptually, through my intellect) would only send me into worm holes and suffering, and eventually throw me back on myself until I was forced to question the existence of this 'self' and what it believed it knew. Initially through the *Enlightenment Intensive* and then through *The Work*, I was able to *experience* my Self separate from the mind-created 'self.' It is a sort of backdrop of awareness, or knowing, that allows things to take place in its context—it's pure consciousness. And I know this is synonymous with who I am because when all thoughts of 'self' were stripped away, this is what remained. It was just pure experiencing. The process is captured nicely by Veltheim in the quotation below:

> Between seeker and sought is Seeing….Isn't it odd that the *impersonal self* is what is sought, yet you think you can find It by means of adding to your *personal* accomplishments? …the question is rarely asked, "How is the experiencing of this possible?"
>
> Simply showing up for life is all that is necessary, and it happens despite you as it always has. Be as you Are, Experiencing, and the mystery of existence is solved. Focus on Be-coming, and you will continue questioning the meaning of life and your existence.
>
> …you continue wondering, "Who am I," wanting a conceptual description of the non-conceptual You. Meanwhile, the source of the question Is the answer.

I would describe the experiencing Veltheim describes above in the paradox of the following personal experience: I would normally be terrified because I immediately see that 'I' do not exist (and this sends my mind into a panic, looking around for somewhere to anchor itself), nor is anything the way I thought it was, except that there is such a feeling of rightness and assuredness and exhilaration to experiencing myself with no limits that there is no 'one' there anymore to question what is happening or to suggest it isn't real or possible. Perhaps it is best summed up and simplified in the delightful quote I heard not long ago: *Now and then it is wonderful to pause in our pursuit of happiness and just be happy.*

Intentional Creativity

I've noticed over the years (10+) of being a mom that somewhere along the path between child and adult, I learned or believed the idea that creating *intentionally* (as opposed to unconsciously, which is what I seem to be doing as an adult) is not valuable. I learned to stop playing, which really means that I learned to not be creative. I adopted the belief that using my brain was really the most important thing I could do—to think, to develop complex ideas, to be logical, to learn (add knowledge to my stored memory). And I notice that when I've been given exercises in the form of actions to do (from a therapist or even a self-help author in a book, etc.), I fervently resist them within. It's as if they don't feel real, that they're not going to exact any real change for me, that I'd rather be given *information*, something my brain can chew on. It occurred to me that 'the world of my head' is what I have been trained to feel is real. The world of ideas, thinking, and knowledge—trained by society, but especially by school. In the same vein, I notice that when my daughter asks me to play, something in me resists quite violently: my mind says *it is a waste of time, it's silly, I don't know how, it takes too much energy, I'm safer to stay in the world of my concepts* (i.e. my head), etc. These thoughts happen so rapidly, of course, that it registers at the time only to me as 'I don't *feel* like it.' (The mind is so rapid that I am aware of the byproduct of thought—the feeling—but not of the thoughts.)

Yet for the times when I'm able to overstep this voice and play with her anyway, I enter the moment. Just like that. I experience it as joy, as laughter, as presence with what I am doing. Because creativity requires us to be right here, right now—by definition. It's a place of not knowing what's coming next—and that's where all the excitement comes from. This is the space children inhabit *naturally* as I've noticed by watching them. They understand the joy of the present moment—not cognitively, of course— they just do this naturally, innately. This is the grand excitement of life: not-knowing what comes next, and waiting with baited breath. What could be more exciting? It's that feeling of anticipation I have felt when I suspected—highly expected—that something good was going to happen, but I didn't know exactly how it would play out. This is the state I believe we were meant to inhabit—this is life as described by those who live entirely from this place, even when something supposedly 'bad' happens. I am not saying that my childhood consisted only of this, of course, but that I do not experience the same phenomenon now as an adult (unless it is deliberate, like in my experiences doing *The Work*). My own experience and observation of children is that we're born with it and more or less gradually coaxed out of it.

For example, Byron Katie, when faced with the experience of someone holding a gun to her stomach and threatening to kill her, wondered with great excitement, "Is this how it ends?" (personal communication, October 2013). Because, as she says, she does not have a story that opposes 'what is'—she cannot find any reason he should not be holding a gun to her stomach; she is not playing God, but is instead in the 'don't-know' mind of not knowing what is best to occur. For her, even that staying alive would be better is not a given. And of course, there is no *trying* to make this happen (certainly it would be an appealing way for any of us in the same situation to get rid of fear)—it happens on its own as a result of perceiving the truth of who she is and the truth of what life is.

I can often remember, as a child, feeling this sort of background excitement or anticipation, in the same way that I now have a background feeling of dread or doom: same mechanism, opposite feeling. It felt like excitement at just being alive. It felt like living in a mystery where good things awaited around the corner but they weren't even my concern. They just arrived and I got to experience them. The felt memory of this is vague, and I have to reach for it, but it's there. The more I focus on it, the more it expands in my awareness and I can grab hold of the feeling better.

Even by the time I was in grade six, I can remember still possessing a feeling of certainty, absolutely knowing that I was exactly where I was

---

* I write in detail about four people in particular in a companion book, *Wide Awake: Anatomy of Awakening*, which you can downoad for free from my website, Kathryn jefferies.com/educationforenlightenment.

supposed to be, doing what I was supposed to be doing (only cognizing this in retrospect). I remember with great clarity spending a long time walking home from school with my best friend. I would describe the feeling now as 'the pin-prick of the universe,' meaning I was at the centre—it is difficult to get across in language, but I would say it felt like being fully myself. I was expressing my essential self in those moments of freedom of creation, in snow banks as we took our time walking home from school. With the further experience and language I have now, I would explain that perhaps what I was experiencing was the one consciousness expressing itself through me. In other words, I didn't have a story that opposed it so I was merged with it. There was no 'Kathryn' outside of the experience—it was straight experiencing, pure expression. There was certainly a quality of timelessness to it: I had nowhere to go, nothing to be other than what I was in those moments. I was not witnessing, I was the experience. Simply put, I was present. In the absence of the concept of 'I,' there was only presence.

It is apparent that we each have had these experiences as children. We are not yet identified enough with any story that would take us away from that experiencing. It is no wonder that these moments stand out so strongly for me—set against the backdrop of a life canvas that had exponentially fewer and fewer of these as I was taught—conditioned—to inhabit more and more of my conceptual mind. Those moments of presence and acute awareness remain like beacons or bright stars in the night sky, as a 'place' it's possible to find my way back to.

Awareness of Conditioning

To begin looking at conditioning's specifics, then, and how they play out, is to begin the process of stripping away that which we are not. Moody captures a nice definition below of conditioning and sums up Krishnamurti's intent of his schools in the process:

> Conditioning is essentially the weight of tradition, the burden of past generations, the accumulated patterns of thought and judgment imposed on the individual by society. Education in the traditional sense is an agent

and facilitator of the conditioning process. In a profound reversal of convention, Krishnamurti proposed instead that education become the process of unconditioning the human mind. (Moody, 2011, p.34)

So conditioning, then, for example, is when we cried and our parents tried to get us to stop crying because it was upsetting them, and so we formed a belief (for example), *Crying is a negative thing. It must mean I am doing something wrong. I am bad and if only I could understand how to be better so I wouldn't upset my parents.* If they also got angry or in another way manipulated us to stop we also learned behaviour from their modeling at how to get others to bend to our will. Many thousands, millions of incidents occur like this that condition our minds. They don't have to be 'negative' concepts either; positive ones equally condition. For example, my daughter got the "Courage Award" for her Grade 3 class during the month that recognized that character trait at school. That was before the Christmas holidays. It's now into the new year. She's been back to school for a week and commented this morning how neat it was that she got that award. I couldn't help but wonder how that added concept to her 'self' identity will manifest in coming years. The first-blush, quick, surface answer would be to suggest that this is a great self-concept to have—courageous! But a closer look makes it easy to see that it could just as easily play out adversely: her mind has already begun to search for ways to both prove this and disprove it in the hopes that she will avoid being courageous-less, lest everyone find her out for the fraud that she is. Ultimately, positive and negative concepts work the same way, since they aren't real—that is, based in reality—but are *ideas.* The mind will self-protect this belief and cause problems for her either way unless she has a tool to question what's true about herself.

Also, the concepts that are not on a personal level can be taken for granted and not easily questioned. Concepts like, *Murder is wrong. But it is okay if governments decide to do it en masse and we will call it war instead of murder. And we will give medals and the highest honours to soldiers who are especially good at killing.* Or, *Democracy is ideal. We should force nations to become democratic.* (Despite being blatantly hypocritical, the above examples are generally accepted as legitimate.) And so we accept these beliefs and try to organize ourselves around an understanding of them by creating a mental chart or tally in our heads, so that we can always try to stay on the side of 'good.' Tolle explains that since thought is an energy form(ation), it can be there for years—one particular belief, way of looking at reality:

> Then you look at everything through one particular thought form, not realizing that it's an illusion. It totally distorts reality. It could be a collective thought form in which case several million people have got the same thought stuck in their heads and look at reality through the same thought form (ex. religion, political ideology). 'Totally conditioned' is another way of putting it. The fundamental dysfunction: humans are possessed by thought, possessed by the conditioned mind.

We reject certain things and accept others, but always with an idea of the 'me' in mind that we want to create or mold—the ideal 'me' that exists in my mind who is in a perpetual state of becoming. And from this, it's easy to see how this 'me' can never be enough; if one is always in a state of be-coming, of being formed, then by definition, this cannot come to an end. And this 'me' is all based on thought—on ideas, on beliefs. It is an image. Where, in reality, can one find it? Nowhere, because this 'me' does not really exist. And yet we think we are this image. *Who am I if not this image*—this carefully crafted image that I have spent my life building up, shoring up, defending, embuing with life…it must be real. It feels real. I can see her in my mind's eye. And yet, all she is, is thought. Any 'doing' that I would do would be from this me-made 'self' that doesn't even exist. So it would serve to perpetuate her existence as if she were real.

The linear model of growth, in any way (ex. child to adult, self-devel-opment), is a fallacy in my experience—it's just an idea that comes out of the 'me' identity. It has been the strongest block to my own peace because I am aware of the concept of enlightenment and then there is me over here not being enlightened with the implication being I cannot rest until I am. It is a concept created by the mind, like time, as a way of taking me out of the present moment. I realized that my belief that I was inadequate until I was awakened to the truth, kept me unawakened to the truth because it meant I couldn't keep my version of myself and also be in the present moment. Attaching to the thought meant I was in the past or future. It was really that simple. And then I could watch the behaviours I would carry out that did not serve me, because I did not self-judge—which is another way of saying I did not identify with my behaviour. I saw it for what it was: learned, but not who I am in essence. Only then could I change it. Only now do I finally understand the emphasis all of the spiritual teachers place on *the present moment.* There really *is* only now, but my mind could not know this—not ever. Simply by definition.

Feeling bad in any way (which comes from believing a negative thought) takes me out of the present moment. If I'm aware of it, I notice the mind claims that it is making me feel bad so that I can then work harder to understand that which I do not understand. Then I look more closely. I watch. *Is this true?* (That I need to think badly of myself or see that can I can be better in order to be better. Does change ever arise this way?) I know by how I feel. *Do I feel at peace with this thought?* What makes me feel at peace is *seeing*[14] (not accepting) that I am doing all I can in this moment, in each moment, that all is all right in each moment. So, for example, if I am angry and accept this, ironically I move into peace. To reject it and say to myself it would be better not to be angry but to be kind keeps me in my anger and increases it.

This, I believe, is what Tolle means when he says to say yes to the present

---

[14] "Seeing" is how I describe what happens in inquiry: asking the four questions and doing the turnarounds of The Work, I am shown what is true. Cognizing is bypassed. The truth is just given. It's as simple as that. Which is what, in my experience, makes it so profound.

moment, accept reality as it presents itself in *this* moment, and align with the present moment, or how he sums up his teachings: one with life. It is what Krishnamurti means when he cautions against ideals. We think that to create better circumstances (more humane, non-violent, cooperative, etc.) we must first imagine this better reality (and therefore also the problems with the current reality by default) so we can move towards it. However, this is the paradox I get into more fully in Part 2: change comes in acceptance of what is, not in the struggle to bring about change.

The Mirror of Life

When I first read Krishnamurti's statement, "You are the world," many years ago I did not understand what he meant. Now I believe I do. Everything that is in my head—in my belief system, in the thoughts I think—is represented in the external world that I perceive. In fact, this is *all* I can experience. This is the great gift of phenomenal life—we get to see ourselves in the mirror of the world and thereby find out who we're *being*, what this *human being* is. We think we are seeing something separate from us, something that has nothing to do with us—that we are a pure witness to events (though they may affect us and we are at the mercy of them). Yet if we inquire, we will quite easily see that what we are seeing is ourselves—that is, who we believe ourselves to be—an image created through thought. This is not an experience someone can give another any more than someone can give someone the experience of riding a bike. Katie (2002, p.12) explains it in this way: "When you do The Work, you see who you are by seeing who you think other people are. Eventually you come to see that everything outside you is a reflection of your own thinking. You are the storyteller, the projector of all stories, and the world is the projected image of your thoughts." Veltheim (2000, p.208) echoes this insight in relating her own awakening:

> ...the most dramatic *relative* change I experienced. Until then, I had spent my life feeling the world was hostile. I thought I was experiencing everyone else's emotions and pains. Clearly, "others"

> were simply a reflection of the emotional holdings in my own
> body....I suddenly realized that the phenomenon that surprised me
> most was that I no longer experienced anyone in my environment.

In other words, everything—every experience—points back to the self. This is a radical insight and one that has profound implications, including (especially, in my view) both interpersonal dynamics and one's *response-ability*—that is, one's ability to respond to life.

For example, when we're looking at something like teaching children kindness and empathy towards others, it's a real shifting away from the focus of morals and ethics (which are intellectual/conceptual) onto the *experience of how being 'mean' and how being 'kind' feel to oneself.* I think this is a very important point. We routinely admonish children with, "If I did that to you, how would you feel?" Yet this question makes it difficult for a child to even go within to consider that because she/he is feeling guilt and shame.

Rather, in a spirit of open inquiry a child can notice what the action does to herself/himself and what thought she/he was believing in the first place that compelled the action. It's a process of self-understanding. It leaves one free which means in the deepest sense in control of themselves (so-to-speak, as we'll see in a minute) and not at the mercy of actions stemming from emotion that in turn stems from believing a painful thought.

This is the symbiotic and mirrored nature of life: if we want to feel good, we must treat others kindly, because in the deepest sense, others *are* us. It also applies to when people feel that they can't—and need to—control their outside circumstances in order to feel safe (or good, etc.). This feeling of being out of control and needing to be in control is what is responsible for the various levels of violence.

Yet, in the realization of the paradox that 1) in a sense we *do* each 'control' life, that it is always a mirrored response to ourselves, then the belief in the need to control others drops away, replaced by the desire to simply understand oneself and 2) ultimately, peace comes not from being in control of one's circumstances (because then of course there's the ever-present fear of losing control) but by realizing it's impossible and unnecessary.

I have seen this insight for myself, and the more I look, the more I see it. I see it most clearly in my daughter, likely because I am most attached to (or we might say, 'invested in') her emotionally/psychologically—the one whose experience I care the most about, the one I feel responsible for, and the one I spend the most time with.

She mirrors back to me the relationship I have with everything in the world: with myself, with people, with things, with life and death. I may think she is the problem at times, that I must control her behaviour, teach her to act differently, when in fact if I look to see where I do this in my life—as if I were her and acting out her behaviour—I always find it. And when I see it, I know how to treat her.

For example, if she cries, I hate it. Something within me reacts violently, and that something is a reaction to the thoughts I am thinking but am not necessarily aware of—thoughts like, "She is suffering; she is suffering and she shouldn't because she's only a child and fragile; I need to stop her suffering because I'm her mother; if I had been a better mother, I would have prevented this suffering.'

So the story I'm telling myself, unconsciously, about what it means that she's crying takes me out of presence (and an ability to be there for her which I have come to see is enough and is ultimately what it is that I want) and into a story about how it affects *me*. So I have projected onto her all my stories about crying and aloneness and suffering and future pain, etc. But if I do not have the story (i.e. the thoughts) going on, then I notice that I can be completely present for her, with an open mind and heart about what is happening for her in her experience. I am curious about her experience; I don't have a voice in my head assuming I know that crying or suffering is bad. It is a being there for her fully. This is ultimately exactly what I want. It is completely selfish and selfless (absence of the 'I,' the needy one) at the same time.

Inner Reality

One of the first steps for me was bringing to full conscious awareness the existence and validity of my inner reality, and then recognizing my power to make the choice to turn my attention to my inner reality, as opposed to keeping it turned outward (i.e. to the world of phenomena). It's the decision to find out the truth for myself, to become aware of what is true for me. In other words, it's a way out of the conceptual mind. It's within this context that I can make sense of what I would describe as a feeling of pressure inside myself, that I carry with me all of the time, that seems to want to 'get out'—that is, that it wants to express itself. It's a level of existence that seems true, that feels like the *ground of being* that spiritual teachers speak of, or *pure consciousness*; it feels like it underlies the more superficial (in comparison) experiencing. This is my inner reality; the real world to me— what I see outside me confuses this inner reality, because it distracts me. We can use it to see ourselves more clearly (because, as I stated previously, the outside world is merely a reflection of our inner world), but most of us go in the opposite direction and use it to separate ourselves from each other in a deluded attempt at self-protection. So, grasping that whatever I happened to be seeing or experiencing externally was actually only possible because there is *me*, allows me to return again and again to the reality of my self, my inner world.

When I clear away all thought (and this only happens for me during inquiry, for brief moments), I have experienced that I am limitless, literally: I am not this body, but have experienced being a vastness that does not end. I experienced it powerfully at one point in my Enlightenment Intensive through the symbol of the Sphinx (which I have never seen, but still knew immediately what it was). I was that Sphinx, looking through its eyes and I could see as far as the eye could see and it was apparent that it kept going infinitely. The words that came were, "The world is my oyster." I understood somehow that the message was that the world is whatever I want it to be, that in fact it *is* me. It is created by my choosing. Now I am beginning to understand how the mechanics of that seem to work: it is through desire that I summon something into being; I am choosing how I want things to appear to me. But only if I allow it through believing that it is possible; if not, I will block my creation. I *have* to because my conceptual reality won't allow for it. We do this as humans all the time and wonder why we can't create the life we want for ourselves, the life we've imagined. We just *know* there's a life inside of us that wants to be lived—I have felt this my whole life, and I know this must be a universal human experience, instinctively. It would seem that it would be accurate to say that I am the one somehow being lived—the control ends up being illusory. This is so because my perceived control is in the hands of the one I think of as 'me.' In the absence of the conceptual me there is just what is. And in that space, a knowing.

It is my experience that if I sit and listen, an answer shows itself to me. In my experience, things arise, and then dissipate, or disappear. In inquiry, images arise and then disappear; I can watch them internally. No amount of grasping can make them stay—it seems that this is their nature. I have also noticed that my emotions arise and then fall away—but only if I am present for them and allow them. If I am afraid and resist them, then my very act of trying to push them away is what keeps them stuck next to me; they cannot fully arise, so they cannot dissipate. Through this contemplative inquiry I have seen what I believe to be the nature of energy (which is to say, life) that it is always in constant flux.

When we believe our thoughts, we must act as a result of our beliefs. But if we can realize that we do not have to believe our thoughts, we are free. Most of us do not realize we can attach or un-attach to thoughts and beliefs. (Actually, the reverse is ultimately true: they attach or un-attach to us, as we inquire; it is not possible for us to be the doer in this regard but we can create the conditions for it to occur through inquiry.)

The simple way to realize this is notice how we react when we are believing our stressful thoughts, and then ask ourselves, *Who would I be without that thought?* We see immediately that if we did not have any thoughts, 'we' would still exist. The only way to know this for ourselves is to inquire ourselves—it gives the *experience* of the ground of being, of no-thought, of the knowing or intelligence that is already there. So this 'us' that is still in existence without thought—since it is all that remains and that it does remain—must somehow be us. And noticing this is when we start to see that in the absence of a thought that we *must* or *have to* do something, which is to say in the absence of the doer (the 'thinker,' the 'decider'), that we actually are *being done*. Decisions get made as a noticing in retrospect that a decision was made. This, I believe, is the right action that Krishnamurti was talking about. He explained that there isn't the perceiving and then the action, but that the perceiving *is* the action, and what I explained above is how this is possible.

Conclusion to the Autoethnography:
Influences from Education

The repercussions of living without awareness of how one's conditioning of mind is affecting one's life are immense. In my own life, my attempts to navigate a major life crisis demonstrated this clearly to me. I came to see that my crisis was not because of my life situation but in fact was caused by my *deep fear that I could not trust my perceptions of things*, of life. When I saw this fact, I could also clearly see the origins of this throughout my upbringing and education: the paradigm whose ultimate implied lesson was *You cannot know, you cannot trust your own knowing. You have no innate knowing. We have the answers, you do not. How could you arrive at what's true* [non-conceptual knowing] *about this when you have no knowledge of it* [conceptual knowing] *and we do.*

Through trying to relieve my suffering by understanding what caused it, I realized I have a fear of saying "no," a fear of (outside) authority, a constant fear of repercussions, and a background anxiety of getting life 'wrong,' of getting in trouble (because the accompanying emotions were so painful). I came to see that my fear of being wrong was really about my fear of not being able to know that my own perceptions were valid.

I see a direct link between these conclusions and an education paradigm that a) acts as if there is no innate knowing but all knowledge is located in external or conceptual knowledge, b) acts as if children should have no authority (and, indeed, have no innate authority) but need to acquiesce to adult authority, c) fails to recognize the truth of paradox and instead subscribes to a view of right and wrong, d) sees ideals as motivators for right behaviour and e) asserts *knowing* (answering) above *not-knowing* (questioning) as a way to arrive at truth.

Further ramifications of being conditioned in this way are in the following examples of my own life. I began to see my confusion over other people's *certainty*. I had always taken this as a sign that they must be right, because I myself did not feel certain of anything. I had not yet conceived of the possibility that there isn't any right and wrong, only what's real and true for someone in her or his experience.

I was ever aware of the wrestling and ambiguity within me, and this to me felt like weakness. I did not yet see that it came from the struggle between habitual subservience to outside authority and my own quiet voice of my truth.

Only very recently have I come to see *my ability to question* as a strength of being able to engage in the tension of living the questions, as a measure of being in touch with an innate intelligence that questions the validity of imposed structures, and that, likewise, this sort of intellectual certainty I was perceiving in others is the sign of a closed mind. (This is not to say that knowing can't exist, that any demonstration of certainty means a closed mind.)

I also came to see how my conditioning gave rise to aggression within me. I saw that aggression (through frustration, getting louder, etc.) arises because someone is not open to, or is rejecting my perceptions and I feel I must convince them of their (my) validity. What I came to see through doing The Work is that it was I who was not open to my perceptions and that I was waiting for myself to trust *myself*. There is only me; there is only one of us here. I project it all from inside me.

The negative impact of my conditioned mind can also be seen in my experience in years of psychotherapy. I approached my weekly sessions as if I was learning everything possible about how my mind works. I summoned weekly courage to delve into what I thought was 'wrong' with me—why I couldn't be at peace, content, and make my life work. What I came to see was that I was still adhering to the belief that I was in need of an external authority or 'expert' to instruct me. Being in therapy kept me subservient not only to this outside authority but to my intellect as the means of problem solving. Ultimately, any insights I may have gleaned were secondary to the detrimental effects of perpetuating the belief that I could not rely on my own perceptions, that I would always be at the mercy of my ego but that a trained expert could guide me. In finally seeing the fallacy of this, I see the absolute necessity—as did Krishnamurti, and as does Katie—of one finding their own answers. No one can give them to someone else. It's not possible and its attempts are catastrophic. I liken this now to an abuser-abused relationship in the sense of an inherit power dynamic that is abused yet there is at least one difference: I do believe my therapist was well-intentioned and just deeply confused. After writing the passage above, I recently came upon the following from Krishnamurti that speaks to my experience:

> It is comforting to have someone to encourage us, to give us a lead, to pacify us; but this habit of turning to another as a guide, as an authority, soon becomes a poison in our system. The moment we depend on another for guidance, we forget our original intention, which was to awaken individual freedom and intelligence.
>
> All authority is a hindrance, and it is essential that the educator should not become an authority for the student…
>
> The student is uncertain, groping, but the teacher is sure in his knowledge, strong in his experience. The strength and certainty of the teacher give assurance to the student, who tends to bask in that sunlight; but such assurance is neither lasting nor true. A teacher who consciously or unconsciously encourages dependence can nev-

er be of great help to his students. He may overwhelm them with his knowledge, dazzle them with his personality, but he is not the right kind of educator because his knowledge and experience are his addiction, his security, his prison; and until he himself is free of them, he cannot help his students to be integrated human beings. (1953, p.107)

Through this experience, I can also see why Krishnamurti asserts that "all life is learning" as opposed to the mistaken belief that learning happens only in school. It's this experiential learning—that happens through my uncertainty and ability to question, to inquire—where learning happens. I moved from intellectual understanding to experiential understanding and back. I resonated with Krishnamurti's writings but didn't really understand them until life brought me the experiences. I couldn't force the understanding. For example, I obviously needed the experience of not being helped by therapy so I could fully examine this possibility for myself and discover how it is lacking and is a dead-end. I followed it to its ultimate conclusion.

In the above I use the word conditioning but if the word indoctrinating is used, it might help make the meaning more explicit. It can't be said that what we are doing in schools is not indoctrination.

Throughout this chapter, I have communicated as deeply as possible through language my own experiences of meeting mind (self), and ultimately transcending or absorbing/dissolving mind to reveal the Self. I delineate between self and Self in this way much like the Buddhist terms *Little (or Small) Mind* and *Big Mind*: the former is the identity we have put together through thought that has no basis in reality; the latter is who we are without thought. Using mind in this way can be problematic, because of our tendency to associate the term *mind* with *brain*. On the other hand, I like the term because it is accurate in the sense that we also associate *mind* with intelligence, and as far as I can tell, this *Big Mind* refers to that pure intelligence (as opposed to the limited intellect that can be put together by *Small Mind*). I have left out other personal experiences and insights in the interests of length and focus of purpose: I believe I have shed enough light through what I have written to make my point.

As I wrote at the beginning of the chapter, I wrote this autoethnography in the context of—and in hopes of revealing—the following, with the purpose of connecting my experience to the broader purpose and potential of education:

1. My claim that education focuses on training the intellect, which in turn:
   a) intensifies mind identification and conditioning, and
   b) ignores the (transcendent, or 'real') Self, or consciousness

2. My claim that education is lacking the clear intention of educating for creative problem-solving (which is the logical concluding purpose of educating for giving the tools and knowledge that children need to both succeed in the world and become positive contributing members of society)

3. My claim that creativity and therefore creative problem-solving does not arise out of the intellect but out of the Self, or pure consciousness.

Chapter 3

Introduction

This chapter looks at the phenomena of mind, self, consciousness and its transformation through those who have gone through it. I go more deeply and specifically here into the creation and dissolution of the 'I' identity that I began in the first two chapters. I think of it as a real slowing down and going deeply in; the mind needs to slow down in order to understand. I also look at 'phenomena' itself. In other words, while I consider this investigation ontological—the exploration of being—I can't conceive of studying it without studying the things that arise in relation to being, or, phenomena. It is being that makes phenomena possible, so looking at one can help explain the other.[15]

~

As is probably the story of so many, what brought me to these teachers of 'oneness' or 'spiritual teachers' was what they seemed to so clearly emobdy: peace, joy. In truth, I think it was more what they *didn't* exhibit any sign of: suffering, anxiety, fear—any hint of the pain or confusion that seemed my constant companions in life. As life would have it, I've now had the privilege of spending considerable time in the presence of one of these teachers, Byron Katie. What I can tell you is that the same held true in person and

---

[15] Of course, the experience of being could be considered a phenomenon, yet I think it could be helpful to describe being as the absence of phenomena, or, what allows phenomena to exist.

on a profound level: that is, what struck me when I looked into Katie's eyes more than anything was what *wasn't* there. "There was *no one* there," I've since described it to others. It was like looking into infinity, in that piercing blue of her eyes—she was all and nothing at the same time.

At the first worldwide convention of The Work in January 2015, I found myself partnered with her for a brief activity as part of a presentation of those moving The Work in the world. Katie turned to me and immediately answered the question the assignment put to us with her quick mind, and there was nothing—no one—else. It's difficult to put into words. It seemed as though there was just no 'one' to hold a story about herself; I could say she exhibited an absence of ego. Only totally. Almost two years before that moment, I had found myself on the small stage next to her amongst the group of people who had acted as staff for her school. We were in the back row. She had melted back to be part of us rather than remain out front. The three hundred or so participants in the room were acknowledging our contribution through applause at the time. And what struck me was her humility, which is perhaps the wrong word since that makes it sound like she had some agency around it. I had my arm around her shoulders and hers was around mine, and yet there was no one there, no sense of her being special. I recall something Katie said about her husband Stephen Mitchell, that he was brave enough to be married to the impersonal. And I really felt I understood what she meant, in those moments I describe above.

There's truly something profoundly alive in this absence—losing her 'self' gave her everything it would seem. It's for this—this peace, this joy, this truth that I write the below, that we may all learn firsthand what it is to be liberated from the self.

Biographies

The true value of a human being is determined primarily by the measure and the sense in which [one] has attained liberation from the self.

Albert Einstein

~

I have chosen the subjects for this exploration because I have personal experience of them and/or they were the first examples of awakened people I encountered[16]. They have clear, direct knowledge of what they are speaking and writing about that is apparent simply by reading or watching them. Their humility—their complete lack of ego—and compassion are also clearly evident. They have all experienced what is known as an 'awakening experience' (Taylor, 2005); that is, they went from existing in a state of consciousness that most humans seem to apparently inhabit to a state of consciousness where they were no longer identified with their minds; they transcended thought and pierced the veil of conditioning to have a direct experience of themselves and life beyond any *thought* about themselves and life. Furthermore, this state of consciousness remained permanent for each of them. Also, all four have become what we could

---

[16] Other awakened people exist of course; some are well-known and there are perhaps many more who are not. Jeff Foster (lifewithoutacentre.com), for example, has recently attracted notice as a young teacher (Bentinho Massaro is another) who is making generous use of social media to connect with people. Jo Dunning is another. This teaching is really not new at all, of course, though it is relatively new in the West. It has been a part of Eastern culture for ages through many sages such as Nisargadatta Maharaj and Ramana Maharshi. Spiritual awakening was brought to the West through the teachings of Jesus that were eventually turned into doctrine and dogma, through the mistaken belief that the truth was something the mind could grasp. There is evidence that First Peoples (see Steve Taylor's *The Fall*) in the West and throughout the world exhibited the awakened consciousness of which I write. There seems now to be a real impetus towards this awakening throughout the world: many people seem to be awakening to a new consciousness.

call teachers of awakening—through their words, but mostly through their example. Given this, they often have things to say about communicating the ineffable to others, about the role of a teacher, about assisting others to awaken—the possibilities and the impossibilities—despite not being involved in formal education (with the exception of Krishnamurti).

Krishnamurti, Tolle, and Katie[17] are quite well known and have been very prolific in terms of audio, video, and written data by them[18] so there is a lot of material to draw on. Veltheim is not as well known but I have included her as I found her book, *Beyond Concepts*, to really focus on the specifics of the process of transformation for the individual (her), which is also the focus of this book; she meets the reader where they are in the 'old' consciousness, addressing blocks they are experiencing and how to surmount them, based on her own experience. Furthermore, Vetheim's awakening was a gradual process, perhaps more akin to Krishnamurti's— which she is able to describe articulately and walk a reader through— unlike the apparently sudden awakening of Tolle's and Katie's[19]. I think this diversity proves helpful.

Krishnamurti[20]

Jiddu Krishnamurti was 'discovered' while he was playing on a beach

---

[17] In terms of personal contact with the subjects, I have attended talks or workshops with both Tolle and Katie; in addition, I have engaged in numerous processes of doing "The Work" as facilitated by both myself and others.

[18] In Krishnamurti's case, while he personally wrote only a handful of books, many more have been created through transcribing his talks, both before and after his death.

[19] It is interesting to note that although Katie and Tolle seemed to suddenly 'be awake,' they also suffered through years of depression beforehand like Veltheim which she actually includes as an essential part of the process because that is how she experienced it. Krishnamurti went through an acute depression before his awakening, brought on by the death of his brother. All of them spent time integrating the awakening experience afterwards.

[20] There are numerous books and articles written about Krishnamurti so I will not go into many facts about him here. I refer the reader to *Krishnamurti's Notebook* which contains his own account of his awakening process. Evelyn Blau's book, *Krishnamurti 100 Years*, gives witness accounts, as well as an overview of his life.

with his brother near Madras (Chennai), India by Charles Leadbeater, a Theosophist, who claimed that Krishnamurti had a "pure aura," uncontaminated by any selfishness. Together with Annie Bessant, then head of the Theosophical Society, they proclaimed Krishnamurti the awaited "world teacher" (or second coming of Christ)—a title that he would famously disavow when at the age of twenty-one he dissolved the order that had been set up to support him to bring his teachings into the world:

> I maintain that truth is a pathless land, and you cannot approach it by any path whatsoever, by any religion, by any sect. That is my point of view, and I adhere to that absolutely and unconditionally. Truth, being limitless, unconditioned, unapproachable by any path whatsoever, cannot be organized; nor should any organization be formed to lead or coerce people along a particular path. ... This is no magnificent deed, because I do not want followers, and I mean this. The moment you follow someone you cease to follow Truth. I am not concerned whether you pay attention to what I say or not. I want to do a certain thing in the world and I am going to do it with unwavering concentration. I am concerning myself with only one essential thing: to set [humankind] free. I desire to free [humankind] from all cages, from all fears, and not to found religions, new sects, nor to establish new theories and new philosophies. (Krishnamurti, 1929)

Prior to this, Krishnamurti had gone through a three-day intense process of spiritual transformation that resulted in an experience of mystical union and immense peace (Lutyens, 1975, pp. 158-160). "The process" as he came to call it continued throughout his life but with decreased intensity. In his journal, he wrote that he "...woke up early with that strong feeling of otherness, of another world that is beyond all thought..." (Krishnamurti, 2003, p.38).

Krishnamurti spent his life traveling and giving talks and writing. He also founded eight schools: six in India, one in England, and one in California. His concern was psychological freedom:

All authority of any kind, especially in the field of thought and understanding, is the most destructive, evil thing. Leaders destroy the followers and followers destroy the leaders. You have to be your own teacher and your own disciple. You have to question everything that [humans have] accepted as valuable, as necessary. (1969, p.21)

Eckhart Tolle

Eckhart Tolle is fairly well known currently as a spiritual teacher and the story of his awakening experience is well documented. In brief, Tolle recounts how he had suffered terrible depression for years and during one painful night, he thought to himself, 'I can't live with myself any more,' feeling that he must end his life. That thought was followed by another in which he wondered who was the 'I' and who was the 'myself'—that is, how there could possibly be two of him. In that moment, his mind suddenly let go and he heard a voice in his head telling him to "resist nothing." He fell into sleep and when he awoke, he was in a deep state of peace. Although he didn't realize it then (because he had no way of knowing what had happened, not having a context for what he experienced), his continuous flow of thinking had stopped, enabling him to feel at peace. He has described an immense silence and knew that he was experiencing his real self, and that everything before this moment was life as experienced through *ideas* of his self and life.

In the subsequent two years, he said he mostly sat on a park bench, completely in awe of the experience of pure being. He has since said that he was integrating his experience at this time—without any idea, literally, of himself or life, and no idea of a past or future, he was content to just 'be' and did little else. In trying to make sense of what he was experiencing, he turned to books. He has said that he "quickly realized academia did not have the answers I was looking for" and turned instead to the great wisdom traditions and/or religious texts where he began to piece together what had happened to him. Eventually, as people came to him for help with their personal suffering, he began to host groups of people in his home, giving talks.

In time, he had the sense that he was to move to the west coast of Canada (he was living in Europe), which is where he wrote his first book, *The Power of Now*. He has acknowledged that there was a field of consciousness on the west coast (in the United States as well) that enabled the book to come "through" him. He has also written *A New Earth* and *Stillness Speaks*.

Byron Katie

Byron Katie has a similar story to that of Eckhart Tolle. She had been in a deep depression for several years, the last two of which she rarely left her bed, despite being a working mother to three children. She had checked herself into a halfway house and recounts how the women there were all terrified of her because she was so volatile and angry. One morning while there, she awoke on the attic floor (where she had been sleeping because she was too dangerous to share a room with another and her self-hatred had her believe she did not deserve a bed) when a cockroach ran over her foot. Like Tolle, she found herself in a deep state of peace. "Then the mind hit," she has said, and she immediately realized that with thought, there is stress, while without thought, there is no stress[21]. She describes this moment as when what she calls "inquiry" was born in her. Essentially, this is the questioning of what we think we know to be true—questioning the mind—as a bridge into the unknown and psychological freedom.

Katie describes how, shortly after this dramatic awakening she would enter other people's homes, knowing they were hers—as her experience that she was one with everything was so complete—and experience with delight how the people in them would "lie" and say that she did not own this home. Her family would get her and take her home. And so, slowly she learned "how not to alienate people" when she expressed disbelief in their stories. For example, she describes going along with her family and friends'

---

[21] To be clear, the equation is: believing stressful thoughts causes the suffering. Believing thoughts that are kind does not cause suffering; this works for us. The question of their truth is another matter—one, incidentally, that The Work also accesses.

assertion that she was a "Katie" because although this had no meaning for her and was therefore not true in her experience, she had no reason not to let them have their story; it was causing no harm.

She has said that she realized that everyone was entitled to have this ability to question their mind through inquiry and willingly helped people who came to her. She describes her early interactions with people, after her awakening experience:

> People used to ask me if I was enlightened, and I would say, "I don't know anything about that. I'm just someone who knows the difference between what hurts and what doesn't." I am someone who wants only what is. To meet as a friend each concept that arose turned out to be my freedom. (2007, p.30)

Esther Veltheim

Esther Veltheim's transformation began with her experiences with Reiki where she experienced that "thoughts cut off during it" (p.216). In 1989, Esther founded, with John Veltheim, the Reiki Network, which still exists today and cofounded PaRama, a "school of philosophy and life sciences."

Veltheim describes her process of awakening in detail in the final chapter of her book *Beyond Concepts* (2000) called "Satsang: What is Enlightenment?" in the traditional question and answer form. In it, she recounts how she too, spontaneously emerged from a two-year depression like Katie and found herself (also spontaneously; that is, not as a decision), again like Katie, "investigat[ing] every concept that people think of as significant, such as control, sin, enlightenment, illusion[22]" (p.200). She did this by writing a book (though she never published it): "The writing was, I guess, the mind's way of finding explanations and processing the dissolution of dualistic thoughts" (p.200). This investigation of concepts

---

[22] Katie has also noted that stilling the mind requires writing the thoughts down, at least for considerable time initially.

she calls "jnana yoga" (pp.200, 216) which she undertook in her own way.

She describes what has also been my own personal experience, that "I figured that my mind was too active to meditate....Other than Reiki, I didn't relate to other forms of meditation. As my mind was sharp, I decided to use the power of discrimination constructively. I investigated and unraveled concepts and beliefs" (2000, p.216).

At the end of her transformation, Esther describes how she felt/feels in identical terms to that of Tolle: "Very natural and absolutely ordinary are the best way of describing it. All desires to be other than I am have gone. The desire to become special has dissolved in ordinariness" (p.206). Esther's answer to the question, "So, is your mind still active?" gives us a sense of the mind post-awakening:

> When I'm writing, it's active: but very peaceful and thinking is effortless....But I am noticing that when interaction is necessary, it's often rather like coming up to the top of a deep ocean. The mind is really very peaceful—that is its nature after all. You weren't born with a stressed-out mind. So sometimes, it's almost hard to interact. (p.215)

Esther developed something she calls the "BreakThrough System"—"a dynamic process of self-investigation." She conducts advanced workshops internationally and in the U.S. as well as gives instructor training programs for BreakThrough.

The Nature of Thought

The highest form of human intelligence is to observe yourself without judgement.

J. Krishnamurti

~

This first section examines the nature of thought—how it works, its origin, its function, its relationship with emotion, and consciousness, what it is both capable of and not capable of, how and why it puts together the "I" identity and the external world we experience with our senses, etc. This exploration takes place in the context of perceiving education as primarily a developer of thought (as the paradigm currently exists, as explored in *Awake*) and questioning whether this is ultimately a helpful or harmful orientation for education. This section is the largest because once the nature of thought is understood then the major hurdle (i.e. being identified with thought) has been overcome.

Inability of the Mind to Know the Whole

The base nature of the mind is "the desire to know, understand, and control" (Tolle, 2003, p.15); in short, to be right. Given that this is so, it develops "opinions and viewpoints" which it "mistakes...for the truth" when in reality, this is an *interpretation* of life and only "one of many possible perspectives." By definition, thinking cannot apprehend reality because "reality is one unified whole, in which all things are interwoven, where nothing exists in and by itself" whereas thinking's task is to fragment reality—"it cuts it up into conceptual bits and pieces." Veltheim (2000) uses different language to describe the same phenomenon, describing Tolle's "whole" as "an absolute" and referring to his "opinions and viewpoints" as "concepts," agreeing with Tolle that concepts/thought/the mind will never contain the truth: "Because all concepts are dependent on the existence of their contradiction, no concept is an absolute. When the paradox of life is deeply understood, duality no longer poses a problem" (p.3).

Veltheim introduces the concept of *duality* here—the existence of something only in relation to its opposite. So the paradox comes, then, when we begin to entertain the idea of 'both/and' instead of 'either/or'—something that the mind is not capable of.

Byron Katie describes the same "no concept is an absolute" in recounting her "awakening" experience: "I saw that nothing was true..." She goes on to explain a bit about the function of the mind, that it was never a vehicle meant to capture reality: "Then the mind hit and I saw that the mind wasn't true and I saw that people *believed* their thoughts...because the mind immediately is giving them all the proof and all the images; that's how the mind works" (Katie, 2008).

In her awakened state, Katie initially had no thoughts, she had no beliefs operating through which she was mediating her experience. Then thought began operating within her again but she did not identify with it, she observed it. In other words, the reason nothing can be *true* is because things known are in the realm of knowledge, which as we've explored is only thought taking a position on something—one perspective out of many possible perspectives.

The second part of Katie's statement describes, however, what the mind *is* excellent at: picking out of all previous experience the things that line up with this position, by way of making this perspective stronger, and more stable. This definition of mind is in line with Krishnamurti's description of the mind being made up of the past, whether through one's personal experience (in actuality, thoughts interpreting the experience) or through someone else's stored knowledge and experience transmitted through teaching—none of which can be said to be true.

Krishnamurti refers to this information gathering process as *conditioning* the mind. The mind, in other words, is incapable of seeing what is true; to access reality, we must go to somewhere other than the mind/thought.

The Mind Does Not Think, It *Is* Thought

In terms of the relationship of *consciousness* with the mind: it has become a habit of the mind to absorb all human consciousness, that is, to make humans believe that thinking and themselves are one and the same. We don't leave room for consciousness to observe thought. (Eckhart Tolle)

> The gravitational pull of the old mind structures and the mental habit of absorbing all your consciousness into thinking is very strong and old. So there is a momentum there or a heaviness, old pull of the mind that is used to possessing your entire consciousness and continues transforming your entire consciousness into thinking and it wants to come back in there. It wants you to give your total attention to thinking, become one with the thinking. (www. eckharttolletv.com, August 2011)

So, Tolle points out both the tremendous habit of absorbing consciousness into thinking, and also that humans *are not* that thinking but instead *the consciousness* that has been absorbed into the thinking; they are not one and the same. This point might seem obvious to you, yet this is how most of us live, and think that it's normal—i.e. at the mercy of thought. Katie describes the phenomenon of "becom[ing] one with the thinking mind" in a simple way: "Most people think that they are what their thoughts tell them they are" (http://thework.com/downloads/little_book/English_LB.pdf).

Veltheim agrees that one of our biggest impediments is misunderstanding the mind as a distinct source of intelligence itself—that is, believing that when we access the mind, we are accessing a distinct entity that is capable of insight. "What needs to be understood is that the mind does not think—it IS thoughts. To most, the mind is considered the enemy and something to be battled with. But your involvement with thoughts and identification with them are the only 'problem'" (p.36). This is a tremendously important point.

So humans, then, in being identified with the mind and unable to see the whole (of life and/or any aspect of it) forego a lived experience of their connection to all life and their place in it.

Or, as Tolle describes it, "a sense of the miraculous...was lost a long time ago when humanity, instead of using thought, became possessed by thought." (Dec. 2011, www.eckharttolle.com)

The implications of losing a lived experience of this sense of the miraculous in life are astronomical and involve all aspects of someone's experience; in short, it is what is responsible for allowing people to be capable of hurting themselves, one another (both on a small and grand scale), other creatures, and what we call the environment or the 'natural world.' (I outline the implications more fully—especially as they relate to education—in the final chapter of *Awake*.)

Inability of Controlling Thought

In the following quotation, Krishnamurti uses the word "awareness" to describe a state where one's consciousness is not entirely absorbed in thinking and is thus able to witness thought, alleviating the impulse to try to control it:

> And it is only in silence that you can observe the beginning of thought *not when you are searching, asking questions, waiting for a reply.* So it is only when you are completely quiet, right through your being, having put that question, 'What is the beginning of thought?" that you will begin to see, out of that silence, how thought takes shape[23].
>
> If there is an awareness of how thought begins then there is no need to control thought. We spend a great deal of time and waste a great deal of energy all through our lives, not only at school, trying to

---

[23] What Krishnamurti describes here, which could be called a process, is also the process of the Enlightenment Intensive and The Work of Byron Katie that I describe in detail, through my own experience of it, in *Awake*. It is a process of observing rather than entering the thinking mind and analyzing through thinking.

control our thoughts—'This is a good thought, I must think about it a lot. This is an ugly thought, I must suppress it.' There is a battle going on all the time between one thought and another, one desire and another, one pleasure dominating all other pleasures. But if there is an awareness of the beginning of thought, then there is no contradiction in thought. (Krishnamurti, 1969. pp.103-104, italics mine)

In addition to pointing out how and why we try to control thought, Krishnamurti also here offers a great description of how perception or insight—an aspect of his definition of "intelligence"—occurs for someone through something other than through thought. It's more like an *observation* of the answer. (I'll come back to this further on.)

Byron Katie also points out that while one might logically conclude that if we could control thinking (as in the belief in the efficacy of using positive affirmations as popularized by the self-help movement) that this would be the solution to the problem of being mind-identified, this is not possible. "…you can't stop mental chaos, however motivated you are. But if you identify one piece of chaos and stabilize it, then the whole world begins to make sense," and, flying in the face of convention, Katie suggests that not only is it futile to control thought, but to actually meet one's thoughts with awareness turns out to be a path to their freedom. I have found the same thing: doing The Work relieves suffering *and* insights are revealed to me I couldn't see otherwise.

For me, thoughts are the beloved. Thoughts are not to kill or avoid or dodge or meditate down or medicate down; they're to be met with unconditional love, as though they were children just screaming to be understood and that's what The Work brings us to…the mind…to a complete understanding of itself and…enlightened to itself—mind enlightened to itself, mind in love with itself, the love affair with itself. You know, terms like self-love…when the mind loves the mind it loves everything it sees. (online interview with Bill Harris)

And:

> People try to "let go" of their thoughts. That's like telling your child you don't want her and kicking her out onto the street....Of course, I would never ask people not to believe their thoughts. Not only would that be unkind; it isn't possible for people not to believe what they believe. We can't help believing our thoughts until we question them. That's the way of it. (2007, p.29)

So Katie here makes a clear distinction between *thinking* and *believing*; while we may think something, the important thing to realize is that we do not have to believe it. This distinction points to the origin, that in fact we are not doing the thinking because it is not a personal act of agency; thoughts just happen. It would be more accurate to say we are being thought. Whereas believing requires personal agency, by default we are our thoughts.

Katie explains how one *does* get free of thought: "No one has ever been able to control his thinking, although people may tell the story of how they have. I don't let go of my thoughts—I meet them with understanding. Then they let go of me" (http://thework.com/downloads/little_book/English_LB.pdf).

So, having the experience of seeing for oneself the reality or truth of a situation, through inquiring into it, allows the thought to complete itself and it then is free to leave; before, it seemed to have unfinished business with a person. The thought was there to cause pain until questioned; it was there to wake one up to reality. I recently found myself describing the experience of The Work to my daughter as like unwrapping a present, that people think The Work is for alleviating suffering by getting rid of the unwanted thoughts, but that this is not my experience. Inquiry actually comes bearing gifts.

It would seem that the very nature of thought is to arise and fall away, *if we allow it*. In addition, it would seem that thought can be used by us as a tool once we have the experience that we are not it.

Tolle recounts how, since his awakening, he has long stretches of his days where no thought crosses his mind. Then, if he requires the use of it, he uses it. He is not *controlling* thought, as there is no thought there to be controlled. This is in dramatic contrast to how most of us feel imprisoned by our thoughts, unable to *not* be used by thought. Indeed, for most of us, it is an unfathomable experience—to imagine no-thought.

Impersonal Nature of Thought

Esther Veltheim (2000, p.45) offers a succinct description of our experience of thinking: "No thought arises because of you, and you don't know how thoughts happen, or where they come from" and "...you have no idea how thoughts appear in your mind, or where they come from. Despite this you take delivery of them, think they are personal to you, and you act on them. Does that make any sense to you?" (p.95).

That thoughts are not personal is really a paradigm-altering statement, since it seems that our education paradigm hinges on the belief that thoughts *are* personal—that is, that they can be generated, controlled, and manipulated by the individual; indeed, we consider those the most intelligent who have the most detailed and sophisticated thoughts, the greatest amount of knowledge, and the highest ability to manipulate concepts.

Yet, Katie has said that no one is wiser than anyone else; we all have the same amount of intelligence—indeed, the same intelligence (2006b). So, the difference between her and others, for example, could be explained by saying that she is 'awake' to the true nature of life and thought while most of the rest of us are 'asleep' to our true nature and our reality as aware beings separate from thought. That is, we are just not *aware* that we have access to the same wisdom.

Katie explains how one might notice that thoughts cannot possibly be personal; that is, not generated by an individual person:

One day I noticed that I wasn't breathing—I was being breathed. Then I also noticed, to my amazement, that I wasn't thinking—that I was actually being thought and that thinking isn't personal. Do you wake up in the morning and say to yourself, "I think I won't think today"? It's too late: You're already thinking! Thoughts just appear. They come out of nothing and go back to nothing, like clouds moving across the empty sky. They come to pass, not to stay. There is no harm in them until we attach to them as if they were true. (http://thework.com/downloads/little_book/English_LB.pdf)

We believe that the thoughts that cross our paths are true—which we do, I believe, because we feel we have had agency in generating them. The fact that we don't know we're doing this is what causes all the harm in the world, to ourselves and to others. We have simply to observe what happens when we are acting as if a stressful thought is true for us to see it.

Katie also alludes here to what we could call a passiveness or receiving experience where she is not the 'doer' but, rather, is *being done*. This is a hint at what Krishnamurti refers to as intelligence that is not of the mind. It is the beginning of being willing to consider that 'we'—this idea we have constructed of individual identities and individually generated intelligence—are not in charge. At base, it requires only a simple recognizing or noticing that if we cannot control thinking, if it just appears unbidden by us, then perhaps there is an agency or source of intelligence *different from thought* as Krishnamurti, Tolle, Katie, Veltheim and others claim.

Thought and Emotion

Finally, a discussion of thought would be incomplete without also discussing emotion, for they are intimately connected. I would argue that the common understanding of emotion is that it arises separately from thought—in the sense that one would say a given experience *just makes one feel a certain way*. However, Tolle and others posit that emotion almost always follows thought: "Be aware that what you think, to a large extent, creates the emotions that you feel. See the link between your thinking and your emotions. Rather than being your thoughts and emotions, be the awareness behind them" (Tolle, 2008, p.5). Katie explains the link between thought and emotion:

> A feeling is like a mate to a thought appearing. It's like a left and a right. If you have a thought, there's a simultaneous feeling. And an uncomfortable feeling is like a compassionate alarm clock that says, "You're in the dream." It's time to investigate, that's all. But if we don't honor the alarm clock, then we try to alter and manipulate the feeling by reaching into an apparent external world. We're usually aware of the feeling first. That's why I say it's an alarm clock that lets you know you're in a thought that you may want to investigate. If its not acceptable to you, if it's painful, you might want to inquire and do The Work. (Katie, 2006b, p.15-16)

The re-framing of emotion as something that can change, based as it is on thought and not independent of thought, has important implications for self-experiencing and self-understanding, which in turn has significant ramifications for interactions between individuals.

In brief, if people are not governed by their thoughts and emotions they are free to choose peaceful interactions: they can be capable of real listening, which is real empathy and real compassion. (The consequences of this sort of freedom are discussed further in *Awake*.)

While Tolle advises *Rather than being your thoughts and emotions, be the awareness behind them*, this isn't so simple, in my experience, without some guidance given that it is not an intellectual exercise but an actual experience one is after.

Katie's The Work gives this consistently and reliably, in my experience. When one disengages from their current thoughts, the emotion created from these thoughts also lets go, and what remains is "the awareness behind them." Katie gives a good summation of the process below:

Through inquiry, we discover how attachment to a belief or story causes suffering. Before the story there is peace. Then a thought enters, we believe it, and the peace seems to disappear. We notice the feeling of stress in the moment, investigate the story behind it, and realize that it isn't true. The feeling lets us know we are opposing what is by believing the thought. It tells us that we're at war with reality. When we notice that we're believing a lie and living as if it were true, we become present outside our story. Then the story falls away in the light of awareness, and only the *awareness* of what really is remains. Peace is who we are without a story, until the next stressful story appears. Eventually inquiry becomes alive in us as the natural, wordless response of *awareness* to the thoughts and stories that arise. (Katie, 2006, p.10-11; italics mine)

The Work allows us the experience of awareness rather than keeping it as an intellectual exercise, something that has never changed anything, ever.

Construction and Destruction of the 'I' (The 'Knower') *or* Thought Becoming Identity

Esther Veltheim (2000) touches on something that I think the holistic education paradigm, progressive as it can be, is still susceptible of falling prey to and that is taking all this information on the mind and self and presenting it to students conceptually rather than allowing them to have their own experiences of self and the mind (etc.). The point, then, is to continually point students back to their own experience by reminding them that anything that is said about the self is meant to act as a theory until it is tested *by them*. "You think you are a body, a mind, and perhaps a spirit and a soul" (p.3) writes Veltheim. "You weren't born with a mind full of concepts. Before they entered your mind, no limitation was experienced. There was simply the pre-personalized awareness of being…. Before you learned to describe yourself as "I am some-one," "I am this," "I am that," there was awareness only of being" (p.9).

Veltheim describes here the birth of the "I" identity that is so compellingly real for most of us that we never think to question or verify its reality. And yet, as Veltheim describes, it is merely an image put together by thought; it doesn't exist in reality. Furthermore, the belief in its existence prevents knowing the true or actual Self. "This self-image is the only thing inhibiting you from knowing who you really are" (p.17).

At this point, the mind, still actively trying to know, tries to see oneself then outside its (the mind's) filters. Veltheim explains clearly why this is impossible:

> You cannot think of yourself in terms of a non-concept, because the mind IS conceptualization. If you understand this deeply, you will realize that via the mind you can never know who You are, in reality. Via the mind, you can only discover who you are not. (p.98)

Krishnamurti also advised that we not try to know things but to unknow; that is, approach the reality of things by determining what they *are not*. Others have dubbed this approach of his as *negation*.

Seeking the Feeling of 'Safe'

Why we seek psychological security is because this "I" believes it is real (i.e. that it's alive, an entity unto itself) and therefore that it can perish (die). So it identifies with whatever it can identify with: a body as identity is an easy one; a mind is another. It seeks constant reassurance of its existence through observation of contrast (ex. I'm *this*, not that; we're *us* not them). It's easy to see how this is the root of violence based on race, religion, nationality, ideology, gender identity, etc.

But what is this "I" who seeks security because it feels threatened? What is that entity? And what happens when we question it? In my experience, it is possible to experience myself outside of thought *but not through thought*; that is, thought is outside of this experiencing. Which is to say: thought cannot apprehend reality. Veltheim (2000) confirms that this quest for "intellectual understanding" of the Self to "fall away" (p.5) as a natural result of seeing what the mind is.

Peter Ralston[24] (1991) points out the subtle path of transformation of consciousness and how we initially try to make this happen within our "I" identity:

> ...we notice with overwhelming and devastating clarity that absolutely nothing we do or achieve, no matter how apparently powerful or happy it is, changes our fundamental condition at all, not even slightly. This is so because the essential context is not even touched. All that we do is done within the context of "self," so the sense of "I" always remains. "I" may identify with different things, and this identity may change radically, but don't be fooled into thinking that this has changed the existence of "I" in the least. The true practice of Being is to understand this, and recognize that "I" does not exist; then the dissolution of "I" occurs simply through the direct-experience of the nature of Being. (p.74)

So, the "I" cannot be gotten rid of, but dissolves naturally upon seeing clearly, which is to say, seeing reality, 'what is.' What this means is that there is no longer a 'thinker/knower'—one is not *doing* anything, not *trying*, not *thinking*—the central "I" disappears, as there is now nothing holding it together. Thought was the mechanism that was holding the idea of an 'I'

---

[24] In 1978, Peter Ralston became the first non-Asian ever to win the World Championship full-contact martial arts tournament held in the Republic of China. Consistent with Zen studies, his investigation into martial arts also came to include a questioning of reality. Long periods of intense contemplation resulted in many enlightenment experiences regarding the nature of self and reality, which greatly influenced his study. To communicate his understanding, Ralston founded the Cheng Hsin School in 1975. In 1977 he opened a centre called "The Cheng Hsin School of Internal Martial Arts and Center for Ontological Research" in Oakland, California. His main focus in his facilitation work is to uncover the truth of things, to break through assumptions and beliefs, and to assist others in having a direct, authentic, and experiential increase in Consciousness. (chenghsin.com)

together and thereby keeping a separation between itself and anything else (—this is the "optical illusion of separation" that Einstein refers to that I mentioned in *Awake*).

Creation of External Reality

Just as the mind creates the "I" for each of us, it also creates external reality, or the world of form. Byron Katie describes how this manifests, how powerful our minds are, and what happens when we are identified with 'the thinker':

> The world is your perception of it. Inside and outside always match—they are reflections of each other. The world is the mirror image of your mind. If you experience chaos and confusion inside, your external world has to reflect that. You have to see what you believe, because you are the confused thinker looking out and seeing yourself. You are the interpreter of everything, and if you're chaotic, what you hear and see has to be chaos. Even if Jesus, even if the Buddha, were standing in front of you, you would hear confused words, because confusion would be the listener. You would only hear what you thought he was saying, and you'd start arguing with him the first time your story was threatened. (Katie, 2006b, p.28-29)

And:

> When you do The Work, you see who you are by seeing who you think other people are. Eventually you come to see that everything outside you is a reflection of your own thinking. You are the storyteller, the projector of all stories, and the world is the projected image of your thoughts. (2002, p.12)

If this is the case, then it follows logically that in order to experience things as they are (which we call reality) then we would need to step outside of thought. Krishnamurti famously said, "You are the world." I believe that this is what he meant—that is, that we project our own beliefs out and create the world of form, including everything we see in everyone else. I also believe this is what Krishnamurti meant when he said, "All life is relationship." That is, we encounter ourselves—who we are—through our relationships with others; they literally mirror us back to ourselves. Krishnamurti, too, points out that thought is matter—that is, that there is a form that results from it, that it is not neutral or inert:

> Those who think a great deal are very materialistic because thought is matter. Thought is matter as much as the floor, the wall, the telephone, are matter. Energy functioning in a pattern becomes matter. There is energy and there is matter. That is all life is. [like Eckhart's "There is space, and there are things in space."] Thought is matter as an ideology. Thought has set up this pattern of pleasure, pain, fear, and has been functioning inside it for thousands of years and cannot break the pattern because it has created it. (1969, pp.101-102)

In this, I see a reframing of what I might call the 'status' of thought from its position on a pedestal in education (i.e. *"There's no such thing as thinking too much"*) to thought as 'being caught up in *things*' as one is whom we call "materialistic." Furthermore, Krishnamurti makes the same case as Katie when he claims that our unawareness of our attachment to thought makes us attempt to use thought to cut through the patterns created by thought— an obvious impossibility.

Thought Transcended

To leave home is half the Buddha's teaching.

Milarepa

~

There has to be at least a bit of willingness to leave the known—that is, one's dearly held beliefs. There has to be at least a tiny openness to consider that what one feels one *knows* could perhaps be incorrect. This is what it is "to leave home."

Going *Through* Thought: Self-Inquiry/Experiencing

Moving beyond thought to an experience of oneself as the *awareness* behind thought happens experientially (that is, not conceptually):

> If you can recognize, even occasionally, the thoughts that go through your mind as simply thoughts, if you can witness your own mental-emotional reactive patterns as they happen, then that dimension is already emerging in you as the awareness in which thoughts and emotions happen—the timeless inner space in which the content of your life unfolds. (Tolle, 2003, p.14)

Tolle distinguishes here between the content of one's life and "the timeless inner space" or "awareness" that is life itself—that is, who we are. We have confused the two, and therein lies the problem.

Yet when we are able to witness or watch emotions arise within us as reactions to thoughts, then we can start to be able to pull the two (awareness and content) apart and the result is a natural identification with the witness, or timeless inner space, as who we truly are. Using oneself as the means of inquiring into the truth is not only a valuable tool, it is the only way through to direct experience, given that the only thing we are sure of is our individual experiencing (i.e. that we, as an individual, are here, experiencing):

> Catholic Saint Francis: "What we are looking for is who is looking." If you have ever wondered if you really exist, close your eyes, direct your attention within, and ask yourself, "Who wants to know?"
>
> The power of asking "Who wants to know?" as a way of knowing God is called self-inquiry. Vedanta teachers say that all religious practices for knowing God are postponements, because no ritual or activity will bring you closer to what you already are. The teacher Gangaji describes self-inquiry as "an intense concentration of attention on the *source* of this attention and awareness itself." (Katra & Targ, 1999, p.153)

Katra and Targ use the word "God" whereas Katie says she refers to God as "reality because it rules" (personal communication, 2012). So when we say we want to know God, what we are really saying is we want to know reality; we know intuitively that this is where our minds can rest, in this truth of how things are, how life is. The source or witness of attention can (only) be experienced/known outside of any ideas or thought (about the source or witness).

Seeing that the mind is not who we are, then, leads us to find the freedom we are in continuous search of; we are no longer trapped by the limits of what we think. Furthermore, in my experience, when I realize who I am and that it is not my mind, I realize my true nature is love, peace, kindness, compassion, etc. In this is the "choiceless awareness" that Krishnamurti speaks of, as well as Byron Katie. Freedom, ironically, comes from realizing that we do not have a choice when it comes to who we really are; we do not need to choose, we just 'be' who it is that we are, which is the great truth and freedom we are all searching for. This is what the ancient Tao Te Ching means, as well as Tolle, Katie, Krishnamurti and others, when they talk about being in harmony with life, with The Way things are—perceiving 'what is.' Tolle sums up the human condition as "lost in thought" and its salvation as "One with life" (2003, p.13). In my experience, there is a great freedom in not having to choose and great suffering from believing I can—and must—make choices, when in fact on one hand I am ruled by what it is I believe and on the other hand I am being lived—the paradox of life. In neither do I actually have agency. So action springing from this state of consciousness—where one is not ruled by thought—is much different than action springing from a state of consciousness where one is completely mind-identified.

When we believe our thoughts, we must act as a result of our beliefs; but if we can realize that we do not have to believe our thoughts, we are free. Most of us don't realize we can attach or unattach to thoughts and beliefs (actually, as we have seen above, we cannot let go of thoughts, but they can let go of us). The simple way to realize this is to ask yourself, 'Who would you be without <a given> thought?' Since it is possible to answer this question, then we must not be our thoughts.

In other words, if we did not have any thoughts, we would still exist. The only way to know this for ourselves, though, is to inquire into it *experientially*. This is why Krishnamurti, at the beginning of every one of his talks, implored his listeners to *inquire into* the subjects under discussion *with him*. The words are useless unless each person takes the journey. Otherwise, it remains in the realm of the conceptual—a fantasy world of the imagination that we mistake for the real.

Both Tolle and Katie have echoed this and I have experienced it for myself. Katie puts it, "I cannot wake you or my friend up with my words… you both can do that" (blog post, http://www.byronkatie.com/ April 9, 2011). If words do not teach then, but only life (i.e. personal experiencing), then we need to take a good, hard look at what we think we are doing with education. For in our current paradigm, we certainly believe that words can and do teach; I would argue that this premise forms the basis for our current education paradigm, that's how pervasive and dominant is this belief. To reiterate what I've said earlier, this is not to say that forms of knowledge are not communicated through words, but that the most essential understandings cannot be; and through our current education system, we are perpetuating the belief that all things can be understood (or accessed) through thought, because of course, the paradigm believes this to be the case.

This self-experiencing, or, self-inquiry is crucial—in fact, is the source of all learning—as Katie makes clear in this remarkable claim: "*Teacher* implies that we all don't teach equally or have equal wisdom. And that's not true. Everyone has equal wisdom. It is absolutely equally distributed. No one is wiser than anyone else. There's no one who can teach you except yourself" (Katie, 2006b, p.32). There is a correlation, then, between experience (or 'experiential education' we could say) and transcendence of thought/non-conceptual intelligence—i.e. not accepting others' beliefs and ideas but experiencing the truth for yourself. Consider Veltheim: "Unless all concepts have fallen away, your investigation of self must continue. There are no levels of progress and no degrees of enlightenment. Either you know, beyond a shadow of a doubt, that you are not a concept, or you are identified with a concept" (p.130). So concepts, then, have nothing to do with the experience of reality. You cannot *think* yourself into knowing.

Finally, Krishnamurti explains it in the following way:

> …any amount of seeking truth, of talking valiantly and in most scholarly ways, or interpreting the innumerable sacred books has no value at all. So you might as well just throw away all the sacred books and start over again, because they, with their interpreters, their teachers, their gurus, have not brought enlightenment to you….So you might just as well put them all aside and learn from yourself, for therein lies truth, not in the "truth" of another. (1971, pp.97-98)

What Krishnamurti says here (along with Veltheim and Katie above) could be very provocative for many people, as it certainly goes against our current paradigm for gaining intelligence. In essence, he is saying that 1. Each of us contains the truth (or 'answers') of life 2. Scholarship cannot bring you to truth, and 3. The belief in the efficacy of this scholarship is a severe impediment to real learning. Instead, Krishnamurti says, look within:

> You must ask questions, not only of the speaker but of yourself, which is far more important. Ask yourself why you believe, why you follow, why you accept authority.... Question that and find out the answer; and you cannot find out the answer by asking another. You see, you have to stand alone, completely alone.... Therefore you must endlessly ask questions. And the more you ask of yourself, do not try to find an answer but ask and look. (1971, p.109)

So, we learn about life through ourselves—not as a personality, but as a generalized 'self' (as in, *What is this thing we call a 'self'?*). Self-inquiry is the portal, the way through. What is meant by *questioning* or *inquiry* is covered in the next section.

Questions versus Answers: the Open Mind

"Unless the individual is abiding at least 51 percent in that state of not knowing the mind it will be impossible to affect any degree of perfection, which is the true expression of the ultimate source of being..."(Cohen, 1997, p.27)

In the dominant education paradigm, *answering* is deemed particularly important: finding the right answers, knowing the right answers, etc. However, in my experience finding the right *questions* serves to open the mind and lead to insights; the "truth" (see Ralston below) presents itself in response to penetrating questions. Peter Ralston sums this up beautifully in the following:

Questioning serves to lead us to the truth. It is always appropriate. The truth is what is. Directly experiencing this, no question needs to be asked. If there is a question then something is still unknowing, isn't it? And there is always something still unknown. The goal is to be conscious of what's true; the goal isn't to be certain about some conclusion or other. (Winter 2012 Cheng Hsin Newsletter, p.16)

By distinguishing between being conscious of what's true and being able to be certain (or know), Ralston points to the difference between *seeing* or *knowing directly* rather than through the mind, for only the mind can feel it's sure about something. The Tao Te Ching explains the paradox this way: "When they think that they know the answers, people are difficult to guide. When they know that they don't know, people can find their own way" (Mitchell, 2009, p.65).

So, essentially what this says is: One must find her/his own way, and it starts with asking, not answering—with not-knowing, not knowing. According to Byron Katie (2007),

To think you know something is to believe the story of a past. It's insane. Every time you think you know something, it hurts, because in reality there's nothing to know. You're trying to hold on to something that doesn't exist. There is nothing to know, and there is no one who wants to know it. It's so much easier to know that you don't know. It's kinder, as well. I love the don't-know mind. When you know that you don't know, you're naturally open to reality and can let it take you wherever it wants to. You can drop your identity and be who your really are, the unlimited, the nameless. (p.236)

So, of course, Katie is speaking from her experience of this. To adopt this as a belief does no good. Test it. This leaving of the known is is such profound opposition to the very foundation that our education paradigm rests on. In the following, Katie offers a good description of the mind by metaphorically creating various 'parts' of the mind (which I've highlighted in bold) in order to help describe how it functions when it is allowed to question what it thinks it knows[25]:

> As we question what we believe, we come to see that we're not who we thought we were. The transformation comes out of the infinite **polarity of mind**, which we've rarely experienced, because the **I-know mind** has been so much in control. And as we inquire, our world changes, because we're working with the projector—mind—and not with what is projected. We lose our entire world, the world as we understood it. And each time we inquire, reality becomes kinder.
>
> The part that is doing the questioning is the **neutral part of the mind, the center**, which can take one polarity of mind to the other. The neutral part offers the confused, stuck, I-know mind the option to open itself to the polarity of mind that holds the sane, clear, loving answers that make sense to the I-know mind. The neutral part doesn't have a motive or desire, a *should* or a *shouldn't*; it's a bridge for this polarity to cross over. And as the I-know mind is educated, it dissolves into the polarity of wisdom. What's left is absolutely sane, undivided, and free. Of course, all this is just a metaphor, since there is only one mind. The bottom line is that when the mind is closed, the heart is closed; when the mind is open, the heart is open. So if you want to open your heart, question your thinking. (2007, pp.25-26, bold mine)

Katie's final statement here about the open mind is a profound reversal,

---

[25] It's appropriate to note that to anyone reading the following quote, it's unlikely to make sense unless one has experienced this for oneself. In my experience, the "polarity" to which Katie refers, is essentially the opposite point of view; when the mind starts to see something from multiple perspectives, as it does through inquiry, it realizes it can't rest in just one perspective any longer and becomes flexible or unstuck.

I would argue, from what we now commonly believe: normally we understand (and therefore teach) that if someone is not being kind, for example, there is something they *don't know*—as in, they don't know to be nice; yet Katie is saying the opposite, that it's precisely because they firmly believe they *know* something in relation to that situation that they are being unkind. Their mind, in other words, is closed. So, for example, Katie doesn't say, "So if you want to open your heart… "…become kind," or "…try to be nice," or "…see the other as yourself" which is how in our current education (and generally speaking) we usually try to 'teach' children to be kind and compassionate. (This is the modus operandi of what's called Character Education.) In other words, Katie explains that an open heart—kindness, compassion, presence, empathy, a desire to help, give, understand, and comfort—is our natural way but is covered over by thinking that would cause us to act otherwise, and therefore can only be uncovered by investigating this thinking, not by piling on more concepts such as "be nice." I have experienced this over and over in my experience of inquiry, that my true nature is pure love and this is self-evident. Veltheim (2000, p.127) says, "Your mind can't conceive of neutrality because it's locked into dualistic thinking. Either there is peace or there is strife. Either there is freedom or there is limitation." And yet, questioning serves to allow the mind to experience this elusive neutrality. So, continuing the example above, the mind might say, "I am not kind" and the pain of this causes one to act unkindly. However, through questioning this, one can see for oneself that one can be both kind and unkind which begins to loosen the duality (either/or thinking); questioning further, one can discover that without any painful thinking, one is always kind.

Attention (Listening, Seeing) as Intelligence
In this section, I go into the nature of attention so that we can see what is meant by it and discover what its function and capability is, in assisting awakening. Nisargadatta Maharaj (the Vedanta sage) said, "Intelligence is

the door to freedom, and alert attention is the mother of intelligence" (in Katra & Targ, 1999, p.136). So, attention is required for intelligence to be present, but what is it exactly?

Krishnamurti (1969) goes into detail on the nature of attention. Firstly, he distinguishes it from concentration: "Attention is not the same thing as concentration. Concentration is exclusion; attention, which is total awareness, excludes nothing" (p.31). Furthermore, he equates "whole attention" with awareness, saying that anything can be seen and understood if this is present. Finally, he maintains that only in authentic caring is one able to give full attention:

> If you want to understand the beauty of a bird, a fly, or a leaf, or a person with all his complexities, you have to give your whole attention which is awareness. And you can give your whole attention only when you care, which means that you really love to understand—then you give your whole heart and mind to find out.
>
> ...Such a state of attention is total energy; in such awareness the totality of yourself is revealed in an instant." (1969, pp.31-32).

So then, the wholeness of something is "revealed" when total attention is given—it is not a 'doing' by the observer; in other words, thought is not present. So it is attention that reveals the self, not thought. Not only is true perception only possible outside of thought, but the 'self' idea also disappears in a state of complete attention: "Have you ever noticed that when you are in a state of complete attention the observer, the thinker, the centre, the 'me,' comes to an end? In that state of attention thought begins to wither away" (1969, p.102).

Since it is thought holding together the "I" *and* preventing clear seeing, then in a state of total attention where there is *only* seeing, there can be no "I" and no thought; there can't be total attention and thought simultaneously. As Krishnamurti says, "Verbally we can go only so far: what lies beyond cannot be put into words because the word is not the thing. Up to now we can describe, explain, but no words or explanations can open the door.

What will open the door is daily awareness and attention…" (1969, p.33)…
i.e., more knowledge cannot "open the door" to clear seeing, or awakening;
only total attention, which is awareness, can do that.

In the following, Krishnamurti explains that learning comes from
observing and seeing clearly, not from accumulating knowledge, which is
thought. This is so essential to understand in light of our education's focus
on accumulating knowledge.

> If we can observe very clearly, that in itself is a form of discipline.
> We are using that word *discipline* not in its orthodox sense. The very
> meaning of that word is "to learn." The root of that word means
> "to learn"; not to conform, not to control, not to suppress, but to
> learn and to see very clearly what is happening outwardly, to see
> that this is a unitary movement, not a separate movement; to see it
> as a whole, not divided. (p.118)
>
> If discipline means to learn, what is the **quality of mind** that is
> capable of learning? **Attention is the essence of learning**. Attention
> means hearing, listening; hearing with the ear as well as "behind"
> the ear. Attention is a natural function of the nervous system; it
> cannot be so much cultivated as denied. It is denied when the brain,
> or mind, is occupied with a problem, a goal, or with any prolonged
> particular object of attention. (Krishnamurti in conversation with
> David Moody, 2011, p.254; bold mine)

Interestingly, the word *disciple* has the same root word and meaning,
which is *to learn* and not, "to follow" as the word seems to have become
in common usage. And especially in light of what Krishnamurti says below, we seem to mistake following what someone else says (whether that
is a teacher, a parent, a textbook, etc.) for learning; indeed, in my view of
our current education paradigm, we equate the two. Krishnamurti explains
that, not only *can* we learn from/through ourselves, but that we must—that
that is the true learning:

First of all, I would like to say how important it is to find out for oneself what learning is, because apparently all of you have come to learn what somebody else has to say. To find out one must obviously listen, and it is one of the most difficult things to do. It is quite an art, because most of us have our own opinions, conclusions, points of view, dogmatic beliefs and assertions, our own peculiar little experiences, our knowledge, which will obviously prevent us from actually listening to another. All these opinions and judgments will crowd in and hinder the act of listening.

Can you listen without any conclusion, without any comparison and judgment, just listen as you would listen to music, to something you feel you really love? Then you listen not only with your mind, with your intellect, but also with your heart; not sentimentally—which is rather terrible—or emotionally, but with care, objectively, sanely, listen with attention to find out. You know what you think; you have your own experiences, your own conclusions, your own knowledge. For the moment at least, put them aside. (1969, pp.116-117)

Krishnamurti says at least three important things here:
1) That one can discover independent ouf others' knowledge by asking oneself
2) That listening (and therefore real learning, as opposed to say, memorizing) can only happen outside of thinking/knowledge
3) That the heart has something to do with real listening/learning[26]

Finally, in the following, Tolle agrees with Krishnamurti that the 'self' or in Tolle's case, the "perceiver" dissolves in a state of total awareness, and that the clear seeing or "knowing" happens because the "I" is *united* so to speak with that which she/he is giving her/his full attention to:

---

[26] I go further into the nature of the heart in the next section on pure intelligence.

Wisdom is not a product of thought. The deep *knowing* that is wisdom arises through the simple act of giving someone or something your full attention. **Attention is primordial intelligence, consciousness itself.** It dissolves the barriers created by conceptual thought, and with this comes the recognition that nothing exists in and by itself. It joins the perceiver and the perceived in a unifying field of awareness. It is the healer of separation. (Tolle, 2003, p.16; italics mine)

Again, this 'knowing' that we call wisdom is not a result of thought.

World Beyond Thought:
Non-Duality, the Absolute, Unity Consciousness

There is no approximation in direct experience.
Jane Katra & Russell Targ

~

The Direct Experience of Pure Intelligence
In this section, we look at the experience of intelligence that one is able to have once it is understood that thought has nothing to do with true intelligence and that its presence at all can only stop one from encountering the intelligence that is innate to each of us, that is, who we are. Likewise, it also explains why staying on the level of thought (which includes logic) in an effort to either validate or invalidate someone's words (including this book) can never penetrate to the truth, for it rests *beyond* thought.

In his book *The Living Universe*, Duane Elgin references our direct experience[27] and its reliability as "knowingness," as "wisdom."

---

[27] A reminder to the reader that *direct experience* is that which is encountered, we might say, unmediated by concepts. It's experiencing the phenomena directly, as it.

The wisdom of creation is directly accessible to us as the hum of knowing-resonance at the core of our being. When we relax into the center of ordinary existence, we penetrate into the profound intelligence out of which the universe continuously arises.

If we look within, we will discover immense wisdom within our direct experience....The direct experience of life carries its own meaning and requires no intellectual explanation....When we allow our ordinary experience of knowing to relax into itself, we find a self-confirming presence. When we rest in the simplicity of "knowing that we know" without the need for thoughts to confirm our knowing, we directly enter our stream of being. The nature of the soul is knowingness itself; when we rest within our soulful knowing, there is no distance between the knower and that which is known. (2009, pp.108-109)

Elgin, as Tolle above ("...joins the perceiver and the perceived"), echoes Krishnamurti's probably most famous idiom here, "the observer is the observed." It seems like the meaning of this is such a puzzle, which it is for the intellect: it certainly cannot be understood by the rational mind but only by experiencing it. However, I can explain through logic that if there is a 'knower' and 'that which is known,' it stands to reason that there is a space there; that is, until they are unified, there is distance. So in other words, there is separation or what Krishnamurti calls "fragmentation," and thus what we are calling 'the known' is not really known at all but *thought* ('thought' being used here as a verb). Katra and Targ explain the illusion of separation between knower and known, or observer and observed, in the following way:

...self-knowledge comes from experience, not books, authority figures, or religious dogma. When we directly experience who we are, from the spiritual perspective of consciousness, we realize that the perception of ourselves as a separate entity has no real independent existence, because our consciousness has no boundaries. (1999, p.23)

Byron Katie is also referring to the illusion of separation below, and describes then how a mind that is not attached to any idea can "go anywhere" or, in Krishnamurti's terms, it can give its *total attention*; that is, it can unite with anything and *be that*. This is what it means to *know directly*:

> As the mind realizes itself, it stops identifying with its own thoughts. This leaves a lot of open space. A mature mind can entertain any idea; it is never threatened by opposition or conflict, because it knows that it can't be hindered. When it has no position to defend or identify to protect it, it can go anywhere. (2007, p.25)

It's logical to see that if a mind is needing to see things a certain way in order to feel secure (as in *This is who I am; This is the way things are; This is scary; This might hurt me*) then it can't go everywhere—it must have boundaries to maintain a sense of security. But a mind that realizes that in this very act of identifying with certain beliefs (ex. with ideas of safety) is the creation of its opposite (ex. the opposite of safety, or, danger), then the mind can see that its needing—or ability to create—safety is an illusion, and it's free to wander into any territory, to entertain any possibility.

The Heart as the Seat of Intelligence

Above, Krishnamurti asks, *Can you listen with your heart?* Byron Katie and Esther Veltheim also clearly state that the heart literally is the place in the body that contains the voice of wisdom, as opposed to the brain, which, as the mechanism of thought, is where we usually attribute wisdom, or answers. (Below, Katie refers to the heart as the "gentler polarity of the mind"):

> This work is meditation. It's like diving into yourself. Contemplate the questions, drop down into the depths of yourself, listen, and wait. The answer will find your question. The mind will join the heart, no matter how closed down or hopeless you think you are:

the gentler polarity of mind (which I call the heart) will meet the polarity that is confused because it hasn't yet been enlightened to itself. When the mind asks sincerely, the heart will respond. You may begin to experience revelations about yourself and your world, revelations that will transform your whole life, forever. (http://thework.com/downloads/little_book/English_LB.pdf)

In saying that "The answer will find your question" (i.e. as opposed to "The question will find the answer"), Katie makes clear that the answers already exist 'inside' us—the answers appear to precede the questions.

Veltheim agrees with Katie: "Only when the mind ceases judging, aiming, and censoring, can the silent voice of the heart be heard. Therein lies the Truth" and "If these words trigger an understanding that you can't put into words, then don't even try. When all tears and questions temporarily subside, it means the words have by-passed the mind. The heart has 'absorbed' what is being communicated" (2000, p.239).

Katie also exposes that we cannot access our hearts' wisdom if we cannot let the mind ask its questions. The directive of "Quiet the mind" doesn't work because the mind is the 'one' who takes that directive and attempts to quiet itself; clearly, there is a problem there. The quiet mind (or transcending thought) comes as a result of clearing the mind, so to speak:

We buy a home for our children, for our bodies; we get a garage for our car; we have doghouses for our dogs; but we won't give the mind a home. And we treat it like an outcast. We shame it and blame it and shame it again. But if you let the mind ask its questions, then the heart will rise with the answer. And "rising" is just a metaphor. The heart will reveal the answer, and the mind can finally rest at home in the heart and come to see that it and the heart are one. That's what these four questions are about. You write down the problem and investigate, and the heart gives you the answer you've always known. (2006b, p.53)

Summary of Part 1

Part 1 consisted of my own awakening experiences (Chapters 1 and 2) as well as a distillation and detailing of the the awakening of four spiritual teachers along with their insights from the awakened mind (Chapter 3).

Autoethnography of Consciousness Transformation (Chapters 1 and 2)
The first two chapters are a reflexive autoethnography that uses my own experience with structures of consciousness. Using my own experience is a process that mirrors the content of my research: I am researching the possibility of consciousness transformation from identification with thought to knowing directly, without the use of the intellect. Logic dictates that I, as the researcher, need to find out if this is true directly, and not only through research subjects who claim to have direct knowledge of this, which would seem second-hand or once-removed, as it were. Krishnamurti (1953, p.16) offers justification for the study of myself as research subject:

> Systems, whether educational or political, are not changed mysteriously; they are transformed when there is a fundamental change in ourselves. The individual is of first importance, not the system; and as long as the individual does not understand the total process of himself, no system, whether of the left or of the right, can bring order and peace to the world.

So, can *I* do this, 'understand the total process of myself'? Can I do what I am suggesting we need to make the central focus in schools? This moves this research from the theoretical into the practical. Data—in the form of my own and others' examples—is important because it gives you a way to go along for the ride. The examples of consciousness transformation found here take you into the subjects' and my experiences, stepping into experience, out of theory. Of course, you still have to take the journey yourself.

The Question of Objectivity

I began this book long before I began writing it. I set out to inhabit that which I would eventually write about—to not just write about a transformation of consciousness, but to live it. The reasons for this were two-fold: 1) I believe that my own transformation of consciousness is the most important thing I could contribute in life, and 2) I knew of no other way to accurately conduct research for this book.[28]

In research jargon, this would be in the realm of "truth value." Inherent in this research topic is experiential (as contrasted with conceptual) learning. As tempting as it was in some ways to keep this learning at a distance and let it be about other people, this does not ultimately even make logical, scientific sense: my writing about the essentiality of going beyond the thinking mind from the thinking mind is akin to a human writing about what it's like to be a fish—in short, impossible.

There are many who might disagree with me and say that through our sophisticated underwater data collection devices and so on, we can ascertain everything we need to know about what it's like to be a fish. I agree we could find out a whole lot of information about 'fishdom', but the one thing we could never know is what it's actually like to *be* a fish.

Or, to leave the metaphor, I want to know the experience of a trans-formed consciousness. Not only that, but as a researcher, I feel this is in the highest integrity: it seems to me that one can only claim knowledge of something if one has direct knowledge of it oneself. This is not to say that I'm not corroborating my evidence but I'm corroborating it with other 'fish' (those who speak from the unconditioned mind of presence), not with the 'underwater devices' (the conditioned mind of intellect).

Autoethnography acts as an example of how people might inquire for themselves. Since words do not teach but the journey one takes individually does, this is as close as we can come (i.e. to 'teaching' using words). However, I believe my use of autoethnography seeks to go a little deeper

---

[28] This book started out as my Ph.D. dissertation.

than the conventional use of personal narrative as research. It is also why I like the terms "autoethnography" and "self-study" rather than narrative for what I am trying to do in my research. I think narrative inquiry is most important in a way unintended by its proponents in that it demonstrates the extent to which—and the infinite ways in which—the human mind creates meaning from (which is to say, analyzes and judges, *decides*) life, thereby establishing the world of duality in which we live: i.e. this is good, this is bad; this wanted, this is unwanted, etc.

Yet I also think its *intended* ways have been helpful in that narrative has opened up social science research to writing very personally from experience—elucidating the human condition from the first-person perspective and bringing the reader along for the ride, in the vein of a novel or painting—an antidote for academic prose which is often very difficult to penetrate. As well, narrative has challenged the possibility of truly researching 'other,' revealing the fallacy, the myth, of objectivity as research has used it. I see the narrative methodology as significant to the academic world and also to this book for all of the above reasons.

However, the precise strengths of narrative also give rise to its weakness, which is why, in my view, it can only be a stepping-stone of inquiry. I go beyond the narrative to expose the very mechanics of the narrative-teller in order to ascertain whether or not there is *something other than* the story and storyteller. In other words, the narrator, the meaning-maker... *who or what is that?*

I agree with David Carr who observes, "coherence seems to be a need imposed upon us whether we seek it or not" (in Ellis & Bochner, 2000, p.746) but I disagree that narrative can ever give us such a coherence we are looking for. The implication is that the one in need of coherence is the narrator; instead of looking for the narratives, we need to ask, *Who or what is it that is creating these narratives?*

I have found in the course of my own research that the telling of any stories about myself and/or from my own perspective have been helpful in a sort of purging way: getting the stories 'outside' myself, I seem able to see them more clearly: created objects that are fastened out of my mind as if out of clay by a ceramicist. Separated from me in such a way, they can be seen for what they are: stories. And these stories have nothing to do with my essential Self. Another way of explaining this is,

Can I look at myself without the label of 'me' that exists through my stories? Can I see the limiting nature of labels, of stories, thereby seeing what's left?

Bochner (2000, p.747) writes: "The crucial issues are what narratives do, what consequences they have, to what uses they can be put"—however, can we also see the limits of its ability?

Bochner also writes—in a profound but simple observation—of the influence of the researcher on the researched:

> If you couldn't eliminate the influence of the observer on the observed[29], then no theories or finding could ever be completely free of human values. The investigator would always be implicated in the product. So why not observe the observer, focus on turning our observations back on ourselves? And why not write more directly, from the source of your own experience? Narratively. (200, p.747)

Up to a point, I agree. The only problem is that there isn't the consideration that the observer and the observed might be one and the same; the observer who *is* the observed is not-two and therefore cannot observe the self. What if the one telling the story *is the same as*—*is*—the story?

To me, Bochner seems on the right track but only got halfway there. What Bochner and others fail to question is where the story is coming from—who is the narrator? That is all that is left to us when we strip everything away. Perhaps the narrator is 'unreliable' (a literary term and device), and so any story coming from 'her' or 'him' would also be unreliable.

---

[29] That "the observer is the observed" is one of Krishnamurti's most oft-repeated statements.

What if the story and the storyteller are the very impediment to the truth?

Unwittingly, Ellis captures this when she writes, "The truth is that we can never capture experience" and when she quotes Bochner: "Narrative is always a story about the past" (p.750). Experiencing happens in the present moment, whereas a story by definition is always about the past. So, the story of our past cannot lead us to an understanding of the present moment. By definition, there is no story of the present moment; it just is.

Phenomenon of Consciousness Transformation (Chapter 3)

The third chapter is an examination of consciousness and its transformation through first-person accounts in the literature. In essence, it seeks to answer the question put by the late Advaita Vedanta sage Sri Nisargadatta Maharaj: "The mind by its very nature, divides and opposes. Can there be some other mind, which unites and harmonizes, which sees the whole in the part and the part as totally related to the whole? ... ending the mental process as we know it" (in Katra, 1999, p.138). It was a question Krishnamurti put to his audiences many, many times: is it a new kind of mind possible? It is "...a state of consciousness we may call stillness" (Tolle, 2003, xi).

I discuss the significance of the transformation of consciousness to education throughout the book. Krishnamurti informs a large portion, as he not only claims to undergo his own transformation of consciousness and claims to directly perceive its structures and the nature of reality, but what sets him apart from the others in the literature is that he directly applies his insights to education. He sees both the dangers of conditioning the mind through education as well as the possibility to break free from conditioning through a different type of education.

Ashwani Kumar, in his doctoral thesis (published as a book in 2013) largely on Krishnamurti and education, argues for what he calls *meditative inquiry* as a new type of curriculum in light of the "limitations of thinking, analysis, system, and authority" (2011, p.117). Kumar (2011, p.122) argues convincingly for self-inquiry:

> What is…significant is that each one of us goes to the very depths
> of our psychological reality—its contradictions, conflicts, and
> problems—to understand how we are part and parcel of this
> exploitative social reality, and how, knowingly or unknowingly,
> we are inheriting the existing system and contributing towards the
> increasing chaos.

In other words, he argues for the necessity of experiencing our conditioning, which in its very course, gives us also the experience of who/what we are in the absence of our conditioning. He continues: "It is important for each one of us to realize that no outside agency can bring about a total revolution of the psyche but the individual him or herself, and unless there is a revolution in the psyche there can be no fundamental change in society." By extrapolation, then, the next step would be to perform this, to undertake it, to go "to the very depths of our psychological reality" within a scholarly study; otherwise, we stay within the realm of theory and the intellect rather than move into actuality, which is precisely the case for which Kumar is arguing against.

To clarify, then, the case has been extensively made by Krishnamurti, other sages and scholars, and again by Kumar for moving beyond the intellect into *something else* (and I, too, will support these claims here with an experiential set of data); now let us examine that 'something else' in those who claim to have experienced it, and by my own experiential examination of it. It is not enough to argue for it: Krishnamurti did not care that there were many who seemed to intellectually understand him; of course, that is antithetical to the point. Likewise, we do not need someone to repeat and corroborate what he is saying (which is the sum total of a theoretical investigation) because this is endless; the mind will always ask for further clarification, further proof and explanations. It is akin to saying, "I will point out what everyone needs to do, but I will not do it myself."

The question is, *can one set sail and leave the shore without a new shore in sight* (to use a Joseph Campbell analogy)? *Can one actually make the journey? What exists after one has left shore, what does not exist? How does one know?*

So, for example, Kumar talks about "fragmentation," as does Krishnamurti. What is that, *fragmentation*? What is that like to experience? Can we discuss fragmentation through experiencing it, rather than theorizing about it with the intellect (which can only know terms, that are symbols *pointing to* fragmentation but they are not fragmentation itself)? Let us go into these terms actually and not theoretically.

The following excerpt from a novel by Aldous Huxley, quoted here by Ken Wilber, nicely demonstrates what I am trying to say. It is a conversation between two characters:

> "I like the words I use to bear some relation to facts. That's why I'm interested in eternity—psychological eternity. Because it's a fact."
>
> "For you, perhaps," said Jeremy.
>
> "For anyone who chooses to fulfill the conditions under which it can be experienced."
>
> "And why should anyone wish to fulfill them?"
>
> "Why should anyone choose to go to Athens to see the Parthenon? Because it's worth the bother. And the same is true of eternity. The experience of timeless good is worth all the trouble it involved."
>
> "Timeless good," Jeremy repeated with distaste. "I don't know what the words mean."
>
> "Why should you?" said Mr. Propter. "You've never bought your ticket for Athens

This book aims to give dispatches from those in Athens. That is, I am concerned with exploring the phenomenon of the awakened or expanded consciousness from those who are able to speak about it—and who model it—from experience, from living it.

~

Of course, using literature that is not necessarily considered 'scholarly'—
that is, not using corroborated empirical evidence to any real extent to
support one's claims—already felt risky to me in the context of a PhD dissertation. To then increase said literature's importance and relevance to my
study by using the authors (Krishnamurti, Tolle, Katie, and Veltheim) as
the subjects, seemed like something I was not sure I was prepared to take
on. However, it became clear to me that in order to study the phenomenon
of consciousness transformation, this felt like the best way to proceed.

Any valid scholarly study asks that its findings be judged by the fruits
of the tree, so to speak, by testing the claims against logic and against other
claims in the literature and I did not see how this study should be any
different. In other words, we should not discard any claims even if they
are based solely on personal experience until we have subjected them to
our own academic rigor as researchers. As Katra and Targ (1999) point out,
"...many of us have learned...that if something isn't verifiable or falsifiable
by the scientific method, we should consider it unworthy of our attention,
or even nonsense. But science itself is based on the unverifiable premise
that it is the most appropriate method for discovering truth" (pp.13-14).

In their book, Katra and Targ (1999) tackle this very problem of sci-
entifically exploring individual, personal experience, specifically about
what one can know about the nature of reality. They reference scholar,
philosopher, author, and Buddhist Ken Wilber, who asserts that "although
physics will never explain spirituality, the spiritual realms may be explored
by the scientific method" (p.7). They also cite Ludwig Wittgenstein and
Alfred Ayer, "Early in the twentieth century, two of the world's greatest
logicians," (p.6) who countered their early findings—that "nothing meaningful could be said about God, because no experiment could be
designed to either prove or disprove, verify or falsity, whatever one might
say"—at the end of their careers, realizing that "the experience of mystics
might actually be considered data—something observable in an experiment" (p.7). Indeed, "in Wittgenstein's last book, *On Certainty*, he gave pri-
macy to experience over theory" (p.7).

Using the Buddha as an example, Katra and Targ (1999) explain the process of using personal experience as data for "scientific empiricism":

> For thousands of years wisdom teachers such as the Buddha have presented a worldview to all who will listen. They have described a practice that is available for all to observe and experience. They then invite us to compare our experience, and see if it corresponds to with [sic] their teaching. Ultimately, this seems to us like an acceptably scientific, empirical approach to spirituality.

They point out that such an approach "...invite[s] us to look beyond our thinking mind to discover who we are" (p.7). In other words, this is not scientific empiricism as we're used to it; we are not theorizing. It is worth pointing out that Krishnamurti himself is not considered a scholar in the common usage of that term: his insights were not arrived at by conducting studies and analysis; he does not have degrees from institutions of higher learning; he is not an academic. His insights were arrived at by his own direct encounters with life and with himself and yet should be able to bear the test of scrutiny and more importantly, of replication through experience. That is the whole point of this book, really: to elucidate the possibility for insight that is not arrived at through analysis and furthermore, to explicate the absolute necessity for each one of us to experience insight that is not arrived at through thought, for only then is this transformation of consciousness possible.

PART 2

EDUCATION FOR ENLIGHTENMENT

What is missing from education is where all learning begins and ends: the self.

~

We are limited by the questions we are not asking. It is the questions that enlighten...

Kathryn Jefferies

Chapter 4

As far as I can tell, there are internal inconsistencies in all conceptual systems.

Robert Kull, PhD

~

Education as Transformation of Consciousness

This book is an exploration into the means of inquiring into—and discovering—the true nature of s/Self, mind, and life in the context of exploring the purpose of formal education (that is, schooling).

In this sense, I see it as primarily an ontological inquiry—an investigation into *beingness*. As in, *What is it to 'be'?* Yet there is also an element of epistemology in the sense that I am inquiring too into the nature of *knowing*—this thing that education seems to concern itself so doggedly, so imperatively with. So, then, what is *being* and what is *knowing* and how are these two phenomena related? "Jiddu Krishnamurti (1895-1986) is regarded globally as one of the greatest thinkers and educators of all time" according to the website of one of the schools he founded. I agree. "To understand life is to understand ourselves, and that is both the beginning and the end of education," (1953, p.14) he said. Illuminating what this enigmatic statement means is one of my purposes here.

Krishnamurti's (1953) central claim was that for any outward change (i.e. in the world: in any social, institutional, or personal structures) to occur there must be an inward shift in the consciousness of the human mind.

For example, if one wants peace in the world, one must first learn to create or allow that environment inside oneself.

He characterizes this shift in consciousness as moving from a conditioned, limited reality to a transformed state of awareness that is total or unlimited. The former exists through defining thought as originating and embodying the highest potential of intelligence whereas the latter recognizes an intelligence that does not originate in thought. Intelligence in Krishnamurti's usage refers to an ability to recognize things as they are, or simply, reality; in other words, to be one with the truth of life.[30] Krishnamurti explains that humans for the most part do not encounter life (including ourselves and others) as it is or as they are, because we encounter life only through our mental concepts. So, the transformation of the human mind away from identification with thought to a broader state of consciousness that includes but is not limited to thought, involves both a superior intelligence than what we are currently aware of and a superior life experience; the two are inextricably related. This is so because a mind identified with thought is a confused mind since it is unable to see the whole; whereas in an unmediated life, one can finally be at peace, resting as one is in reality and in one's true nature. Therefore, it seems important to examine consciousness—its nature and possibility for change—and the nature of intelligence, thought, and the mind, keeping in mind the broader context of education's purpose.

Krishnamurti was advocating for an idea whose time has now come, it would seem.

As any great visionary, Krishnamurti was ahead of his time; humanity was evidently not yet prepared to be able to see the insights he so readily perceived. He was not the only well-known public figure who saw the central relevancy (and indeed imperativeness) of consciousness transformation to all of life, as evidenced by the following: Carl Jung: "In the history of

---

[30] I go into a detailed discussion of intelligence as Krishnamurti uses it at various points throughout the book.

the collective, as in the history of the individual, everything depends on the development of consciousness"; Teilhard de Chardin: "evolution is an ascent towards consciousness"; Sri Aurobindo: "A change of consciousness is the major fact of the next evolutionary transformation….An evolution of consciousness is the central motive of terrestrial existence." Einstein said that we only experience ourselves as separate from each other because of an "optical delusion of consciousness" while astrophysicist Sir Arthur Eddington, echoing Einstein, said our minds only appear to be separate because of "the narrow limits of our particular consciousness" (as quoted in Katra, 1999, pp.147-148).

Certainly these last two are especially provocative, mind-bending statements by well-respected intellectuals and yet the idea hasn't really been picked up on or broadly investigated with any rigour. It's as if sense could not be made of it and so the statements were put aside and forgotten. These are statements that, if true, clearly have profound implications on how we experience and live life.

Contemporarily, Tolle is one of the most well-known harbingers of consciousness transformation:

> … I speak of a profound transformation of human consciousness—
> not as a distant future possibility, but available now—no matter who
> or where you are. You are shown how to free yourself from enslave-
> ment to the mind, enter into this enlightened state of consciousness
> and sustain it in everyday life. (2004, p.8)

Tolle also points out that at this juncture of our collective human history, transforming our individual consciousness is imperative to the continuation of our species: "Humanity is now faced with a stark choice: Evolve or die. …If the structures of the human mind remain unchanged, we will always end up re-creating the same world, the same evils, the same dysfunction" (www.eckharttolletv.com, Dec.2011) and "The next step in human evolution is to transcend thought. This is now our urgent task. It doesn't mean not to think anymore, but simply not to be completely iden-tified with thought, possessed by thought" (2003, p.20).

Researcher Ralph Metzner concurs with Tolle and points out that Einstein did as well:

> Albert Einstein remarked, "The atomic bomb has changed every-thing except our way of thinking." In a world teetering on the brink of nuclear holocaust, economic collapse, and ecological catastrophe, we are being challenged to examine ourselves. We feel we have to ask ourselves, "What are we?" after all, to have arrived at such an insanely dangerous impasse. It seems to me that two important con-clusions are emerging with increasing certainty: (1) that the evolu-tionary transformation of society and of humanity must take place first in the individual, and (2) that the transformation of the indi-vidual requires a turning inward, toward self – not in narcissistic self-absorption but in aware self-confrontation.

All of the above visionaries shared the same perception that a change in consciousness is necessary for humanity in order to see life and ourselves cor-rectly which, in turn, is evolution in action. The only difference between the message of the contemporary and earlier visionaries listed above is that it seems there is no longer the luxury of time; the same message may be more urgent. Time, it would seem, has run out on a way of life as lived by most of us.

The Perennial Philosophy

Philosopher Aldous Huxley (and close friend of Krishnamurti) is popu-larly credited with coining the term "Perennial Philosophy"[31]—which in-cludes the fact of the human mind being an *aspect* (i.e. not the totality)

---

[31] John P. Miller has pointed out that the term was "first used by Agostino Steuco in referring [to] the work of the Renaissance philosopher, Marsilio Ficino. Leibniz picked up this thread in [the] 18th century" (2006, p.15).

of the larger consciousness and that there is indeed a reality that is not dependent for its existence on human perception of it. He describes it as:

> ...the metaphysic that recognizes a divine Reality substantial to the world of things and lives and minds; the psychology that finds in the soul something similar to, or even identical with, divine Reality; the ethic that places man's final end in the knowledge of the immanent and transcendent Ground of all being—the thing is immortal and universal. (in Miller, 2006, p.15)

Huxley was searching the world's religions and wisdom traditions for the common, underlying thread that united them all, which he described as "a Highest Common Factor which is the Perennial Philosophy in what may be called the chemically pure state" (in Katra, 1999, p.34). He went on to caution "this final purity can never, of course, be expressed by any verbal statement of philosophy." It is this point that is a particular focus of mine, as this seems to be the thing that is overlooked or discarded as inconsequential, in studying the real-world, educational application of holistic education. That is, that the intellect is limited not just in its ability to express but in its ability to even *know* in the first place. Physicist Fritjof Capra (1975) also noticed that "the spiritual tradition's... view of the world is essentially the same [as one another]. It is a view which is based on mystical experience—a direct non-intellectual experience of reality..." (p.133).[32] Katra and Targ (2006, pp.35-36) distil Huxley's Perennial Philosophy into "four enduring elements of the world's spiritual truth":

---

[32] Furthermore, "[t]he most important characteristic of the Eastern world view—one could almost say the essence of it—is the awareness of the unity and mutual interrelation of all things and events, the experience of all phenomena in the world as manifestations of a basic oneness" (Capra, 1975, p.133). This, too, has been the startling discovery and contribution of modern physics—an area of study that is significant but outside the scope of this book. It is an interesting side note that Krishnamurti is one of the dedicatees of Capra's book.

1. The world of both matter and individual consciousness is manifested from spirit. The world is more like a great thought than a great machine.

2. "Human beings are capable of not merely knowing about the Divine Ground by inference. They can also realize its existence by direct intuition, superior to discursive reasoning" (Huxley).

3. [Humans] possess a dual nature: both an ego associated with our personality and our mortal, physical body, and an eternal spirit or spark of enduring divinity. It is possible…to identify with this spirit…with "the Divine Ground" or universal consciousness.

4. Our life on earth has only one purpose: to learn to unite with the Divine Ground and the eternal, and to help others do the same.

Katra and Targ (1999) point out that the core of the Perennial Philosophy is a "message of personal transformation of consciousness" (p.37); however, they go on to explain that while the Perennial Philosophy "tells us that we are here to learn to unite with the Divine Ground, …it neglects to tell us how to do it" (p.37). David Moody (2011), former teacher and director of the one Krishnamurti-founded school outside of India and England, addresses the problem with the questioning of "*how*": "There is no blueprint or method for this process because any prescribed method can only produce a mechanical result. What can be done is to explore the meaning of and the *actual, living reality* of one's own state of mind" (p.34, italics mine). So with this in mind, Katra and Targ's book is an attempt to do what Krishnamurti did his whole life: he pointed a finger towards truth, thereby explaining that it is up to each person to take the journey, because it is the journey itself that is transforming, not the *idea* of the journey or the end point.

While it is true that contemplative practices can give one direct knowledge of the mysteries of the universe, Krishnamurti and other sages such as Ramana Maharshi and Sri Nisargadatta Maharaj seldom, if ever, told one *how* because the one who asks how is looking for somewhere to get to, rather than being willing to notice her own experience. Whenever someone asked Krishnamurti "how?" he would respond with saying that it is the wrong question (1953, p. 111). This is why Maharshi directed people to ask, *"Who am I?"* followed immediately by *"Who wants to know?"* (Katra and Targ, 1999, p.32); in other words, who is this one we think of as the seeker, the one who desires knowledge? It throws the mind back on itself. With the first question, *"Who am I?"* the mind will commence beginning its search for an answer, but by asking the second question, *"Who wants to know?"* the knowing is forced out of the brain and into the experiencer. In other words, the brain can't answer that second one. What is left is the pure experience of being.

I believe that Krishnamurti, Ramana Maharshi and Sri Nisargadatta Maharaj also often spoke of what the universe *is not* (a process of moving towards the truth through negation) for the same reason that Jesus spoke in parables (a sort of riddle). This deliberate tactic is such a strong clue as to the 'way' through to direct experience: they are saying, in essence, *If we tell you what all life is, what you will find there, you will attach to the idea as if you have found the truth and never, ever take the journey—and under-taking the journey is to find the truth.* It's just not possible to come upon it conceptually, though that is all we know. Until it's not.

~

What we can begin by looking at is our own conditioning. Moody sums up the definition of conditioning: "Conditioning is essentially the weight of tradition, the burden of past generations, the accumulated patterns of thought and judgment imposed on the individual by society" (Moody, 2011, p.34). He goes on to say that education, as it exists now, perpetuates the inability of the mind to undergo transformation, and that for a trans-formation of consciousness to occur the mind must be *un*conditioned. In this vein then, education is more about unlearning than learning. This was Krishnamurti's primary insight and both the cause and the focus for his schools: "Education in the traditional sense is an agent and facilitator of the conditioning process. In a profound reversal of convention, Krishnamurti proposed instead that education become the process of unconditioning the human mind" (Moody, 2011, p.34). That there is even a *possibility* for a transformation of consciousness (never mind arguably a *necessity* in order for humanity to evolve), and that education can play a central role in creating conditions for it, was Krishnamurti's extraordinary insight.

Education as Conditioning the Mind

The crucial relevance of the transformation of consciousness to education, argues Krishnamurti along with other philosophers/scholars/spiritual masters, is that it is not through abstract, conceptual thinking—no matter how elaborate, sophisticated, complex, or clever—that we will ever come upon the highest ideals that we seek, either personally or as a global community. That is, whether it is a world free of conflict, relational or community harmony, the experiences of joy, confidence, and love, the ability to communicate clearly, or simply the ability to create the life we envision, we cannot *think* our way there. Yet this is what our current education paradigm is specifically built upon. We believe that developing the thinking mind can, for example, as an ultimate symbol of success (as measured by *mental* intelligence and creative *thinking*), tackle complex problems like global hunger, inter-nation and inner-nation conflict, disease, distribution of wealth, global warming, as well as personal problems like mental and emotional health and interpersonal conflict. Krishnamurti and others argue the reverse of the current education paradigm: that it is only through *transcending* the mind—that is, transcending our conditioning—that we will find the answers and information we seek. Consider Eckhart Tolle from his website:

> There are still many people who believe that the problems of this world can be solved if we just think harder about them, have more committee meetings about the problems of the world and discuss them and eventually the problems can be solved. They don't realize

that the problems of the world are there because we have lost touch
with the source out of which everything came. So by going into
further differentiation we cannot solve the problems, we actually
increase them. So we need to balance now return to the source and
going out into the world. ...We need conscious connection to the
source.

It is the direct experience of ourselves as the source or pure consciousness
that *is* intelligence. It can only come about when identification with thought
ceases. The mind can then be used as the tool that it seems to have been
created to be, in service to something larger and more intelligent than itself.
Indeed, Einstein wrote "Objective knowledge provides us with powerful instruments for the achievements of certain ends. But, the ultimate goal itself,
and the longing to reach it, must come from another source" (in Katra and
Targ, 1999, p.3).

Current education focuses on training what we call the mind, which I
variously refer to as the thinking mind, the intellect, or intellect-mind. I
will elaborate further on definitions of mind and intellect in both the next
section, *Definition of Mind*, and elsewhere and will only give a brief introduction here for the purpose of explaining how current education conditions the mind.

The intellect (as processor and cataloguer of thought) is only a small
aspect of ourselves, and in fact the mind is something we have access to,
but is not, ultimately, who we are. However, in attending only to the mind
as we presently do in education through adding knowledge and ability in
mental manipulation, children quickly come to believe that thought *is* who
they are, which vastly limits how they can respond to life. This is the nature
of identification with thought or "thought-forms" (Tolle, 1997; 2005); in
other words, what we think of as the "I" in each of us has been put together
by thought. People are limited to who they—quite literally—*think* they
are. Naturally, this is not intended by either the teachers or ministers of
education or anyone responsible for designing the curriculum, it is merely

a reflection of how these people experience life and themselves. In other words, they are doing their best. In a paradigm where intellect is God, then setting up an education system where the intellect is 'educated' makes sense.

Yet, what if thought cannot apprehend the totality of life including who we are? What then would that mean for any action springing from thought that by definition cannot see the whole of life, any person or situation? On a personal level, this leads to internal and external conflict. People do not know who they are outside of thought, not to mention their strengths, weaknesses, unique gifts and talents. People are living with a lot of suffering and are ill-equipped to handle it. They act out their suffering on others (and yes, this can also be at the nation-state level not just the personal), and themselves (depression, anxiety, suicide). It's a crisis, yet not one easily seen because the suffering is seen as inevitable. On a global scale, this is reflected in ideological and religious wars of various kinds as the years of conditioning and inability to separate oneself from the thinking mind play themselves out in the adult leaders of the world. Tolle explains it well here, again from his website:

> Humanity is an abstract concept; it doesn't exist. Humanity is the human being. You are humanity. So for humanity to take responsibility, you need to take primarily responsibility for your state of consciousness because only a diseased or dysfunctional state of consciousness produces a diseased or dysfunctional world out there. By world I mean the human made world that has been imposed on the...what's already there—the planet— which is potentially of course a paradise; the planet—pristine, unbelievable jewel, a being of great intelligence... But the—your state of consciousness determines what kind of world you create, what kind of action you take, and what consequences your actions have. So here...this is why my main work is to address the cause of dysfunction which lies in the human mind—the dysfunction of the human mind or as it is sometimes called in Zen, the "sickness of the

human mind." ....If there is no shift in that then the dysfunction will destroy us. ...All you have to do then is primarily take responsibility for your state of consciousness now. Now. And this is what the entire teaching is about: what is my state of consciousness at this moment. Am I generating disturbance? Am I generating negativity? Am I generating conflict and suffering for myself and others? Am I generating inner pollution? Am I polluting the beautiful being that I am with continuous absurd movements of thought producing negative emotions, producing an entire entity that is illusory that I call the "me"?

There's something more primary than what you do: it's who you are. Who you are is your state of consciousness. Whatever you do flows out of that. ... So the change is the transformed state of consciousness.

In either case, since we are all affected by both the personal and global, freedom from suffering and freedom to create the life one desires are only found in realizing one's true nature that is separate from the thinking mind. In my experience it is through *experiencing* ourselves (as opposed to just *understanding* ourselves, which would be through thought)— our mind as thought and what we are without thought—that is essential. As Einstein said, we cannot solve the world's problems from the same level of consciousness that created them. In Krishnamurti's terminology, there must be a total revolution of consciousness. Finally, Katra and Targ (1999) describe an opportunity to "change your mind" that "has been taught for thousands of years. The reason it has fallen into neglect in this scientific age is that the path resides in *experience* rather than analysis" (p.19).

Intellectual skill and analysis is deemed all-important in today's education paradigm, as it has been for years. The results of this type of education (for example, as seen on the world stage) would seem to indicate that the 'great minds' are *not* solving the long-standing and dire problems of today's world. The problems are still here, and arguably getting worse (when we look at epidemic levels of depression in developed countries, the current violent lawless situation in Syria as well as longstanding wars such as those in Afghanistan and Iraq, the Ebola epidemic in west Africa, all while global weather events have escalated almost certainly due to global warming).

Perhaps developed minds are not the source of creativity[33] (from which, I argue, the only solutions are found to seemingly sophisticated, complex problems) and, indeed, *even inhibit it*. Consider Tolle's point:

> Do you need more knowledge? Is more information going to save the world, or faster computers, more scientific or intellectual analysis? Is it not wisdom that humanity needs most at this time?
>
> But what is wisdom and where is it to be found? Wisdom comes with the ability to be still. Just look and just listen. No more is needed. Being still, looking, and listening activates the nonconceptual intelligence within you. Let stillness direct your words and actions. (2003, p.9)

In fact, it is assumed that humans generate their thoughts; that is, that they can initiate thinking. The experience of the people in this book shows otherwise.[34] Thought cannot be creative if it is shown to be only capable of regurgitation and not capable of insight.

Definition(s) of Mind

The words intelligence, awareness, self, mind, and consciousness, are difficult words because we use them conceptually, and without *direct knowledge* of what they are referring to (since words are mere symbols pointing to what we might call a truth beyond themselves) they cannot be pinned

---

[33] Sir Ken Robinson writes and speaks—very humorously and passionately—about creativity. I highly recommend his work. Also see footnote 10 in this chapter.
[34] I go into this further in Chapters 4 and 5.

down. In addition, scholars employ them to mean different things. In fact, according to Dan Siegel (personal communication, Omega Institute, August 2011), "mind," for example, has not been defined by any scholar. Most times it is referred to, the author or speaker means the brain, including Krishnamurti (1969, p.120):

> The mind has been put together through time. The brain cells, which have evolved through millennia, centuries upon centuries, have acquired tremendous knowledge, experience, have collected a great deal of scientific, objective knowledge. The brain cells, which are the result of time, have produced this monstrous world, this world of war, injustice, poverty, appalling misery, and the division of people racially, culturally, and religiously. All this has been produced by the intellect, by thought, and any reconstruction by thought is still within the same field. I don't know if you see that.

If we want kindness, peace, compassion, and understanding, as well as creativity (for solving complex problems, as well as for beauty) to be qualities that are at the forefront of humanity and exhibited on a daily basis in children, it is essential to recognize that these qualities cannot come from *trying* to be these things, which is another way of saying they do not come from thinking about them. In other words, they will not come from "Character Education," for example, that is prevalent in today's main education (i.e. public) systems.

As Eckhart Tolle explains, "You do not become good by trying to be good but by finding the goodness that is within you." And, "*In you, as in each human being, there is a dimension of consciousness far deeper than thought. Love, joy, creative expansion, and lasting inner peace can only come into your life through that unconditioned dimension of consciousness.*"

In other words, we only try to *become* good—and try to teach children to become good—because we believe we are not. Yet have we actually looked deeply within ourselves to find out the truth about human nature?

As Esther Veltheim (2000) puts it, "There is only one reason for focusing on "becoming better," or "more successful," or "more aware." The reason is that you spend most of your life dwelling on what was, what is not, and what might be (p.4)—i.e., instead of looking at what is. Yet an important part of the dominant education paradigm is built upon looking at what might be in the form of ideals, rather than focusing on looking at how things already are.

Krishnamurti talked at length about ideals and idealism (and "becoming") and why they can never work. In brief, they are fabricated concepts. It would seem plausible at first glance to imagine a condition that is better than the one we currently experience and then work our way towards it—this is the concept of ideal. The problem is, this process doesn't work. It can't. One only need try it to see for oneself. *Or,* we can just look at the system of ideals that society, and education, has set up, to see that we have not reached them and arguably, have come no closer to reaching them collectively in the years or even hundreds of years they've been set up. What does work, is to look at what is already in existence—in Krishnamurti's and Tolle's and Katie's words, "what is[35]." So in this process then we find ourselves instead asking why we set up ideals, if they work or not, etc. and go *into* these questions deeply (that is, not attempting to answer them but instead staying with the question). And we look inside ourselves to see if we have, or are, goodness, for example, and if and why there are blocks to being or expressing this goodness.

In essence, what we are asking children to do when we ask them to try and *be* or *become* something is to first of all imply that they are not already that way. The message is: you are not inherently good, you don't inherently have that quality. The ramifications of believing we are inherently flawed are enormous and not to be underestimated. It is the idea of "the original sin," cloaked. You can track it through all the way to low self-esteem, bullying,

---

[35] Byron Katie's first book is called *Loving What Is*—her total message summed up in this one phrase.

depression, suicide, outward-directed violence in its many-varied forms, etc. And secondly, we teach a lesson in hypocrisy: for we cannot do what it is we are asking them to do. We, as adults, cannot 'be good' most of the time. So it becomes, again, *do as I say, not as I do.*

Thus, 'desirable' qualities such as compassion and kindness arise naturally from children seeing for themselves what the mind is and how it works (that is, *their own mind*). In other words, our true nature is kindness and compassion. When we act otherwise, it is because we're not in touch with our true nature. Moreover, seeing our true nature prompts an immediate dis-identification with the mind and a realization that it is an instrument to be used by us. Until this realization, we cannot help but be used by the mind, and the mind is very limited in what it can perceive; it is merely a collecting and sorting instrument of past experience—nothing new comes from the mind.

In other words, thought is not the seat of creativity.[36]

As Krishnamurti explains in an online interview, "…all thought is the action, the response of conditioning" (1970, p.110) and this is why thought cannot come upon or generate anything new—such as an insight required for seeing reality clearly or seeing the solution to a problem—because thought can only record past experience. Byron Katie simply explains it this way: "…there are no new stressful thoughts. They're all recycled. There are not any new stressful thoughts at all from the beginning of the human race. Any story that you tell about yourself causes suffering. There is no authentic story."

Definition of Consciousness

One of the central questions here, is what is meant by the term *consciousness*? I find Tolle's definition helpful: "You are not 'in the now'; you are the

---

[36] For an excellent discussion on the inhibiting and stifling of creativity in education, see Robinson, K. (2001), *Out of our minds: Learning to be creative*, Chichester, West Sussex: Capstone Publishing Limited, as well as his many talks found on TED and other internet sites.

now. That is your essential identity—the only thing that never changes. Life is always now. Now is consciousness. And consciousness is who you are. That's the equation." Or even more succinctly: "...consciousness is the ground of all being" (physicist Amit Goswami).

By its very nature, what *consciousness* is must be experienced to be known; it cannot be known conceptually. While (as Tolle says above) we in fact are already experiencing consciousness because it's who we are, I could say that *directly* experiencing consciousness, as who you are, is possible. It must first be realized that common or what we would call normal experiencing (because most of the human population appears to experience it) is actually conceptual experience, mediated by the intellect. Another way to explain this is the human tendency toward *complete mind identification*. It is Plato's cave analogy: we mistake the illusion for reality.

The illusion is the world put together by thought, the reality is what exists and is experienced otherwise. Still, we must have a working definition or two of consciousness in order to have an initial sense of what we are referring to. One of the best definitions I have found is Eckhart Tolle's above. Tolle (www.eckharttolletv.com, Dec. 2011) has also commented on the brain/consciousness debate that in the scientific world often seems to be a 'chicken and egg' debate—that is, they say it's difficult if not impossible to determine which came first. Of course, what distinguishes Tolle's explanation/definition is that he is not theorizing, but speaking from personal experience: "The brain does not create consciousness, but consciousness created the brain, the most complex physical form on earth, for its expression." He arrived at through direct experience what science has yet been able to determine, let alone prove.

Metzner points out that consciousness has been used in two ways, which I argue is akin to Tolle's pointing out that all existence exists as "space and things in space." In other words, the way I am defining consciousness throughout this book is that of 'space' or 'emptiness' (see Metzner below), and the second example Metzner gives is actually, I would argue, describing thought, as objects or forms in space.

Consciousness itself has been thought of in terms of two analogies. One is as a kind of space, as in Buddhist notions of "emptiness," or in such expressions as "state of consciousness," or context, or field. The other analogy is that of a river, as in the expressions "stream of consciousness" and "stream of thought." We have, then, a geographical metaphor and a historical one, which correspond to the two main dimensions of our experience of reality—space and time.

In the following response Krishnamurti gives to a question asking him to define consciousness, he is actually equating the *content* of consciousness with consciousness in his initial definition. He does this because the content of consciousness is all most of know of consciousness, so we confuse the two. As he explains below, "Without the content, consciousness, as we know it, does not exist." He goes on to explain that this person we each individually think of as "I" is really the essence of the content of our consciousness. It is the sum total. Another way of saying it is that this I is the centre of measurement of the thinking mind. This 'I' at the centre of our consciousness is created by everything that we have ever experienced. Furthermore, experience includes not just events we have encountered with our physical bodies but also with our minds. In this vein, thoughts, beliefs, concepts … all of them are experiences we have undergone and therefore sources of conditioning of our individual, and collective, consciousness.

Finally, Krishnamurti tackles below the question of whether consciousness can be emptied of its content—in other words, be emptied of its "I"—and what remains when this happens. This is the transformation of consciousness that I have referred to in sections above. "Then consciousness can be emptied and when it is emptied one may or may not find there is something more, it is up to oneself." While Krishnamurti reveals that indeed the I, the centre, can be seen for what it is and therefore disappear, to discover both this and what lies beyond such an experience is not something that can be communicated (nor experienced) through words; in other words, an experience of this must be undertaken to be experienced.

While this may appear like an obvious or redundant statement, we expect that everything and anything knowable can be experienced through the mind and Krishnamurti is attempting to disavow his listeners of this notion for this very notion is the impediment to their experiencing consciousness beyond the content of "I."

I quote Krishnamurti at length here, as he goes into some depth on the nature of consciousness, to give the reader a chance to experience Krishnamurti during an example of his method of inquiry. It is its own experiencing of sorts, reading Krishnamurti:

> Question: What is our consciousness? Are there different levels of consciousness? Is there a consciousness beyond the one of which we are normally aware? Is it possible to empty the content of consciousness? Krishnamurti – One may use words and give descriptions, but what is named and described is not the fact; so do not be caught in the description.
>
> What is our consciousness? It is to be conscious of, to be aware of, what is going on, not only outside but inside; it is the same movement. Our consciousness is the product of our education, our culture, racial inheritance and the result of our own striving. All our beliefs, our dogmas, rituals, concepts, jealousies, anxieties, pleasures, our so-called love—all that is our consciousness. It is the structure which has evolved through millennia after millennia—through wars, tears, sorrow, depression and elation: all that makes up our consciousness. Some people say you cannot change consciousness. You can modify it, you can polish it, but you have to accept it, make the best of it; it is there. Without the content, consciousness, as we know it, does not exist.
>
> The questioner asks: Is it possible to empty consciousness of all content—the sorrow, the strife, the struggle, the terrible human relationships, the quarrels, anxieties, jealousies, the affection, the sensuality? Can that content be emptied? If it is emptied, is there a different kind of consciousness? Has consciousness different layers, different levels?

In India the Ancient people divided consciousness into lower, higher and yet higher. And these divisions are measured, for the moment there is division there must be measurement, and where there is measurement there must be effort. Whatever level consciousness may have, it is still within consciousness. The division of consciousness is measurement, therefore it is thought. Whatever thought has put together is part of consciousness, however you choose to divide it.

It is possible to empty the content of consciousness completely. The essence of this content is thought, which has put together the 'me'—the 'me' who is ambitious, greedy, aggressive. That 'me' is the essence of the content of consciousness. Can that 'me' with all this structure of selfishness be totally ended? The speaker can say, "Yes, it can be ended, completely." It means that there is no centre from which you are acting, no centre from which you are thinking. The centre is the essence of measurement, which is the effort of becoming. Can that becoming end? You may say: "Probably it can, but what is at the end of it, if one ends this becoming."

First of all find out for yourself if this becoming can end. Can you drop, end, something which you like, that gives you some deep pleasure, without a motive, without saying, "I can do it if there is something at the end of it?" Can you immediately end something that gives you great pleasure? You see how difficult this is. It is like a man who smokes, his body has been poisoned by nicotine and when he stops smoking the body craves for it and so he takes something else to satisfy the body. So can you end something, rationally, clearly, without any motive of reward or punishment?

Selfishness hides in many ways, in seeking truth, in social service in selling oneself to a person, to an idea, to a concept. One must be astonishingly aware of all this, and that requires energy, all the energy that is now being wasted in conflict, in fear, in sorrow, in all the travails of life. That energy is also being wasted in so-called meditation.

It requires enormous energy, not physical energy, but the energy that has never been wasted. Then consciousness can be emptied and when it is emptied one may or may not find there is something more, it is up to oneself. One may like something more to be guaranteed but there is no guarantee.

Krishnamurti spoke at such length (both in time and duration), because he was attempting to 'walk' his listeners along with him—not out of coercion, but because neither he nor anyone else can take the journey for someone. And by the very nature of his speech—through its detail—he was attempting to show this, and to help. It was all anyone could do and can do. So it is because "The essence of this content [of consciousness] is thought" and "That 'me' is the essence of the content of consciousness" that it is necessary to "First of all find out for yourself if this becoming can end." Anything that anyone can tell you is merely going to be put together by 'you,' by thought, and it is logically self-evident that thought cannot inquire into its own nature.

Chapter 5

Relative to the level of awareness that is possible for us, our ordinary state of consciousness is as far from a direct experience of reality as sleep is from waking consciousness.

Don Richard Riso, Russ Hudson

~

Holistic Education

History, Root, and Purpose

According to Alan Hunter (2011, p.127) in his account of his years teaching at the Oak Grove School (the only Krishnamurti-founded school in North America, located in Ojai, California):

> Many cultures have had a tradition of education for the whole human being: classical Athens and Renaissance Europe, ancient China and Victorian England, the French Lycêe and the German Gymnasium were all influenced by this ideal. The traditional concept of holistic education often included the teaching of a wide range of subjects, both academic and non-academic, physical education, and the cultivation of moral and spiritual qualities. It is often associated with the idea of drawing out latent capacities of the student instead of merely instructing him/her. The Krishnamurti schools subscribe to this idea and attempt to offer a wide range of courses and activities. They also aim to develop the spiritual and emotional qualities of their students.

Hunter also points out that "The harmony of mind, heart and body, which Krishnamurti also cited as a precondition for the awakening of intelligence, is an old idea that can be traced back to Plato" (p.128). This "drawing out latent capacities" is considered one of the original definitions of the words *educate* and *education* from the Latin meaning "to draw out, or *educe*."

Holistic education scholar and long-time director of Brockwood Park (the only Krishnamurti-founded school in Europe), Scott Forbes (2003) contextualizes the more modern roots of holistic education; that it comes as a response to the failing "mechanistic and nationalistic worldviews" of mid-to-late twenty-first century social institutions, including schools. As an alternative paradigm of education, it emerged in reaction to a worldview that reflected our Western world tendencies to "over-value short-term ideas, a calculating intelligence, the high-priced skill, while undervaluing or even ignoring our own deeper instincts, emotions, imaginations and long-range wisdom" (Ball, 1998, p.17). Attempting to address the needs of the whole person, its central premise is that humans are more than the intellect: we have a mind, but also emotions, a physical body, and something else that has been referred to variously as the soul or spirit. To this list comprising the human make-up, J.P. Miller (2005) adds the "social" and "aesthetic" aspects of human nature, while suggesting that "the defining aspect of holistic education is the spiritual" (p.2).

Many (including educators, researchers, and parents) see holistic education as having the potential to succeed where conventional education is currently failing. What success means by those championing holistic education is that education can and should "...prepare students to meet the challenges of living as well as academic" (Forbes, 2003, p.1). It is also important to realize that schools were never designed with students' needs and interests in mind, but rather those of the state (Miller, 2008; Sherman, 2012). "[Schools] were designed to prepare people for the world of work; to give them the skill sets that would help them up the ladder of success" (Forbes, 2003). Indeed, according to Ashwani Kumar (2011, p.31):

During the 1950s while North American curriculum theory and school education was still working under the dominance of Ralph Tyler's *Basis Principles of Curriculum Construction* (1949) and serving the demands of industrialization, militarization, and consumerism, Krishnamurti by means of his *Education and the Significance of Life* (1953) had already critiqued the nature and character of a positivistic, behavioristic, and capitalistic, or more succinctly, materialistic education, centered on the principles of reward and punishment and technical efficiency.

What is missing in our current, dominant paradigm is deemed by holistic educators to be the most valuable part of a student's learning. As Forbes asks, "Why aren't we as humans learning what we need to know in order to live good and meaningful lives" (2003)? Holistic education elements address more fundamental issues other than just knowledge acquisition and skills training, like meta-learning (learning how we learn) as well as facilitating students learning "about themselves, about healthy relationships and pro-social behavior, social and emotional development, resilience, [and] to see beauty, have awe, experience transcendence, and appreciate some sense of 'truths'" (Forbes, 2003).

According to Forbes (2003), holistic teaching and learning emerged from the pioneering philosophical work of Rousseau, Pestalozzi, Froebel, Jung, Maslow, and Rogers. On why he does not include Montessori, Steiner, and Dewey in this list, Forbes explains that they were either inheritors of the philosophies (in the case of Montessori and Dewey) or, in Steiner's case, although "original in both his philosophies and techniques of education ... he has had little to no influence on other forms of holistic education, and cannot therefore be considered part of holistic education's intellectual precedent" (p. 6). Of course, other scholars would disagree with Forbes' assessment and include Montessori, Steiner, and Dewey. Certainly, since the two former were largely responsible for establishing hundreds of schools in many different countries they are helpful in order to put Krishnamurti's work in context.

In general, there is a "dearth of research on holistic education" (Forbes, 2003, p.9). Montessori and Waldorf schools have the highest number of schools worldwide that fall under the holistic education umbrella; as such, they have been subject to a certain amount of research. The same is not true of Krishnamurti education. It is noted by Forbes (2003) that J. Krishnamurti, "along with Rudolf Steiner and Maria Montessori, are the founders of the oldest continually existing schools considered by most to be holistic" (p.10). The first school founded by Krishnamurti, which continues to exist in India, started in 1924.

The main difference between Steiner and Krishnamurti is that Steiner prescribed a very detailed curriculum for every stage of the child's development—a path which Krishnamurti always avoided as he felt any prescription would always lead to dogma. In other words, if there is a system of any kind, then that of course will be the focus, the measurement, and the children will be secondary. Like Montessori, Krishnamurti saw the importance of freedom for the child. Krishnamurti saw the presence (meaning *alert awareness*, as opposed to a physical presence) of the teacher as the most important thing, for a clear mind could facilitate the inquiry of the student to find her own freedom. Krishnamurti's unique body of work continues to influence scholars internationally in the fields of education, philosophy, and religion; however, his contributions are vastly understudied and his ideas remain relatively unknown.

Krishnamurti's educational vision is unique within holistic education because he shows how non-conceptual inquiry (which he sometimes referred to as *perceiving what is* can lead to the experience of integration of oneself. My experience of what Krishnamurti means by *integration* is that an integrated person will experience a "not-two" (Veltheim, 2000)—a non-dualism, or, in other words, a person experiences what we might call "unity consciousness." In my experience, integration is a withdrawing of consciousness from thought, thought being the cause of the internal fracture into a sense of oneself as the thinker (as opposed to the awareness where experience happens). In a further extension of this phenonmenon,

Miller (2006, p.76) describes one of the possible effects of contemplation: "The boundary between ourselves and whatever we are contemplating disappears." I experienced this for myself, which I outline in Chapter 2.

In this book, I outline the nature of thought and its relationship to what we commonly refer to as intelligence, along with what Krishnamurti (and others) refers to as intelligence. Since it would seem that school's believed purpose is to cultivate intelligence, I would argue, then exploring it and determining its nature is highly relevant to understanding education.

The Limits of Knowledge

Holistic educators see conventional primary and secondary education as insufficient to address larger needs of contemporary students in its predominant focus on the student's intellectual growth. As Gord Ball (1998) remarked succinctly over fifteen years ago, knowledge alone is not going to give students what they need to understand themselves and the human condition and to create positive change in the world:

> Increasingly, observers of the human condition are claiming that we have reached a stage in our evolution where our collective choices are becoming quickly limited, and that current global circumstances are calling for a new kind of planetary consciousness among the world's human inhabitants…with children and adults learning not simply new skills but new ways of being in the world. (pp.1-3)

As a unique paradigm within holistic education, Krishnamurti's whole body of work focuses on a "new consciousness" or "way of being."

Education is currently "churning out minds that are clever, efficient, and proficient in some branch of knowledge," (Krishnamurti, 1953) but Krishnamurti asks whether this is a mind that can understand itself and the whole of life. A mind that can meet life as if seeing it for the first time— that is, with clear vision, instead of from the past through thought and memory—is the only mind that is capable of addressing current global problems and issues as well as personal ones, according to Krishnamurti. I am concerned with illuminating these two kinds of mind: the mind that we've created as well as the transformed mind of which Krishnamurti and other teachers of consciousness speak.

Krishnamurti on Education

Jiddu Krishnamurti (1953; 1996) is known variously as a spiritual teacher and a philosopher whose stated chief desire was to set humankind psychologically free; he saw education as the arena that might do this if done properly. His focus was on enabling the clear seeing of life and one's whole self by way of a psychological transformation to a new consciousness that is not limited to identification with thought. His intention in creating his schools was to provide a very different type of school, with a dynamic, organic curriculum that attempted to teach the whole student[37] while it simultaneously asked teachers and students alike to define for themselves what "whole" means—who we each are (both as an individual and as a human being) and what the nature of right relationship is between teacher and student, between student and student.

Krishnamurti's contribution to the holistic education literature is that he goes beyond educating *for* or *about* the various aspects of human nature (i.e. mind, body, spirit) to inquiring directly, *unmediated by the intellect*, into how our own personal components interact so we might understand ourselves completely. The liability, then, for holistic education in general, is that the mind, body, and spirit can also be experienced abstractly, as concepts created and mediated by the intellect.

This point is crucial.

Consider the following statement from Veltheim (2000, p.3):

---

[37] The curriculum at Krishnamurti schools gives significant attention to the arts and athletics as well as to meditation and inquiry.

If you experience personal limitations, it's because you are identified with concepts. You think you are a body, a mind, and perhaps a
spirit and a soul. You weren't born with a mind full of concepts. Before they entered your mind, no limitation was experienced. There
was simply the pre-personalized awareness of being.

Significantly, like Krishnamurti, Veltheim points out the danger of
believing something, *even if one is correct*, because true knowing (an active
experience, as distinguished from knowledge, which is something passive
or dead, as its memory) cannot be born out of anything but experience. In
other words, concepts cannot give reality to us. Thinking we have or are
a spirit or soul, for example, is not the same as directly experiencing this
for oneself. To teach any concepts then, is just adding to the accumulation
of conceptual knowledge within one's mind and does nothing to bring
someone back to the natural, original experience of "awareness of being."
Peter Ralston[38] (2012) puts it this way:

> When I use the word spirit, it most often describes a disposition or
> attitude: "a spirit of honesty" or "a spirit of open inquiry" both of
> which are necessary for gaining real insight. In the way it sounds
> like you use it—as a distinction within the self, or an aspect of one's
> self—the term spirit is much too ambiguous to be useful. Instead, I
> speak of Consciousness. I capitalized the word consciousness to in-
> dicate that what I'm referring to isn't found in the commonly shared
> ways we use that word, and yet is still somehow connected to what
> we call and experience as consciousness.
>
> In Cheng Hsin, consciously experiencing what's true is the goal,

---

[38] Peter Ralston was the first non-Asian to win the World Championship full-contact
martial arts tournament, held in the Republic of China. From his website: "Consistent
with Zen studies, his investigation into martial arts also came to include a questioning
of reality. Long periods of intense contemplation resulted in many enlightenment
experiences regarding the nature of self and reality, which greatly influenced his study."

and beliefs are, more often than not, barriers to this goal. My "direct experience" about the nature of Consciousness—which in themselves are impossible to convey—provide a very different relationship to the human condition, as well as the nature of reality. Yet, although I try to communicate about this matter, and invite others to consider beyond their given assumptions, I don't ask anyone to believe anything I say about it. I invite them to discover for themselves whatever is true.

What else is true is that no matter what I assert in this domain, it will be misunderstood because it can only be "understood" through one's own direct conscious experience. So asking someone to believe in something I say about it would be ridiculous, since they'd be believing in something that is not "it." It would be like asking someone to believe in god, and yet, shy of becoming directly conscious of god, what would they believe in? It would be some idea that is made up to fill the space of not knowing what god is or is really about. What does that have to do with the reality or lack of reality of the matter referred to as god? See how this works?

Alternatively, what is it to know or experience *oneself*, without, for example, the concept of 'spirit' or 'soul'? As Krishnamurti (1953, p.9) explains, one can discover directly (rather than from "books") for oneself what it is to be a 'human being':

> The ignorant man is not the unlearned, but he who does not know himself, and the learned man is stupid when he relies on books, on knowledge and on authority to give him understanding. Understanding comes only through self-knowledge, which is awareness of one's total psychological process. Thus education, in the true sense, is the understanding of oneself, for it is within each one of us that the whole of existence is gathered.

Krishnamurti is making a profound statement here: that education in its essence is *understanding the self*; and, furthermore, that this is so because *who we are is all of life*—in other words, who we are *is* that which we are trying to learn and understand through acquiring knowledge. Krishnamurti explains that not only is it possible to directly inquire into the nature of thought, mind, emotion, and spirit *within ourselves*, but it is essential to understanding life. Furthermore, for Krishnamurti, this process of inquiry and insight is the very meaning of education.

Interestingly, Byron Katie makes the same statement as that of Krishnamurti, taking the explanation even further here:

> Until there's peace within you, there is no peace in the world, because you are the world, you are the earth. The story of earth is all there is of earth and beyond. When you're in dreamless sleep at night, is there a world? Not until you open your eyes and say "I woke up," "I have to go to work," "I'm going to brush my teeth." Until "I" is born, no world. When the I arises, welcome to the movie of who you think you are…. If you investigate it, and the I arises, there's no attachment. It's just a great movie. And if you haven't investigated, the I arises, it's body-identified, you think it's real, you think there's an "I." Pure fantasy. And if you attach to it, if you think you're that, you may want to inquire. (Katie, 2007, pp.177-178)

She explains this phenomenon through her own experience, describing "…the absolute fulfillment of watching everything unfold in front of me as me" (p.40) and "I'm a woman without a future. I live in the open space where everything comes to me. Reality is a very fine place to be" (2007, p.144). Likewise, in the introduction to the classic spiritual text, *I Am That*, the writer echoes Krishnamurti and Katie when he describes Indian sage Sri Nisargadatta Maharaj as "…not a man with a past or future; he is the living present—eternal and immutable. He is the self that has become all things" (1973, p.xiii—author unknown but likely by the editor, Sudhakar

S. Dikshit). It would seem that it is only our concepts that prevent us from knowing-experiencing ourselves as "the self that has become all things" or "everything unfolding in front of [us] as [us]" or "the whole of existence."

Self-Integration Versus Fragmentation

It is through understanding ourselves that what Krishnamurti calls self-integration takes place. As I mentioned earlier, in self-integration, one is not separate from what one is experiencing—there is not the experience and the experiencer but only the experiencing. From this state of integration comes awakened doing where the doer is no longer the decider, but rather is one who *allows* the action to transpire through her or him; so, in essence, the doer is a *non-doer*. Krishnamurti describes a perceiving, awakened awareness that he calls intelligence, or *"choiceless awareness."* Other spiritual educators including contemporary teachers Eckhart Tolle and Esther Veltheim refer to this intelligence as Truth (with the capital 'T') and 'What is' or Reality often employing capitals to attempt to engage the reader to interact with these words in new ways that break them out of their old, conceptual ideas and serve to act instead as pointers beyond the words. According to Krishnamurti, it is the job of education to put students in contact with this intelligence within themselves: "The function of education is to create human beings who are integrated and therefore intelligent." (1953, p.181). Indeed, he goes on to say that without this awareness of one's total psychological process, which is integration and intelligence, education has no value or significance:

> Though there *is* a higher and wider significance to life, of what value is our education if we never discover it? We may be highly educated, but if we are without deep integration of thought and feeling, our lives are incomplete, contradictory and torn with many fears; and as long as education does not cultivate an integrated outlook on life, it has very little significance. (1953, p.11)

In fact, Krishnamurti titled his first book *Education and The Significance of Life* because, for him, it was impossible to talk about one without talking about the other. It seems at once both a profound and perhaps an obvious statement to make, that life has a deep meaning to it—though our systems of education do not appear to address this significance of life with much, if any, deliberate attention.

Furthermore, Krishnamurti suggests here that it is through integration of thought and feeling that life's deep significance makes itself known to us. He is saying that we are living incomplete lives because we are not in touch with life's deeper meaning and that, without it, the only alternative is to live in fear. Finally, Krishnamurti insists that if education doesn't engender this deep life meaning in its students, it has little significance at all.

The opposite of integration is fragmentation, which is the result of our current education system according to Miller in his book *The Holistic Curriculum*: "Education specifically has done much to sever the relationship between head and heart" (2007, p. 3). Krishnamurti (1973) also uses the term fragmentation when he explains the effect of teaching only through—and for—thought: "Thought does produce chaotic action, fragmentary action....[I]t is not an activity of wholeness. The activity of wholeness is intelligence" (p. 523). Clearly, then, intelligence has no relationship to thought, according to Krishnamurti.

Education's sole focus on the teaching of technique through thought produces the fragmentation. However, Krishnamurti argues that there is an antidote for fragmentation and substitute for thought: "The right kind of education, while encouraging the learning of a technique, should accomplish something which is of far greater importance: it should help man to experience the integrated process of life. It is this experiencing that will put capacity and technique in their right place" (1953, p.20-21). Krishnamurti is saying two things here: 1) *that life is naturally integrated and that we can align with this process within ourselves, to experience it for ourselves* and 2) *that learning of a technique* (which we could summarize for now as any typically traditional school subject) *is not to be done away with;*

in fact, it is necessary and can only be understood as information properly in relation to experiencing the integrated process of life.

Although Krishnamurti believed it was important to develop our mental faculties and increase our skills and knowledge to the point of excellence, the crucial point he was making was to insist that not only are these capacities secondary, but that education is pointless and dangerous without situating this secondary knowledge within the wider context of understanding life as a whole. "If we are being educated only to be scientists, to be scholars wedded to books, or specialists addicted to knowledge, then we shall be contributing to the destruction and misery of the world" (1953, p.11). This is an extraordinary statement because it absolutely opposes what our whole education system is oriented towards: "scientists," "scholars," and "specialists" are considered high praise in our current society. Furthermore, he is pointing out that this sort of education is not just neutral, but contributes to the suffering of the world. A different paradigm would explore students' perception of fragmentation and integration through their education, as Krishnamurti intended when he founded the school, and to understand the nature of this integration of thought and feeling that allows for intelligence beyond mere training of the mind.

(Non-conceptual) Intelligence

One way in which Krishnamurti tries to help us see that there is something other than thought as well as to point out the limited nature of thought, is to distinguish between thought and something else—Krishnamurti calls it "intelligence." "Thought is of time, intelligence is not of time. Intelligence is immeasurable" (1973, p.375); "thought is a pointer. The content is intelligence....So intelligence is necessary. Without it thought has no meaning at all" (p.521). He goes on to say:

> When (thought) sees that it is incapable of discovering something
> new, that very perception *is* the seed of intelligence, isn't it? That *is*

intelligence: 'I cannot do.' I thought I could do a lot of things, and I can in a certain direction, but in a totally new direction I cannot do anything. The discovery of that is intelligence. (p.411).

So Krishnamurti emphatically explains that though we may be aware of something other than thought, we will try to get to this awareness *through* thought, or by way of thought, because that is the nature of thought. It is once we (as thought) realize that we cannot get to this intelligence through thought, that intelligence is immediately present. There is an arising of something other than thought.

Krishnamurti (1953) continues to point to this awareness beyond thought by pointing out the result of an education system that focuses solely on thought; in other words, he is trying to make it obvious what it is that we are doing in order to see the fallibility of it. The problem of solely developing the mind to the exclusion of the other aspects of oneself creates a highly evolved thinking mechanism that is not in harmony or alignment with other aspects of self. It is as simple as pointing out, as Eckhart Tolle does, that it took great intelligence to split the atom but great stupidity to build the atom bomb. He explains the conundrum this way:

> Thinking that is not rooted in awareness becomes self-serving and dysfunctional. Cleverness devoid of wisdom is extremely dangerous and destructive. That is the current state of most of humanity. The amplification of thought as science and technology, although intrinsically neither good nor bad, has also become destructive because so often the thinking out of which it comes has no roots in awareness. (2003, p.20)

Krishnamurti explains it this way:

> We may take degrees and be mechanically efficient without being intelligent. Intelligence is not mere information; it is not derived from books, nor does it consist of clever self-defensive responses and aggressive assertions. One who has not studied may be more

intelligent than the learned. We have made examinations and degrees the criterion of intelligence and have developed cunning minds that avoid vital human issue." (p.14).

He elaborates on the point by explaining that, "We cannot understand existence abstractly or theoretically. To understand life is to understand ourselves, and that is both the beginning and the end of education" (Krishnamurti, 1953, p.14).

Presumably, the opposite is also true: once one understands oneself, life is also inherently understood. What I understand being said here is that there isn't anything else *to* life than to understand life and ourselves (in essence, these two are the same thing) but we do not understand this and hence do not frame life—and certainly not education—in this way. We distance ourselves from life and from ourselves by way of mental abstractions. We essentially create concepts and live through these, taking our thoughts to be some sort of truth. In this way, we never experience existence directly.

Krishnamurti's point here is very significant because he is describing our academic system as it still currently exists. Our society continues to consider "degree" and "cunning mind" a significant and reliable reflection of intelligence.

Of course, I am all too aware of an irony of this topic for a PhD dissertation—in education no less—which I address in my first chapter. It might be a contradiction that is ultimately insurmountable. That is, attempting to establish and legitimize the existence of a non-conceptual intelligence through a conceptual, rational forum of a PhD dissertation could indeed be antithetical. Tolle himself uses the example of the liability of having written a PhD in confusing that with actual knowing:

> You can write a PhD about honey, or you can write poems about honey, but if you never tasted honey…In other words, if honey has not merged with you, then you don't really know honey. But the moment you taste honey, then you know honey. And all the other

stuff beforehand, even your Ph.D. about honey if you wrote one, is not knowing, not true knowing....It's only conceptual.

To my mind, it does require a paradigm shift in terms of imagining a further possibility and purpose of a PhD dissertation—even if just to allow for paradox.

Research on Consciousness

History of Formal Research
Ferrari and Pinard (2006) trace the formal study of consciousness since the ancient Greeks and Romans. I reference it here because my book contributes to this body of work. However, it is interesting to note that for my work, I only draw tangentially from a portion of this body, namely transpersonal psychology. For the most part, I draw from non-disciplined or non-formal studies of consciousness through first-person accounts in the literature.

According to Ferrari and Pinard, "The ancient Greeks and Romans had notions of inner experience, but no term exactly equivalent to even the seventeenth-century notion of consciousness as it emerged among the English natural scientists and theologians of that time" (2006, p.75). They go on to say that

> ...only in mid-nineteenth century do we find the first attempts to study consciousness as its own discipline. But from the very beginning opinions divide over whether consciousness should be studied: (1) as a basic biological process, within physiology, (2) clinically, within medicine, (3) as a sociohistorical process; or (4) as ultimately metaphysical, remaining beyond the reach of third-person natural science (pp.77-78).

Since that time, metaphysics has made great strides and it is this fourth option that my study can most closely be associated with, in its study of the fundamental nature of being (ontology) and (its relationship to) the world.

Two people and their ideas "encompass virtually the entire nineteenth-century science of consciousness," namely, Wilhelm Wundt and William James (Ferrari, 2006, p.78). Interestingly, Jame's godfather was the transcendentalist Emerson, whose work James followed and his later work involved examining atypical states of consciousness including mystical experiences (Ferrari, 2006, p.79). Ferrari suggests that Jame's "overall vision of a 1st person science of consciousness had its nearest echoes in clinical and transpersonal psychology" (p.81). I would consider my work in this book to follow somewhat in this lineage.

It seems the idea that emerged in the 1950s that the mind is like computer software (p. 84) is indicative that the study of consciousness was focused on what I would call the *objects* of consciousness, or the content of consciousness—the knowing—rather than on consciousness itself. Tolle has pointed out that the objects of consciousness are often confused with consciousness itself.

In transpersonal psychology, we find the continuation of the "Jamesian tradition of a transcendental psychology" (p.86). Ferrari describes it this way:

> Thus, transpersonal psychology, like cognitive psychology, aimed to return the study of psychology to human experience and human meaning—but goes beyond basic information processing to document and explain states of consciousness that represent the highest levels of human aspiration.

He goes on to say that Ken Wilber's 'integrative [integral] psychology' today is a similar approach to consciousness studies and in my view, set the stage for a new, mainstream study of consciousness that has arisen in the last 10-15 years, including the first-person science of consciousness.

Ferrari cites David Chalmers, John Searle, Max Velmans, and Eleanor Rosch, who say that "our phenomenological 'first-person') experience is an undeniable fact that must be integral to any science of consciousness" and Ferrari goes on to say that

The systematic first-person study of inner life has at least as much rigor and dedication to it as does neuroscience. One of the most innovative new approaches is 'neurophenomenology,' pioneered by Francesco Varela…. It aims to reconcile or at least coordinate (third-person) neuroscience and (first-person) phenomenology… (2006, pp.88-89)

Varela had the idea to use Buddhist methods of mindfulness to meditate on the nature and contents of the subject's own experience.

Realization Beyond Thought:
Direct Experience, Pure Intelligence, Essential Self

In order to understand, we have to remain in the darkness of not-knowing.

~ Tao Te Ching

In addition to Krishnamurti, contemporary spiritual teachers (Tolle, Katie, Ralston, Foster, Veltheim, Liberman), mystics, spiritual lineages (notably Zen Buddhism, Taoism), poets and authors (Rilke, Huxley, Redfield), philosophers, psychologists, doctors, and scholars (Jung, Miller, Chopra, Kraft, Needleman, Campbell) among others, point out something beyond knowledge, thinking, and the faculty of conceptual manipulation that they name variously as intelligence, pure consciousness, pure awareness, the unified field, the knower, natural mind, Divine Ground, Ground of Being, deeper self, big mind, no-mind, don't-know mind, and intuition. In short, they are describing an experience of an entirely different nature that the typical state of consciousness or awareness that most of us seem to be in and/or have access to. Of course, we can't know for sure that they were referring to the same thing as one another, but the fact remains that something other than thought has been held up as not only an alternative, but a decidedly better alternative for pure and accurate insight into the nature of life, as well as a way of being.

Tolle (1997) writes: "...since every person carries the seed of enlightenment within, I often address myself to the knower in you who dwells behind the thinker, the deeper self that immediately recognizes spiritual truth, resonates with it, and gains strength from it" (p.8). What Tolle sees clearly is that there is a recognizing faculty within us that doesn't have to *process information through thought* in order to ascertain its truth; not only this, but it is that recognizing faculty that *already knows* the truth. In Part 1, I explain that I have had this experience of "resonance" many times, including when I read Krishnamurti for the first time, many years ago. My experience is that there is indeed one in us who 'knows.'

Zen scholar Kenneth Kraft refers to a non-conceptual intelligence that he calls "intuition": "...one of the goals of Zen Buddhism is to go beyond the senses and beyond thinking. Intuition—the source of insight—sneaks up on you from somewhere else when you're not thinking about it. You need to be receptive and responsive to this possibility" (in Goleman et al., 1992, p.49).

Holistic educator and academic J.P. Miller also makes reference to "our deeper knowing and intuitions" (2007, p.4). Aldous Huxley, noted admirer of Krishnamurti, also references intuition: "Human beings are capable of not merely knowing about the Divine Ground by inference. They can also realize its existence by direct intuition, superior to discursive reasoning" and echoing one of Krishnamurti's most well know aphorisms, writes, "This immediate knowledge unites the knower with what is known" (pp.35-36). In other words, there is no longer a concept of 'the knower' to know anything; there is only direct experience.

Kraft explains that Zen Buddhism (considered the mystical arm of Buddhism) also distinguishes between two types of 'mind:'

> In Zen they use the word *mind* in a very interesting way. The word
> is also a symbol for the consciousness of the universe itself. In fact,
> the mind of the individual and the mind of the universe are regarded
> as ultimately one. So by emptying oneself of one's smaller, individual

mind, and by losing the individual's intense self-consciousness, we are able to tap into this larger, more creative, universal mind. (in Goleman, 1992, p. 47)

These two minds are commonly known as "Big Mind" and "Little Mind" in Zen. Contemporary spiritual teacher Byron Katie refers to this "smaller, individual mind" as the "I-know mind" and to this "universal mind" as the "infinite polarity of mind."

> As we question what we believe, we come to see that we're not who we thought we were. The transformation comes out of the infinite polarity of mind, which we've rarely experienced, because the I-know mind has been so much in control. And as we inquire, our world changes, because we're working with the projector—mind—and not with what is projected. We lose our entire world, the world as we understood it. And each time we inquire, reality becomes kinder. (Katie, 2007, p.25-26)

What Byron Katie describes above is a profound transformation, akin, I believe, to Krishnamurti's psychological transformation, which is possible when we inquire into the fundamental nature of our thinking mind (out of which come our beliefs).

Consciousness researchers Jane Katra and Russell Targ (1999) follow physicist David Bohm's term *nonlocal mind*, referring to "this extended awareness that transcends time and space" (p.15). They also point out that Buddha's term was "'no-mind,' meaning the absence of thoughts disrupting an awareness of indivisible unity" while Jesus used the phrase "the peace that passes all understanding" (p.5).

Chopra (1993) describes the phenomenon of intelligence in language that replaces 'thought ' and 'concept ' with their by-products—words and language—as a product of thought: "When we transcend, we know nonverbally without the use of words. We obtain knowledge directly, without the distracting intervention of spoken language" (p.67). He also explains the necessity of transcending thought to arrive at pure consciousness:

> This source of all material reality is pure consciousness. It is pure awareness. It is the unified field. It is the field of all possibilities. We cannot know this field just by thinking about it because, by definition, it is transcendental to thought. We can, however, have experiential knowledge of this field by transcending to it and knowing it intimately as our own nature. (1993, pp.66-67)

Philosopher Jacob Needleman echoes Krishnamurti's assertion that we live in a reality created by our minds when he writes: "The thought 'I exist' is not the same thing as the awareness of one's own existence....Thought is not the same thing as consciousness." Redfield (1997) too, points out how we are so used to living through mental concepts that we try to "intellectualize" our way to awareness, which, by definition, we cannot do:

> ...we are all overcoming the temptation to merely intellectualize this journey. Loving the idea of mystical transformation, being intrigued by it, keeping it in mind, is great as a first step. But, as we all are coming to recognize, believing intellectually is not the same thing as actually living the experience.
>
> I mention this again because the old materialistic paradigm constantly keeps us thinking and analyzing and relating to places and things from that perspective....What we are seeking is more than just the intellectual appreciation of the beauty of a special site, or the comfortable relaxation of prayer and meditation...
>
> We all must find that spiritual experience we have never felt before that expands our sense of self from within, transforming our understanding of who we are, opening us to the intelligence behind the universe. (p.96)

Redfield lays out the contrast between intellectualizing the spiritual journey and actually undertaking it. In so doing, he points out, a transformation can happen that is a paradox of allowing us to see who we are beyond thought and therefore transforms who we know ourselves to be. Furthermore, this action journey, or transformation, leads us to an awareness of the "intelligence" behind all that is.

The recognized scholar on myth, Joseph Campbell, writes of "transrational insight" (1972, p.141) that is a "mental state" both expressed and "provoked" by Zen koans. Campbell describes the way that koans function: "Such conundrums cannot be reasoned upon. They first focus, then baffle, thought…. Suddenly, the intellect lets go and an appropriate retort breaks spontaneously forth. It has been said (I am told) that the ultimate koan is the universe itself."

By way of example, Tolle references the Zen saying, "There's a blind Buddha in your belly, make him see," which Tolle explains "you can't reason this; it forces you into feeling your body." Tolle goes on to explain that the "Focal point of their being is not in their head but in their belly" (referring to the common Buddha statues with big bellies). Campbell also goes on to describe "Buddhist 'wisdom of the yonder shore'—that shore beyond reason, from which 'words turn back, not having attained'" (p.141).

Carl Jung (1963) writes of the natural mind: "The 'natural mind' is the mind which says absolutely straight and ruthless things. That is the sort of mind which springs from natural sources and not from opinions taken from books; it wells up from the earth like a natural spring, and brings with it the peculiar wisdom of nature."

Adding "natural" to mind distinguishes it from what we normally think of as mind, which is our thinking mind (for some, equated with the brain). Jung (1963) describes the phenomenon in an anecdote which ended with the following excerpt: "I came to the conclusion that there must be something the matter with these philosophers, for they had the curious notion that God was a kind of hypothesis that could be discussed" (p.62). In other words, that which we call God is something that can only be directly experienced, not experienced *through* thought, otherwise there is no real knowing[39], only mental conjecture.

The poet Rilke (1984) refers to the same phenomenon of a knowing that is located within oneself, which is a deep "feeling" accessed through intense quiet. Here he gives advice on how best to live in a letter to a young admirer of his work:

> ...finally I want to add just one more bit of advice: to keep grow-
> ing, silently and earnestly, through your whole development; you
> couldn't disturb it any more violently than by looking outside and
> waiting for outside answers to questions that only your innermost
> feeling, in your quietest hour, can perhaps answer (p.11).

Krishnamurti (1975) echoes this need for quieting the mind to access no less than "the origin of everything:" "That quietness is necessary because a mind that is really very quiet, not distorted, understands something which is not distorted, which is really beyond the measure of thought. And that is the origin of everything" (p.100).

Ken Wilber (2004) points out that who we are as humans cannot logically be any of those things that we can experience (such as thoughts, or the body) because by definition we are that which is aware of the experiencing. He calls it the "Witness:" "I am not objects in nature, not feelings in the body, not thoughts in the mind, for I can witness them all. I am that Witness—a vast, free, spacious, empty, clear, pure, transparent Openness that impartially notices all that arises."

While the above authors may have used different language from each other to describe the phenomenon, what these different descriptions have in common is a pointing the way to a sort of omniscient presence in the

---

[39] I use the term 'knowing' throughout the book to delineate between stored knowledge as memory and that which is other than this, other than thought.

universe *and within ourselves* that *is*, or *is the source of*, intelligence and insight *but we need to put thought aside in order to uncover it*. It is this phenomenon of direct awareness, or, consciousness, or, natural intelligence (there are many different terms that these writers employ, which I actually find helpful because it makes it more difficult for the mind to pin the phenomenon down to a concept—it remains a bit elusive) that I am looking at in my research.

Krishnamurti (1953) states, "Intelligence is the spontaneous perception which makes a man strong and free" (p.103) and "Intelligence is the capacity to perceive the essential, the what is; and to awaken this capacity, in oneself and in others, is education" (p.6). In other words, humans have the ability to encounter life directly, unmediated by the mind; this is what Krishnamurti describes as "spontaneous perception" because it is not calculated, it is not 'pre-experience' through thought, as it were. It is perceiving essence, "the what is." It is a perception, not an analysis. Described in this way, seeing is really a passive act rather than an active one—analysis is an active state. Moreover, "awaken" suggests a sort of dormant state—that is, it's innate to each of us but lies unaware and unacknowledged. Krishnamurti is suggesting here that there is a reality that exists independent of our concepts or thoughts about it and that the ability to see this reality is the definition of intelligence. Indeed, he not only equates direct perception with intelligence, but with education—what its purpose is as well as what it is in essence.

Recent studies (see especially Taylor, 2010) have looked at awakening experiences outside the context of education—how they happen, what they are, and their implications. Chris Bache (2008) has written about consciousness transformation within the context of education. However, I am not aware of any autoethnographic studies on consciousness transformation and its implications for education.

Empirical research on consciousness or spiritual transformation within the context of education include a study on collective consciousness (Bache, 2008), transformative experiences with the labyrinth (Compton,

2007), and on positive psychological characteristics with a new relaxation response curriculum in high school students (Benson, 1994).

There have been numerous studies on the effects of meditation on students' lives. The nature and results of meditation is a closely related area of study, although this study includes both a larger scope (i.e. the phenomenon of non-conceptual intelligence) and more focused outcome, intended to cover not just the effects of a formal spiritual practice on students' experiential knowing but the effects of any and all educational practices in a typical, current Western school and their effects on helping or hindering students to know themselves, and to perceive 'what is.'

Chapter 6

The true measure of a person seems to lie in the standard
of their conscious and free emotional relationship to others.
It is not found at all in their beliefs, their opinions, or their judgments.
It is not found in their philosophy, their intelligence, their skills, or abilities.
It is not found in their type, their make-up, or their particular temperament.
Rather, it is in their intention, their presence with others,
and their emotional orientation to the truth.

Peter Ralston

~

Theoretical Context

Intellect versus Intelligence

> Intellectually you have no energy because you repeat what others
> have said. You are prisoners to theories, speculations, and therefore
> you have no capacity to reason, observe with logical, healthy minds.
> You have mechanical minds. You go to schools where you cram in
> facts and repeat the facts, and that's all. Intellectually you are not
> aware; your minds are not sharp, clear. (Krishnamurti, 1971, p.113)

Contemporary primary and secondary education focuses almost exclusively on developing the intellect (as distinct from Krishnamurti's
"intelligence") or the thinking mind. It does this through adding knowledge or

188 • Kathryn Jefferies

information to memory, and developing skills such as reasoning, measuring, analyzing, and judging. In such a context, intelligence is then measured by the ability to hold knowledge as memory, to analyze, and to conceptualize information. As Krishnamurti (1953) puts it, "What we now call education is a matter of accumulating information and knowledge from books" (p.17) and "the accumulation of facts and the development of capacity" (p.20). In short, we equate intelligence with the intellect—a well-developed thinking mind.

According to Krishnamurti, equating intelligence with the intellect, or thought, is to miss an intelligence that is far superior in its nature than that which we currently think of as intelligence. We give thought central importance, not even realizing that there is anything else, any other place from which to know. "Thought, the intellect, dominates the world. And therefore intelligence has very little place here. When one thing dominates, the other must be subservient" (1973, p. 521). Krishnamurti suggests here that "the other" (i.e. intelligence not of the intellect) cannot be seen because we have placed our emphasis on thought. By virtue of experience, one cannot be in service to thought and experience real intelligence at the same time. Furthermore, he suggests that helping students discover this intelligence is far more crucial in education than developing the intellect. Katra and Targ (1999, p.139) explain:

> Pantanjali taught that an individual's intellect tended to attribute the power of consciousness to itself. He said our illusory sense of our separate selves comes from this egoic tendency, and that thinking is unable to transcend itself to access a higher dimension of truth. According to Pantanjali, our mind is another organ of the body. Like the eye, which is illumined by light but does not create it. Rather, it is consciousness or awareness that activates and informs the contents of the mind. Because an individual's mind and thoughts are so reactive to any sensory input that happens to grab its wayward attention, thinking must be transcended for union with Divine Consciousness.

In fact, experiencing this intelligence, Krishnamurti (1953) contends, is the only way for students to have a deep understanding of life and themselves and therefore live life as whole human beings. Moreover, it is only in being whole oneself that one can then create positive change in the outside world. This is the essence of his claim that revolution originating in society will never create real change but instead one must revolutionize one's mind and this will automatically lead to transformation of society.

Krishnamurti and Education

Krishnamurti questions the very foundation of our education system, the entrenched pillars it stands on. Specifically, he suggests that the knowledge we believe we possess—as individuals, as cultures, as a human race—comes from the movement of thought, and that because the nature of thought is limited, we can never arrive at the whole (we might say 'the big picture' or truth of the nature of life and ourselves) through thought. Krishnamurti boils this down to very simple terms by way of examples we can all relate to. The examples are so simple that I didn't really understand fully what he meant until years after I first encountered his work. Since I assumed they were complex problems, I assumed they must also have complex solutions.

He points out that we have not ever been able to solve the problems of the world that we say implicitly, as a global community, we would like to solve—things like war, hunger, and poverty. It was at this point—after reading this statement in one of his books that I would think to myself, 'Well, naturally. Of course we haven't solved these problems. How could these issues ever get solved? They can only be improved upon.' But then I would and did miss the point: I missed the simple truth that we have been working for thousands of years to solve these problems and haven't been able to do it. We are so accustomed to living with war and conflict of all kinds, that we don't actually step back and look at this simple fact—that we have not solved these problems by the way we have been going about them. There seems no evidence to suggest that the global situation (war, hunger, etc.) would change (or at least very quickly and without enormous effort given that this is so far how change has occurred) by continuing to attempt to solve the problems in the same way as our current and previous attempts. The way Byron Katie explains it, is

> So, you know, no wonder we continue to have violence and wars on this planet. You know, war in our head, war in our homes, communities, countries and the world. You know, we're still killing each other. Can you imagine a world so ancient that we still argue over who's right as though we are going to win and it...you know, we know from history that it doesn't work.

Krishnamurti has argued that the social movements in the last half century that have resulted in increased power, rights, and acceptability for people of visible minorities, various sexual orientations, and women (to the extent to which these rights were achieved in his lifetime) were a reaction *against* the prevailing dominant norm, which can solve a problem only on surface levels and does nothing to address underlying issues that caused them in the first place (Krishnamurti, 1970b; 1971; 1973).

To put it another way, when something becomes culturally unacceptable, it just drives the tendency (towards discrimination, or violence, for example) underground, suppressed within the mind, but it does not address the psychology of fear that caused people to be violent and discriminate against one another in the first place. So this fear gets turned towards someone or something else, projected outward; it is not a permanent transformation, which would require that one transcends the behaviour completely through encountering the workings and effects of one's own negatively-held beliefs. Thus, rather than being a reaction against, it is coming from a different 'place' within oneself—it is in a different relationship with those occurrences which one doesn't like and wishes to see replaced. Steve Taylor (2010) offers a helpful explanation as to why social activism without personal transformation is insufficient for permanent change, and at the same time why, ultimately, personal transformation is not personal at all, but highly in service of the collective:

> We need to wake up for the sake of the human race as a whole, in order to free ourselves from the social chaos and conflict that have blighted the last few thousand years of history. The only possibility the human race has of living in harmony—without warfare, inequality and the oppression of women and different ethnic and social groups—is through transcending the overdeveloped ego. Only then will the impulse to accumulate wealth and gain power over other people disappear. Only then will we gain the ability to empathize with other people rather than mistrust or exploit them, to sense the shared essence which lies beneath the superficial differences of race or nationality. (p.230)

I would describe the ego as both the self-identity as well as the aspect of the mind that created it. Another way to describe the 'waking up' that Taylor talks about is as stepping out of complete identification with the conceptual mind. In conversation with Sir Ken Robinson, Tolle explains how this is what is required in order for humans to truly know 'others' opening up the possibility for conflict resolution:

> Sensing the consciousness in the other means you are not totally trapped in the conceptual mind because through the conceptual mind you judge the other and it's only when you step out of the conceptual mind into awareness or aware presence that you can sense the other beyond your judgments. It's a modality of knowing the other human...

And,

> Prejudice of any kind implies that you are identified with the thinking mind. It means you don't see the other human being anymore, but only your own concept of that human being. To reduce the aliveness of another human being to a concept is already a form of violence. (2003, p.20)

So we can begin to see how prejudice of any kind forms, and how any attempt to address it (through enforcement, coercion, conformity, threat of consequences, etc., which is what we see happening in society and in education) without addressing the root cause, does nothing *permanently*, which is to say, *at the root*, to effect change. Or, as Einstein said, "Peace cannot be kept by force; It can only be achieved by understanding."

Einstein also said that the world as we have created it is a process of our thinking and that it cannot be changed without changing our thinking. He went on to say that the "rational mind" is a terrible master and that it should be the "faithful servant" to intuition, the "sacred gift." I believe when he says "mind" he is referring to thought or the intellect—we usually conflate the three.

In other words, Einstein supports Krishnamurti's claim that there is an intelligence that is not born of thought that is the real source of creative problem-solving. The way Tolle puts it, is: "The mind is a superb instrument if used rightly. Used wrongly, however, it becomes very destructive. To put it more accurately ... you usually don't use it at all. It uses you" (2008, Harpo Productions). I would argue that most of us (based on the evidence of the world stage) are being used by our minds—the essence of bondage.

Some would say that Krishnamurti is too abstract, grandiose, or naïve tackling these big world problems and would dismiss him outright. Yet to me, he is stating the most obvious, simple facts so that we can start at the beginning so-to-speak, to have a way in—a portal, as it were—to a new understanding.

He starts us with the plain and simple facts because, of course, only a new understanding can see what he is talking about—that it is the limited understanding, the fragmented thought, that has created the problems in the first place. So, that we still have war, hunger, and poverty (among other unwanted things) is a fact that is plain for all to see. Krishnamurti gives us permission to ask why this is so.

This is so important—it seems to me that while there are many organizations and governments working to tackle these problems, the 'who' has not been gone into deeply enough first. The questioning is the important thing, not the answering, as it turns out. To ask, and let the asking be there, rather than the movement of thought that desires an answer, is what produces creative solutions.

So, it would seem a fair conclusion to say that if we still have these unwanted things, then the ways we have been approaching them have not been working. And maybe we can allow ourselves to ask, What if there is something essential about life, about ourselves, that we are missing? And so, the good news is: (and this is always where Krishnamurti brings it back to) more important than accumulating vast amounts of knowledge and the mental examination of issues, is our own awareness of experience of life and ourselves, which, of course, we all have. Can we, then, just look at what our experience is? Can we look, without any attempt to change it? Because we have already attempted to make change without first looking deeply into the nature of life, and it has not solved the problems.

At this point, I would like to bring in some concrete examples in the context of education. The difficulty with discussing Krishnamurti's insights is that it requires such a paradigm shift in our way of perceiving the world and ourselves that I need to lay a lot of groundwork first. This can tend to get into what appears to be the abstract (i.e. remaining within the realm of thought). Yet the difference is that I am writing from my own experience, not from memory of what Krishnamurti or another said. I believe offering actual examples can help one cross the bridge into one's own understanding.

Inherent Authority of Experience

Blind belief in authority is the greatest enemy of truth.

Einstein

It is a simple truth that education did not help spiritual masters to awaken to the truth of their nature and to life. In the case of Sri Nisargadatta Maharaj, he was not educated in the formal sense whatsoever, and yet, reading transcriptions of his talks, one could say that his 'knowledge' or 'under-standing' of the nature of all life is immense, if not total.

His case (and others) begs the question then, if his intelligence has nothing to do with knowledge as memory, where does it come from?

Conceptual intelligence versus the phenomenon of what we might call 'natural intelligence' is why, universally, people tune out or have trouble forcing themselves to pay attention when they are listening to someone speak from memory and can't help but tune in when the speaker is present, consciously speaking. An obvious example of this can be found in any video of Eckhart Tolle speaking with well-known spiritual leaders of our time (for example, Marianne Williamson or Neale Donald Walsch). A viewer of the video can easily spot the distinction between the two people on stage, though she may not know or understand what she is seeing. One is clearly at peace: calm, alert, present, not eager to get a point across, not interrupting or coming across as the passionate speaker, clearly attending to what the other is saying. The other has many ideas to share, many thoughts; the quality of their presence is remarkably different. One can feel the difference between them—it need not be analyzed to be seen, but answering why this is so is the thrust of this dissertation. So the question is, what is Eckhart Tolle *experiencing*? Or perhaps an easier question is, what is he *not* experiencing? And what is happening such that listeners respond to what Tolle is saying? They respond to his presence because the same presence exists within them, within all of us, such that it's an experience of resonance in the body as opposed to logical assessment through thought. A listener seems to respond to thought with thought, and to presence with presence.

What I have come to realize is that the meaning of learning is finding answers for oneself. No one else can ultimately teach anyone anything. The reason for this is that words do not teach—life experience does. The best that words can do is to help to either guide someone to an experience or help them make sense of an experience by pointing to something—but even then, the person needs to, again, experience the understanding for themselves. This is what Krishnamurti meant when he famously declared,

"Truth is a pathless land" when he dissolved The Order of the Star—an organization that had been set up by the Theosophical society with him as the spiritual teacher at its head. But Krishnamurti recognized that such a structure itself *is* the problem, in that it creates a false presumption that someone can find truth through the words or instructions of someone else—in this case, through the wisdom or insight of Krishnamurti. The reason one cannot discover the truth through another's teachings, is that these words can only enter one's mind as concepts, and one cannot arrive at anything real and true through concepts, but only through experience. The difficulty is—and this is further complicated by this fact—what we think of as experience is in fact *mediated* experience, not *direct* experience; it is experience mediated by concepts. Hence, there is a necessity of differentiating between two types of experience: mediated and direct (Ralston, 2010, p.71). People who 'know' through mediated experience do not know the truth of something for themselves—they speak from knowledge stored as memory and not from their own experience. This is the difference from those who speak with true authority.

To be clear, I am not saying that people aren't experiencing things all the time—of course they are, but it is the type of experience I am talking about that is essential. I would argue, and this is supported by the spiritual and mystical literature (Katie, 2002, 2007; Maharaj, 1973; Maharshi, Ralston, 2010; Veltheim, 2000), that one and only one of these experiences is an experience of the truth. It is to say that just because someone experienced something a certain way, does not make it true. So, for example, Katie does not question that someone experienced a particular event in the way in which they describe it, but questions what happens when the events are re-experienced in the mind without the thoughts that are causing stress.

Inherent Drive towards (Direct Experience of) the Truth

According to Krishnamurti, "to see" is the meaning of the word "idea," a meaning that we no longer ascribe to our use of idea (which we use now to mean an abstract thought). Seeing implies an existence unaffected by the perception of the viewer. A reality. It would seem that humans are hard-wired to need to see for themselves—each person for herself and himself—the truth of something.

It is for this reason that The Work* (as she calls it) of Byron Katie is so powerful. Along with the enlightenment intensives, this process is the only one I've found that has given me the truth for myself. As Krishnamurti also emphasized again and again in reference to his own talks and writings, there is no adding on of knowledge with these processes, there is no accumulation of beliefs or concepts. Rather, the opposite is true: beliefs and concepts are exposed for what they are—something made up by the mind—so that the truth of life can be allowed to *be seen unencumbered by thought*. The way I see Krishnamurti's work, like Eckhart Tolle's, is a powerful pointer to the truth, while Katie's process is a tool to take oneself there. It does this because it easily and very simply exposes the thinking process for what it is. Krishnamurti always said that in order for one to understand oneself, understanding the nature—the mechanism—of thought is essential. With Katie's four questions and what she calls "the turnarounds," any person can see quite quickly that thoughts become beliefs and we live through these beliefs to create our realities, but *they are fabricated*.

One obvious question, then, is how do we know the truth for itself and that it, too, is not a fabrication? This answer, to me, is also startling in its simplicity and obviousness: our true nature must be 'goodness' because any thought that opposes this hurts (Katie, 2002, 2007). Katie explains that she's a lover of what is, not because she's a spiritual person but because it argues with reality (2002):

> People used to ask me if I was enlightened, and I would say, "I don't know anything about that. I'm just someone who knows the difference between what hurts and what doesn't." I am someone who wants only what is. To meet as a friend each concept that arose turned out to be my freedom (2007, pp.29-30).

It's my own perception that this answer—that anything that opposes reality hurts—is rejected as a simple and clear definition of reality by so many, including philosophers and scientists, because it is so simple and obvious that we miss it. It is hidden in plain sight, as it were; thought looks for something more complicated, more complex. And like Krishnamurti, Katie, Tolle and other spiritual sages through the ages have done, I invite anyone to test this for herself and himself, because my stating it here cannot give one the experience of it, so one cannot know the truth from my words alone nor do I see it as my job to convince anyone. In my view, no one can be coerced towards the truth; it is up to one to make her way there on her own.

Concerning Katie's use of four questions and "turnarounds" (as she calls them), Tolle has said,

> Byron Katie's work is a great blessing for our planet. The root cause of suffering is identification with our thoughts, the 'stories' that are continuously running through our minds. Byron Katie's Work acts like a razor-sharp sword that cuts through that illusion and enables you to know for yourself the timeless essence of your being. Joy, peace, and love emanate from it as your natural state. In *Loving What Is*, you have the key. Now use it. (Katie, 2002, inside pages)

In all of the research I have done on Byron Katie, I have never come across her describing her work as a "method" or "system"; instead, she calls it "inquiry" or just simply "asking four questions." Likewise, I would not refer to Katie's questions as a method *per se*; that is, anything can be turned into method or dogma when something is treated as method. Importantly, Katie talks about asking the questions for the love of truth, rather than as a means to an end (2002) because having a goal in mind—what one might *get* as a natural result of doing inquiry—is what morphs the four questions into a method. The questions are simply asking someone to consider whether they can absolutely know something for sure, ever, and then asking who they become when they are identified with their beliefs and who they would be without them. Because they are in the form of questions, there is no prescription and therefore no method. To me, this is consistent with Krishnamurti insisting that there is no method to follow—no path—to enlightenment and that the very seeking is the trap. Since encountering Katie's Work, I have indeed wondered that Krishnamurti himself did not come up with something like this. In my view, I can only surmise that it just simply did not occur to him. In any event, although Katie's four questions and the 'turnarounds' could be construed as a method, I do not see it this way, as I have explained above. Indeed, when anyone whom Katie is facilitating in The Work wishes to either debate or go into a story outside of the questions, Katie kindly interrupts and explains that as soon as one leaves the questions, one is not in inquiry. Katie has also responded to people who complain that the four questions and turnarounds are not working for them that they are doing the process with motive. Therein lies the definition of method: it is to get from point A to point B. Katie explains that the only way it works is to do it for the "love of peace" not out of a desire for an outcome. In my experience, while conceptually this may be a subtle difference, it becomes very obvious in experiencing the process for oneself. In addition, method places the authority outside oneself (in the sense that one is following something external to one's own inner authority) whereas The Work locates the authority within oneself, the place the answers arise from.

Experiential Context

Situating Myself as the Researcher: A Study in Paradox

In beginning to articulate how I, as the researcher of this project, fit into the process, consider the following three excerpts from scientists and researchers Jane Katra and Russell Targ (1999), who point out that there is a distinction between *knowing* and *believing*:

> We base our response to Sagan on a description of the *experience* of God, rather than a doctrine of belief. As scientists we are convinced that a person need not *believe* or take on faith anything about the

existence of universal spirit, because the *experience* of God is a test-able hypothesis. (p.2)

Although we are experts in neither philosophy nor theology, we offer our experiences and observations with the hope that readers may become *knowers* as opposed to *believers*, and find new appre-ciation for their innate power of attention. (p.3)

This book did not spring from the author's beliefs in spiritual or theological matters. While we are accustomed to reaching conclu-sions conceptually and intellectually, based on our training in sci-ence and research, the motivation for writing this book is rooted in our experience and our heart-to-heart connections with our teach-ers, rather than in analysis. (p.6)

Katra and Targ point out that there is a jump for them—a sort of wear-ing two hats, if you will—from their scientist/researcher paradigm, which is conceptual/intellectual, to their larger, non-role-identified paradigm, which is knowing/experiencing.

As well, consider the following from Michel Foucault (in Feuerverger, 2001, p.115), who "commented that using your own reason (instead of working according to what others want of you) is essential for becoming conscious of your own inner thoughts and desires and in so doing becom-ing the person you would like to be." Indeed, I feel that I have used my own reason to guide this study which is why it takes the form it does.

It is in light of the above, which all highlight the possibility and impor-tance of personal *experience* in for one's ability to truly know, that I'd like to begin the discussion of the relevance of me to this exploration.

Logically, it makes no sense to me to undertake a research study that depends solely upon conceptual knowledge (i.e. through theoretical re-search methodologies and empirical research) in order to demonstrate that a) there is something other than conceptual knowledge and b) what that is. This leaves me with no option but to use my own experience (in addi-tion to others')—which I would like to make clearly distinct from *stories* or *thoughts about* my experience—as a part of the research. In addition, I would have no leg to stand on if I *didn't* have experience in relation to witnessing my mind and emotions and experience of my non-dual self, for starters. Then what I could offer to this research project would be only secondhand information. One would be able to feel that my language is dead, as it is coming out of concepts and not enlivened by my own experience. It doesn't mean I can't use others' 'research' but it will be writing from their own experience.

Granted, I will still use words and concepts to convey meaning but they hopefully arise consistently out of experience, not concepts, and are to act *as pointers* to the truth (even painting a picture would still be a pointer, though it could have more success bypassing the thinking mind, depending upon the person) and are understood not to contain the truth themselves. It is as close as we can get. The rest is up to the reader (-as-experiencer, not reader-as-abstract-thinker). This is why the first thing the Buddha is reported to have said upon awakening is "This can't be taught." No researcher, no matter how much data she has or how insightful he is, can lay out the truth before one such that one immediately understands; only a person can teach themselves—but not through thinking, through experiencing it for themselves. This is why, I believe, Jesus taught in parables, so that people's minds couldn't hook onto the words and concepts presented as easily, because they were already clearly metaphoric and as such were already pointing to something other than themselves. Tolle explains this when introducing the form of one of his books:

> The form of this book can be seen as a revival for the present age of the oldest form of recorded spiritual teachings: the sutras of ancient India. Sutras are powerful pointers to the truth in the form of aphorisms or short sayings, with little conceptual elaboration. The Vedas and Upanishads are the early sacred teachings recorded in the form of sutras, as are the words of the Buddha. The sayings and parables of Jesus, too, when taken out of their narrative context, could be

regarded as sutras, as well as the profound teachings contained in the *Tao Te Ching*, the ancient Chinese book of wisdom. The advantage of the sutra form lies in its brevity. It does not engage the thinking mind more than is necessary. What it doesn't say—but only points to—is more important that what it says. (Tolle, 2003, x-xi)

This is also why Krishnamurti said, "truth is a pathless land"; neither he nor anyone else can be considered a "teacher" in the truest sense because only we can teach ourselves. In other words, a path cannot be laid out—even the concept of a path is inherently false and misleading. 'Path' creates an idea of a future—somewhere to get to—and this is illusory. But as long as we rely on thought as our identity, we can't see this, because thought is the problem.

In writing and living this work, the movie *A Beautiful Mind* often comes to me—in particular, one exchange between the protagonist who is considered a mathematical genius (in real life, he won the Nobel Prize in Mathematics), and his wife. He has gotten to the point where he has some sense of his mental illness that causes him to be unable to distinguish between 'reality' and 'unreality.' When his wife confronts him about what they are going to do about it, he passionately explains that he can fix it—he can reason it through—given, he thinks, his tremendous ability with mental concepts. She musters all her energy and emphatically states, "No, you can't, because the problem *is* your mind."

This example beautifully (though some would say tragically, of course, based as it is on a real person's experience) exemplifies to me exactly our current relationship with our minds: we don't know we are not them. In essence, they have taken over: the man could no longer distinguish between what was real and what existed as concepts in his head. The fact that his experience of this was *obvious* to the rest of the world does not make it any more problematic than what the rest of us are dealing with. In short, we have all lost sight of what is *real* because what is real cannot be apprehended by thought. Tolle puts it like this: "The ego doesn't know that mind and mental positions have nothing to do with who you are because the ego is the unobserved mind itself. When the shift from thinking to awareness happens, an intelligence far greater than the ego's cleverness begins to operate in your life" (2005, p.121).

I see it as my job as a researcher to unpack what is going on for those who seem to be inhabiting a different 'reality' or state of consciousness than what is considered normal or common. In other words, what did they discover and how, and what is it like to live in their reality or daily consciousness now?

The spiritual teachers (as we might call them) whom I write about here* do not widely quote others (though when they do they are always other spiritual masters) because they don't need to—they are speaking from a knowing that arises from their own direct experience. So as a researcher, I am the one who has to notice this and figure out that this is what is going on and compare these spiritual teachers—their writing and their experiences—to pull it all together for others, as well as for myself. I am synthesizing their lives and work in order to present a wider body of evidence for the phenomenon they have experienced. I know that truly I am only able to do this because of my own awakening experiences; otherwise, I really wouldn't have *direct knowledge* of what they are referring to and this book could be at best about *conceptual* knowledge.

I also see it as my job to try and bridge the non-academic 'world' with the academic, to try and put the research into a context and into language that hopefully can be understood by a wide audience. I don't see it as my job to limit my language to academic language, and by extension to only academicians and scholars. In other words, I see my job to be as much about explaining to (my relevant portion of) the academic community the language of the non-conceptual and non-theoretical as much as I see my job as explaining the scholarly to the non-academic community.

My interest in doing all of my educational research comes out of three main desires: 1) to serve the world to the greatest of my capacity 2) to live my life to the fullest (which to me means expanding my capacity for joy every day by being or expressing fully that which I am) and 3) to experience freedom (which to me, can only come from knowing who I am and what life is, so that ultimately, I am at peace).

Of course, the three items could be seen as all one item, as ultimately I think they are the same thing; one can't exist without the others. My own awareness of my motivations in doing this research work and the importance of stating it here can best be summed up by J.S. Taylor's statement (in Smiley, p.105): "For most of us who attempt to produce some sort of investigative project, the self-development aspect is as valuable as answering the research question."

It is my experience that although my mind knows so much about personal transformation (I have spent years reading, studying, and reflecting upon it, undertaken numerous workshops, not to mention ten years of studying myself and human nature through a sort of metaphysical psychotherapy) this alone does not create change in how I live my life.

In other words, although I understand a great deal intellectually or conceptually about living a life of joy (for example), this in itself does not increase my joy or expression of who I am whatsoever. I would even say that I have gone so far as to corroborate my intellectual learning with my intuition—in other words, my knowledge of spiritual concepts goes beyond understanding a concept at the level of the intellect—but again, this alone does nothing to create actual change. (The intuition operates more as a knowing that what I have deduced is indeed correct.) It is for this reason that I am greatly interested in the *practice*—or *living*—of life. Another way to say this is: How do I take myself from the conceptual to the actual? I am certain that if I cannot do this for myself, I cannot facilitate students taking themselves there.

Maybe the question should be: Why do I not put into practice what I know intellectually? It is my experience that we can understand intellectually how to live non-conceptually—(this statement is obviously contradictory and exposes the problem that we seemed to have glossed over in applied education)—and why this would create a life of joy and full self-expression, and we can write and talk about it ad infinitum, but unless we are living it we have done nothing; i.e. nothing new is created and nothing changes.

Graduate Work in Education: Questioning Academic Authority

Undertaking graduate work with Krishnamurti's revolutionary ideas on education as my centre point or guiding framework has not been easy. I'm sure I'm far from the only graduate student and, likely, professor in education to feel this way, given that our job as I see it is to bite the hand that feeds us.

In other words, we are examining (at the very least in some small way, at most in a very large way) the very process we are engaged in; we are in a system of education whose culmination ends at the PhD. Thus, there are limits, it would seem, to what we can challenge as graduate students about this very education system, for by virtue of enrolling as a PhD student, we have implicitly given our vote for supporting this system—we have in essence said, "I believe in this academic process and the inherent value of the PhD."

For my work, expressly, where I am asking the basic ontological and epistemological questions of the nature of being and knowing, it has seemed to me to be particularly challenging. I have consistently engaged in questioning what this education system we have derived (over many years) considers learning and knowing, and what it considers important to learn and know.

In the meantime, I, too, am subject to being evaluated and having to answer to this same system as a PhD student; I need to jump through certain hoops that the academy has decided are important and qualify me to some degree as 'someone who knows.'

So in effect, I am examining both my own experience and process (how could I not? To me this is essential) and that of others in their own (formal and informal) educational processes. As a result, it has felt somewhat constraining at times, as well as confusing (eg. Who am I studying: me or them, or both? Is it *really* possible to examine anyone other than myself?

etc.), and yet by the same token, it offers me a front centre seat, as it were, as I am not separate from the educational process whereof I speak. Graduate work in education is unique in this way (i.e. as compared to graduate work in other subject areas where students are not reflexively engaged in observing and critiquing a process/environment/system etc. of which they are a part). This is not to say that all graduate students in education are actively inquiring into their own experience, but ultimately I would argue that it is impossible to separate the two.

Accordingly, not only am I a student in the process or system I am examining which can present some challenging orientational/relational and practical problems, but also my specific *topic* of study expressly challenges the very foundational underpinning of the educational system. And now it would seem I really am in a conundrum. Given that my topic for my dissertation includes looking at an alternative mode of being and knowing other than the intellect, it seems to me that I am questioning the validity—not only of the foundation on which our education system is based—but of my own process (i.e. by undertaking a PhD). Another way to put this is, Can I really discover the nature of what I am examining (my research goal) within the definitional parameters of PhD? So, at this point, it is probably apparent the degree to which I have had to engage in active inquiry at every turn, throughout my time in graduate school—paradoxically, as a responsibility to the rigours of academia, as well as a responsibility to my own self. If the process of graduate work has taught me anything, it is the necessity as well as the gold mine that is self-examination. Again, in an example of the researcher being the researched, the topic of self-knowing through Krishnamurti's framework is the topic of this dissertation. The meta-levels of this research endeavour can certainly leave the mind in confusion.

This, too, then represents my dilemma with doing a PhD in education, which I need to discuss here as the dilemma informs this dissertation. I would argue that the academy (which I am meaning here generally as that institution that imparts learning from kindergarten to the final destination of which is the PhD) is based on learning (and ultimately living) as acquiring, and being able to manipulate, conceptual knowledge. Yet, it does not see itself as doing this. The paradigm, by definition, does not see knowledge as being acquired indirectly so it can't see the possibility of knowledge being acquired directly.

This is Krishnamurti's point when he argues that, "We cannot understand existence abstractly or theoretically. To understand life is to understand ourselves, and that is both the beginning and the end of education" (Krishnamurti, 1953, p.). Krishnamurti is pointing to the centrality of one's self-experience (i.e. experience of life as experienced through self). Yet, if what we call learning or education is limited to being able to think abstractly or theoretically and to recall from memory (all domains of the intellect), then according to Krishnamurti, we have not understood anything essential about life and ourselves. Moreover, we are extremely limited in our ability to change ourselves and life in any significant positive way when it is initiated out of only conceptual or intellectual understanding.

Scott Forbes (1999, p.6) briefly outlines how this idea of the central importance of the mind (intellect) goes back to Plato, who holds that the mind develops according to the knowledge it acquires.

> According to Plato, after a certain amount of knowledge of sufficient complexity is acquired by the child's mind, that mind develops the ability to form abstractions with that knowledge…. Developing the best mind is accomplished by having the mind acquire the various forms of knowledge suited to form abstractions, because it is with abstractions that a person finds truth. From this it follows that the point of a curriculum is to present such knowledge in increasingly elaborated forms in order to create the mind that will be able to create the abstractions that can see truth. A good case can be made that this is fundamental to the thinking in many approaches to modern education….the important point is that the nature of the person is seen as determined by the nature of his mind, and the nature of his mind is seen as determined by the knowledge it acquires.

In this vein, if what I am contributing to scholarship by executing this study is founded upon this false premise: in this case, that education can be deeply understood conceptually, then I am not contributing anything of value. In many ways, the process of this PhD for me has been about finding out the answer to this question: Is there a way to research, write, and experience this entire process non-conceptually, especially when it comes to researching others' experiences? In other words, what is there *besides* concept, abstraction, and theory? So I have very deliberately brought myself in as an object of study throughout this process; to not do so would be inaccurate and dishonest, it would miss the richest object of study, and the study would be forced to remain conceptual.

Doing a PhD in education really is a paradox of sorts: how, possibly, can I fully examine or challenge what is being done in education when I am trying to adhere to the codes of what makes a PhD a PhD in the first place? It comes back to the argument of who gets to decide what is education and what is research. It reminds me of modernist prose and poetry which I studied for part of my undergraduate degree in literature. I learned that when modern writers came on the poetry scene trying to find ways to express what was true for them, there were many who said, "This is not poetry. This is not literature. It does not follow the rules of what we recognize as poetry and literature." Who gets to decide? Likewise, is it not my job as a PhD student in education to question what I see as currently accepted and unquestioned in education?

So to give some particulars, in my case I am looking into Krishnamurti's (and others) claims that there is an innate intelligence in each of us that we always have access to—that we don't have to go outside of ourselves to books and to the experts to find answers because *there is a deeper intelligence within us that is not of our own individual mind.* In fact, not only do we not need the mind for the source of this intelligence, argues Krishnamurti, but the mind is the very impediment to this intelligence, because it can only contain knowledge as memory and cannot by its very nature meet anything new. This is not the same thing as saying the mind is not needed, but rather, that the mind is needed, as Einstein said, in *service* to something else (he called it intuition). Of course, what better way—perhaps what only authentic way—to do this but by seeing if I could see it for myself? That is, discover this intelligence for myself.

Using one's own experience as research is tricky in that it is not necessarily corroborated by an outside source, which is the very definition of research in the current academic paradigm. So to put it very simply, if someone says, "This is true because I have experienced it," we respond by saying, "It cannot possibly be, because no one else experienced it too," or, "Prove it." Yet, what if we considered the possibility that they may have experienced and be experiencing what few others currently seem able to experience, or remember experiencing? To be sure, this is part of what gives spiritual teachers or leaders their inherent authority: they have experienced something that most of us do not know as our current reality, or, state of consciousness, yet there seems to be a remembering in us that this state is possible. Perhaps our early childhood experiences where there are initially no concepts and therefore no conceptual identity, or perhaps just an innate knowing, or both. For it is not the higher or expanded state of consciousness alone that gives spiritual teachers authority—it is clear that what they are saying somehow makes sense to us, *even if we haven't experienced it consciously.* It touches some part of people (and it would be difficult to argue that it is our reasoning faculty) so that we feel these so-called spiritual leaders are telling the truth and see something we are not seeing. Indeed, spiritual leaders consistently point out that they are only "re-minding" us what we know but have forgotten (or in other words, are not consciously aware of). This alone can explain the vast following of spiritual leaders like Krishnamurti, Jesus, the Buddha, Mohammed, Sri Nisargadatta Maharaj, Ramana Maharshi, Lao-tse, Sai Baba and others and in present day, Eckhart Tolle and Byron Katie and others. That is to say, these people are not resonating with our intellect—our rational mind—but with something deeper.

This is not to say that the individual perceptions of reality would necessarily diverge or be in conflict. Indeed, Krishnamurti and others have argued that the opposite is true: 'what is' (reality) stands unimpeded by others' awareness of it or not. It just is. Yet, it is arrived at through direct perception by the individual and not mediated through a concept of truth. So for example, although a study may have been corroborated by many (perhaps thousands) of people, it does not make it true. To believe that we can directly experience truth for ourselves (Ralston, 2011, p. 70) challenges the very underpinnings of academia, in a sense. Academia exists because people have spent a great deal of time studying conceptually (people or things or phenomena) such that they then become seen as the experts in their given niches. Yet what would happen if truth were seen to be accessible independent of knowledge, if we could bypass the middle people and experience truth *directly* for ourselves? Where would that leave the experts? In this new paradigm, we each would be an 'expert' on the truth, able to tap into a larger source of intelligence or consciousness. Obviously, this doesn't address the place of the conceptual knowledge-information that is held by these experts—for there is a place for it—it just levels the playing field in the arena we call teaching and learning. As mentioned elsewhere in this book, the above is really best explained by using the examples of Krishnamurti, Tolle, Katie, and others who can speak clearly, knowledgeably, and without hesitation on topics that *they have never studied*. That is, they have no conceptual knowledge of them. What they have is clear seeing. With a clear mind unimpeded by conceptual knowledge, they merely describe what is true. It is apparent to them. It's never assumed, hypothesized, guessed at, etc. It's what is; reality, there to be apprehended.

Paradigm shifts are like this, by definition: something new cannot be accepted by the old because it causes the simultaneous destruction of the old—accepting a new paradigm *is the reason* the old paradigm crumbles. And yet, apparently the academy is open to self-destruction or it would not offer a PhD in education. As I see it, this is the only discipline that has as its task to directly challenge the education system. It is a little (or maybe, exactly) like biting the hand that feeds it. So, the academy is open to self-destruction, in theory. In actuality, it is my experience that structures exist because they have been put there by the human mind, and the academy is no different. As a social structure, its continued existence relies on people upholding it; otherwise, it would cease to exist. And then what would we have to measure anything against? Where would the norm be? How would we know what to accept as real, and as unreal? The standards of research are supposed to be rigorous and exact, so that as consumers of the research, we would know what to believe and what not to believe, or what to accept and what not to accept, as truth. We are supposed to be able to rely on the science of research, on its norms. But what if the structures—the norms—are only that which we put in place, based on the best we thought we could do at the time? If we thought intelligence or truth was to be found 'outside' of us (i.e. in theoretical/empirical research), then we would have to set up an outside structure (i.e. the academy) to measure this.

To me, this is the same sort of thinking that refused to accept that the world was not flat but round, and that the sun did not revolve around the earth but the other way around. In other words, just because the vast majority of people believe that something is true and produce evidence based on one or more of the five senses (or thought structures) that it is, clearly does not mean that it is true as the evolving history of humanity has borne out. And although our measuring techniques may have gotten much more sophisticated since the time of Galileo, they are still measuring instruments. In other words, using measuring devices at all may still be based on a false premise that we can, in fact, measure truth—that truth is something that can be found out through detailed analysis. Perhaps, truth is not something to be arrived at, but something to be experienced for oneself. And again, perhaps it is not only that truth cannot be arrived at through the measuring mind (or, the intellect, or whatever name we want to give it) but that this very measuring mechanism within us is what prevents us from arriving at truth through our own direct experience. So what if the only real way to test for truth is to directly experience it for ourselves? What if truth is something we experience rather than something we know about? In my work, I can produce a conceptual study on or I can give the *what is* of the only thing I know directly, which is my own experience.

To be clear, I am not saying that concepts, communicated through words—others' words or our own words, in the form of insights, stories, research, etc.—cannot help by pointing the way; but, in my experience, realizing for myself what it means to be staying with the words (i.e. experiencing in my mind, conceptually) versus jumping off of the words into my own experience *is done by jumping off into my own experience* and this makes all the difference. It truly is the difference between knowing all about a bicycle—how to ride it, what it's made of, the different kinds and manufacturers, its history and evolution, etc.—and riding one. We would not argue with someone who claims that one who has not ridden a bike does not know what it's like to ride a bike. Of course that is so. And yet our whole education system is based on knowing all about bikes but never riding one. To leave the metaphor, I am saying that we teach *about* life and say that this is all there is, that this is enough. What would education look like if we were teaching/learning *from* life instead? We know from many 'experts' how we *should* live—what is moral, what is kind, what is considered success, etc.—all forms of ideals. But do these take us *into* life or *out* of it, and would we even know how to go about looking for the answer? Katra and Targ (1999, p.22) elaborate on my point, using their own example:

> Just as I can't be a musician by thinking about music, I can't know God or love by simply exercising my intellect. Tibetan Buddhist teacher Sogyal Rinpoche tells us: "The absolute truth cannot be realized within the domain of the ordinary mind." And the path beyond the ordinary mind, all the great wisdom traditions have told us, is through the heart.

We may know, for example, how salmon reproduce and how owls see at night, what pi means and how much fuel it takes to send a rocket to the moon, theories about the beginning of our cosmos and the birth of our solar system; we've examined in detail the various bodily systems, we know in retrospect why that tactical unit failed in that combat mission and what they should do next time if all variables remain the same, etc. What the previous list of things has in common is that it's all information and methods for the mind. We know so much *about* life but is this the same thing as knowing life? As Tolle says, we *are* life, we don't *have* a life. This central misconception is what our education system is currently based on. It is why we focus solely on abstract concepts even when we're dealing with things like freedom and truth—we believe we *acquire* the knowledge of these as opposed to *experiencing* them.

To return to the previous metaphor, is there a bicycle that is able to be ridden that we aren't even aware of? For starters, we could look at the above list and recognize that each word that we seem so sure of—"salmon," "owl," "night," "pi," "moon," etc.—are concepts. We chose those words to *represent* that thing that someone wants to identify and communicate to someone else through language. But can we see or know these things without these words? When we look at these things, are we seeing those things or are we seeing the meanings that we have attached to them through mental concepts—through knowledge—and then say we know what these are. For me, it is easy to see that I don't know these things at all. I can quickly see that I have only attached a concept to them. As Krishnamurti and Tolle both ask, *Can you look at a thing without the word?* Krishnamurti insists that we never see things as they are because we haven't truly looked. This gives rise to the saying: *We see things as we are, not as they are.*

To illustrate my point, I once had a dream years ago that was so extraordinary that I remember it to this day. It was of a snowy owl. I had no real knowledge about snowy owls, nor any other kind of owl and don't remember seeing one live previously (it is possible I did, but the fact that I don't consciously remember it is more to the point). Yet to this day, I can remember the amazing vividness with which I "saw" this owl in my dream state. The owl was not just still, either, it was a living thing that I saw fly, rotate its head, and move its eyelids. In other words, I am saying that I saw an owl in my dream state more clearly than I have ever seen one in my waking life. I seemed to have intimate knowledge of this owl; I could see it in detail. What does this imply? Does the mind get in the way of *real* seeing?

The question occurs: how do we know the difference between learning *about* life and learning *from* life? One tell-tale sign in my experience is the same way we know the difference between the bike expert (in theory) and the one riding the bike: it has to do with the exhilaration, the immediacy, of the experience. Until I went through the process of the Enlightenment Intensive, I only knew intellectually—which is to say I only suspected— that I was missing something essential about life, that my own personal trials and tribulations and attempts in years of therapy and through reading books to understand myself, life, and the working of the psyche, still could not touch some place of experience and understanding that I could only sense were there. When I experienced a breakthrough to what I'll name here as reality in the Enlightenment Intensive, there was no mistaking it (which is not to say that I was experiencing ultimate truth, or really, that I can contextualize it at all)—it was just that I knew I was experiencing in a way I had never experienced before, and the best way to describe it is that I was experiencing *directly*. There was no 'watcher' or 'witness'—and I came to see (in those moments when I was experiencing otherwise) that through this watcher is the way I always experience life. There is a distance there. There is the experience and then what the experiencer is experiencing.

When I saw my daughter immediately following the intensive, I was absolutely amazed to realize I was seeing her for the first time (despite the fact that I had 'seen' her almost every day of her then four years of life). It was clear to me that I was seeing her without the lens of my fears and expectations (and everything else) resulting from past conditioning. No one had to explain this to me and I didn't have to think about it—it was just clear. I knew. This is what I mean when I say 'directly experience' the truth and I suspect that this is what Krishnamurti and Tolle mean when they say 'perceiving what is.' It was no wonder that Krishnamurti died having said that no one understood what he was saying. For in order to truly understand, one had to have already experienced what he was describing in words so that it was beyond the conceptual.

What if we were asked, "What is life?" and instead of trying to answer, *just stay with the question…* "Who am I?" and stay with the question. What if we could each inquire into this for ourselves without turning to an outside source for an answer? Krishnamurti describes this inquiry as "meeting life" and as the essence of meditation itself (a much different idea of meditation as a calming mechanism, which is how it's often conceived and talked about in western popular culture). What if we could actually meet life directly instead of through our mental concepts? This is the 'don't know mind' of Zen Buddhism and Byron Katie.

Personal Inquiry Through Krishnamurti

I came to know of Krishnamurti through a friend I took an undergraduate literature course with. I was majoring in English literature and also doing the concurrent education program during my undergraduate years—a combination which would give me a Bachelor of Arts and a Bachelor of Education at the end of it.

My friend knew I was very interested in education, and the following summer after we graduated she sent me a letter from Bangalore, India from the Center for Learning, an elementary and secondary school founded by Krishnamurti where she had been teaching for the year. She told me I "*must check out this guy's work*" and suggested some titles to look for, including *Education and the Significance of Life.*

As it turned out, this book was the only one by Krishnamurti in my small, local library; it looked like a first edition. There couldn't have been a better book of his for me to start with. In retrospect, it seems a miracle there was one there at all.

To this day, I remember how I felt reading the first page of Krishnamurti's book, though it is somewhat difficult to put into words. The way I think of it now, and the best way to describe it I think, is that I had an experience of resonance—something resonating deeply within me. I have come to learn that this happens when I am hearing truth. I would say that I was reading information that I had not been conscious of knowing, but yet knew to be absolutely true as soon as I read it. In addition, I realized that although I didn't understand everything he said, I still somehow *felt* the truth beneath the words. I had an experience of the truth. I don't really know of any other way to say it. In other words, I knew truth in those moments I was reading, not because I understood what was being said mentally with my mind but somewhere in my being there was a *recognition*.

This recognition is what I would call an experience of no-mind: a non-rational, non-conceptual way of knowing. (It is something I went into in-depth in the previous chapter.) This feeling was unlike anything I could remember experiencing up until that point in my life. Just reading Krishnamurti felt like an awakening of some sort. Krishnamurti was writing (I am quoting from my memory from that time here on purpose) that humans live out of a place of fear, looking constantly for a type of psychological security that they are never finding. Futhermore, they look at life and themselves mediated through the intellect which can only see things in parts, and thus are fragmented beings whose lives of conflict were therefore inevitable, for it is only in the realization of the whole that there is peace. He went on to say that this inner conflict within each human being must then play itself out on every level of existence—from an individual's generalized confusion and/or unhappiness, to confusion and conflict between individuals, to conflict between nations on the world stage.

I saw immediately that this was true—at least certainly for me. My life could be summed up as a constant looking for security from a place of fear—this, despite the fact that I then (and still now) considered myself a very average young person, then in my early twenties with a fairly privileged upbringing. In other words, I was not aware of any significant internal or external fears or struggles at that time, (other than the usual transformation from teenager to adult, moving towards independence, looking for my place in the world). So although I can only speak for my experience, it seemed very evident that this was indeed the human condition: living in inner conflict which breads fear and then a desire to look for security to escape this fear that is within oneself.

From that moment of first reading Krishnamurti, I was never without a Krishnamurti book somewhere close by—on my nightstand and in my backpack, throughout my travels to different countries to work and teach. I quickly saw that rarely was there a book of his (and there are many) where Krishnamurti would not bring in formal education and its relevance to what he was saying about the human condition—both for pointing out the tremendous conditioning of the mind that takes place in schools and for the tremendous opportunity education has to do something different than it has done by helping children understand themselves so that they might be free of this inner fear and conflict.

Chapter 7

*This is true wisdom—the total conviction that the mind
contains no data about the Truth.*

Esther Veltheim

~

Implications and Applications for Education

In my conclusion to the previous chapter, I outlined five things about the
current education paradigm:

1. It acts as if there is no innate knowing but all knowledge is located
   in external or conceptual knowledge
2. It acts as if children should have no authority (and, indeed, have no
   innate authority) but need to acquiesce to adult authority
3. It fails to recognize the truth of paradox and instead subscribes to
   a view of right and wrong,
4. It sees ideals as motivators for right behaviour,
5. It asserts *knowing* (answering) above *not-knowing* (questioning) as
   a way to arrive at truth.

By teaching strictly external knowledge, we teach implicitly that there
is no innate knowing, when indeed it is an intelligence that far surpasses
anything we could imagine. It is one's compass. And not only that, *it is who
we are*. By teaching the importance of (external) knowledge—the voice of
the intellect—we teach a misguided reliance on thought when it is not reliable; we teach a striving for certainty, that it's desirable and possible, when

the only certainty is contained in one's soul/heart/spirit/essence, not in the intellect. In short, the dominant education paradigm does not equip children for life. Krishnamurti (1968) explains,

> We live in a world of concepts, in a world of thought. We try to solve all our problems, from the most mechanical to psychological problems of the greatest depth, by means of thought.
>
> Is thought the only instrument that we have to deal with all our human problems? For it does not answer, it does not resolve our problems. It may be, we are just questioning it, we are not dogmatically asserting it. It may be that thought has no place whatsoever, except for mechanical, technological, scientific matters.

Education/Teaching as Non-Doing, Not-Knowing, Unlearning

Any fool can know. The point is to understand.

Einstein

What do the nature of mind/thought, sense of "I," intelligence, direct experience, etc. mean for education, for the role of the teacher, for the process of teaching, for what is taught?

Neuroscientist Jill Bolte Taylor points out what Krishnamurti has also said, namely that we have focused (in our society, and certainly in education) almost exclusively on developing the logical or "doing" (Taylor) mind, which in Taylor's experience is found in the literal left hemisphere of our brain. The result is our inability to connect with our being-ness prompting the need now (i.e. subsequently) to "unlearn" the dominance of the left brain:

> …our western society honors and rewards the skills of our "doing" left brain much more than our "being" right brain. Thus, if you are having difficulty accessing the consciousness of your right mind

circuitry, then it is probably because you have done a stupendous job learning exactly what you were taught while growing up. Congratulate your cells for their successes, and realize that, as my good friend Dr. Kat Domingo proclaims, "Enlightenment is not a process of learning, it is a process of unlearning." (2006, pp.159-160)

Taylor's comment on western society echoes Einstein's "we've created a society that honors the servant—the rational mind" that I quoted in an earlier chapter. It is not only necessary to unlearn reliance on thought for the sake of balance, but in fact is necessary in order to experience real intelligence, or, enlightenment. Krishnamurti explains it like this:

The moment you begin to accumulate what you have experienced or learnt, it becomes an anchorage which holds your mind and prevents it from going further. In the process of inquiry the mind sheds from day to day what it has learnt so that it is always fresh, uncontaminated by yesterday's experience. Truth is living, it is not static, and the mind that would discover truth must also be living, not burdened with knowledge or experience. (1964, p.161)

So in fact the very thing that we think of as intelligence, i.e. knowledge or experience, *is the very impediment to Truth.*

Tolle uses the words "deeper knowing" in place of Krishnamurti's "Truth"; likewise, he uses "non-conceptual" in place of Krishnamurti's "living." Using different words can help us see beyond the words to the things themselves, where the meaning is the same.

Become at ease with the state of "not knowing." This takes you beyond mind because the mind is always trying to conclude and interpret. It is afraid of not knowing. So, when you can be at ease with not knowing, you have already gone beyond the mind. A deeper knowing that is non-conceptual then arises out of that state. (Tolle, 2003, p.23)

Tolle and Krishnamurti are pointing out the dynamic nature of truth, which is opposite to the paradigm that the current education system understands and perpetuates. Though we might not be aware of it, when we believe that knowing truth through the mind is possible, we are saying that truth—real knowing—is static, that it can be acquired. What is truer is that it is a state that is *accessed*:

> Enlightenment, truth, is a timeless state, and you cannot come upon it through time. And knowledge is time. So, as we said, die every day to every knowledge that you have and be fresh the next morning. Such a mind never says, "I know," because it's always flowering, it's always coming new. (Krishnamurti, 1971, p.111)

"Timeless" is a word that has no meaning for me unless I access that part of me where it does have meaning—experientially. For me, Krishnamurti's words give me a sense of the *quality* of the moment that Krishnamurti is referring to, but only because I have already become aware of this quality as a lived experience or moment within myself. As a concept only, this word usually connotes 'not subject to time' in that its meaning or relevance doesn't diminish over time. Yet, this is not at all what the *experience* of this word is, which is rather that time—and an awareness of it—is absent. With simple logic, we can say that "truth" is what is—it is that that is unchanging—hence, the "timelessness" of it. And what I have found personally helpful (and like Krishnamurti, Katie, and Tolle have suggested), I realize what it is to be 'in time'—i.e. in thought—and know that this is *not* the timeless state of enlightenment. Since the mind can't know it, then this is as far as we can go with the mind; that is, it's as far as we can go to 'understanding' the timeless state.

So where does that leave the role of teacher, if not solely to develop mental skill and knowledge? Looking at what are commonly called "spiritual teachers" is a good starting place, for this title is in reference to those who are teaching about consciousness transformation. Krishnamurti did not consider this teaching of consciousness the domain of spiritual teachers alone, but actually it was the focus of his schools and his raison d'être in starting them at all. Indeed, relating this domain of conscious-ness to education is the focus of this book. Within the context of Taylor's, Tolle's, Katie's, and Krishnamurti's definitions of teacher, we can begin to reimagine what is possible for the role of teacher: to include—along with teaching subject matter—facilitation for *unlearning*.

> A true spiritual teacher does not have anything to teach in the con-ventional sense of the word, does not have anything to give or add to you, such as new information, beliefs, or rules of conduct. The only function of such a teacher is to help you remove that which separates you from the truth of who you already are and what you already know in the depth of your being. The spiritual teacher is there to uncover and reveal to you that dimension of inner depth that is also peace. (Tolle, 2003, ix)

Katie sees the damage that is done when one presumes to know and de-sires to impart this knowing onto another, under the domain of "teacher." Rather, she sees, as Eckhart, her job as solely to direct someone's atten-tion and inquiry for knowing back towards themselves as the source of this knowing through direct experience:

> I don't try to educate people. Why would I do such a thing? My only job is to point you back to yourself. When you discover—inside yourself, behind everything you're thinking—the marvelous don't-know mind, you're home free. The don't-know mind is the mind that is totally open to anything life brings you. (Katie, 2007, p.203)

Again, with the teacher pointing students back to their own experience and their own inquiry, the student can then discover their own depth and expansion of consciousness and learn to stand as their own light to them-selves; this process is what it is to have moved beyond the concepts and beyond the external authority of others. Therein students (and the teachers) find their truth and they can stand—rest—in that. This process gives them the freedom we are all looking for: the freedom to know through our own authority who we are beyond concepts and be that unequivocally. Without the internal conflict that results from the divided mind (that is, the mind that believes it knows—the closed mind—and paradoxically, the mind that needs to get its information from without, from others such as parents, teachers, experts, ones who know), one no longer needs to create conflict in the outer world. In a remarkable reversal of convention, then, what is recommended is allowing people (children) to find their own way:

> I don't know what's best for me or you or the world. I don't try to impose my will on you or on anyone else. I don't want to change you or improve you or convert you or help you or heal you. I just welcome things as they come and go. That's true love. The best way of leading people is to let them find their own way. (Katie, 2007, p.24)

The alternative is to step into the realm of indoctrination and dogma. Katie writes: "Parents can only be wise when they stop teaching" (2006, p.65). This could, of course, also be applied to teachers. In the face of such a provocative statement, it seems crucial to ask then as this book has done: 1) *What is the problem with teaching (i.e. education in the conventional sense) and What is beneficial about teaching/education?* 2) *What else can there be in education other than teaching in the conventional sense?*

The Right Place of Knowledge in Education

Never memorize what you can look up in books.

Einstein

It seems clear logic that indeed the two cannot coexist: one cannot teach that one is the source of one's own enlightenment, and simultaneously say (as the teacher to the student), "Listen to me. I know." I think it's helpful to remember here (as I've stated previously) that Krishnamurti emphasized the importance of learning the traditional subject matter (i.e. mathematics, reading, writing, history, geography, science, etc.) but that learning this subject matter is far and away secondary to understanding oneself—this 'pointing back' towards oneself and the reality of one's own experience. Explains Krishnamurti: "Knowledge is necessary at the functional level as a means of cultivating the mind, and not as an end in itself" (1963, p.13). What he means by the "functional level" is the following:

> Knowledge is necessary to act in the sense of my going home from here to the place I live; I must have knowledge for this; I must have knowledge to speak English; I must have knowledge to write a letter and so on. Knowledge as function, mechanical function, is necessary. Now if I use that knowledge in my relationship with you, another human being, I am bringing about a barrier, a division between you and me, namely the observer. That is, knowledge, in relationship, in human relationship, is destructive. That is knowledge which is the tradition, the memory, the image, which the mind has built about you, that knowledge is separative and therefore creates conflict in our relationship. (J. Krishnamurti Online, 1974, p.27)

I have already outlined in previous chapters that conflict in relationship is the same as conflict within oneself (giving rise to fear, anger, depression, anxiety, etc.) and conflict at the global or nation-state level. Given this, it is clear that *only* teaching subject matter and ignoring direct experience, the nature of one's mind—in short, learning about oneself from oneself—is extremely problematic, as it gives knowledge sole importance. Indeed, there is no opportunity for exploration of the self when it, or the learning of subject matter, are not recognized for what they are. That is, there needs to be a context and this can only be done through understanding the nature of the self. Then acquiring knowledge can be put in its rightful place.

Finally, I want to point out a liability (that paradigms of what we call "holistic education" might be particularly susceptible to), and that is, the teaching of any and all of this material I've written here as concepts. That is, consider Tolle:

> Your child doesn't really need to understand presence, your child needs to see what presence is for her or himself by being with you. And by recognizing that he or she has that also—is already born with that ability that just becomes obscured in our civilization at a very early age. Your presence teaches the child to be present. That's the teacher.

So the teacher's self-awareness, which expresses as presence, then, is paramount. The content the teacher teaches is herself/himself in the deepest sense.

Old and New Paradigms of Education: From Comparison, Compulsion, Coercion to Well-Being and Love

In the current (what I am calling the "old") paradigm, an atmosphere of fear is created at school and, more to the point, within the child through comparison, compulsion, and coercion.

Specifically, comparison happens most transparently through grading and marks being given out. In a more subtle form, teachers point out a student who is doing well, in their opinion, at a task (for example), and whom the other students should attempt to emulate. Of course, the implication is that one student is doing better or is better than the others in that way.

Or, another example occurs when a teacher compares a student against herself/himself by pointing out that they are 'behaving badly' one day when they had 'behaved well' on a previous day, implying that they aren't doing as well on that particular day. Of course, there are numerous of these subtle examples. All of this incorporates an idea of an ideal (which I discuss at length in earlier chapters).

Compulsion and coercion (compulsion being the feeling/belief of having no choice so originates internally, and coercion originating from an outside force externally) occur in most moments of the day in school. They happen in the form of requiring students to do anything from sit still, to being quiet, to looking at the teacher, to learning specific material through the performance of specific tasks, to threats of various punishments. Perhaps the most pervasive and at the same time most overlooked is the prevalent systems of reward and punishment that overlays all of a child's daily experience in the classroom: that is, they are considered 'better' and therefore 'a good child' if they behave and do what they're told. In other words, they are rewarded for good behaviour—for not questioning in any real way—those who are set up as the authority. The opposite is also true: they will be punished if they persist in questioning (that is to say, not following) that which they have been asked to do. Krishnamurti gives a small but significant example of this: "One may compel a child to be outwardly quiet, but one has not come face to face with that which is making him obstinate, impudent, and so on. Compulsion breeds antagonism and fear. Reward and punishment in any form only make the mind subservient and dull..." (1953, p.20). What would "coming face to face with that...[etc.]" look like?

Well, for one, it wouldn't involve giving out points or candy or the promise of a pizza party for being 'well-behaved.' Having a conversation with the student wherein the teacher helps a child towards an understanding of the cause of their behaviour is where the real learning happens. Of course, the practicalities of this option being available must be considered. This wouldn't be an option in classes with a large number of students, which is why Krishnamurti pointed out the necessity of small class sizes. It also wouldn't be an option if the goal was to teach the curriculum, as opposed to what Krishnamurti is arguing for, which is to teach the child.

So essential is the need for a child to be free of being compelled or coerced even in its most subtle ways (those, in fact, can be the most confusing for the internal life of the child since they are not obvious), that in fact, *they cannot learn* at all if these are present: "Learning in the true sense of the word is possible only in that state of attention in which there is no outer or inner compulsion" (Krishnamurti, 1963, p.13). As I discussed above, Nisargadatta Maharaj, Krishnamurti, and Tolle all agree that "attention" is what needs to be present for real learning to take place. Krishnamurti explains the relationship between attention and comparison, compulsion, and coercion:

> It is attention that allows silence to come upon the mind, which is the opening of the door to creation. That is why attention is of the highest importance....How is the state of attention to be brought about? It cannot be cultivated through persuasion, comparison, reward or punishment, all of which are forms of coercion. The elimination of fear is the beginning of attention. Fear must exist as long as there is an urge to be or to become, which is the pursuit of success, with all its frustrations and tortuous contradictions. You can teach concentration, but attention cannot be taught just as you cannot possibly teach freedom from fear; but we can begin to discover the causes that produce fear, and in understanding these causes there is the elimination of fear. So attention arises spontaneously when around the student there is an atmosphere of well-being, when he has the feeling of being secure, of being at ease, and is aware of the disinterested action that comes with love. Love does not compare, and so the envy and torture of "becoming" cease. (Krishnamurti, 1963, p.13)

So if attention can arise only in the absence of fear, and the methods and practices that are currently used in education (because of the nature of its focus) produce fear, then clearly the focus—or paradigm—needs to change. In fact, we are now *using* fear as an entrenched tactic to try to get students to "pay attention." As in, "Pay attention or I'll send you to the principal's office." The focus now is on results, on the measuring of students through comparison (to each other and to tests, etc.), and on consistently 'improving' and becoming 'more'; yet, for students to experience well-being—and therefore to learn—all of this must cease. The "disinterested action" Krishnamurti refers to above is on the deep level of the teacher not needing the students to exhibit or be anything in order for the teacher to feel secure. The teacher cannot feel love for the child and at the same time feel that they should become something else (kinder, smarter, quieter, more efficient, more productive, etc.), slight and subtle though that 'something else' might be. Tolle writes: "The longing for love that is in every child is the desire to be recognized, not on the level of form, but on the level of being" (2005, p.105); that is, children want to be seen for *who they are*, not who they should be in someone's idea of an ideal person. This 'being seen' is what creates this atmosphere—this feeling—of well-being. It gives a sense of belonging, of being lovable and acceptable just as one is. Following the threads of this, the outcomes cannot be underestimated: non-violence (since violence comes out of a deep need to be loved for who one is but experiencing the opposite of this); freedom for exploration to discover creative problem-solving (when one's attention is no longer on trying to please the teacher—to live up to the idea that she/he has for her/him), etc. Krishnamurti sums up what happens inwardly to a child who is encouraged to adhere to an ideal (which is what, I would argue, our current paradigm of education not only includes *but is based on*):

> The right kind of education consists in understanding the child as he is without imposing upon him an ideal of what we think he should be. To enclose him in the framework of an ideal is to encourage him to conform, which breeds fear and produces in him a constant conflict between what he is and what he should be; and all inward conflicts have their outward manifestations in society. Ideals are an actual hindrance to our understanding of the child and to the child's understanding of himself. (1953, p.16)

As I outlined in my autoethnography chapter, this was certainly the case in my own life. And discovering and undoing the effects of growing up in a culture and education system of applauding conforming to ideals has taken years and is still ongoing. Its effects are nothing short of almost totally and permanently crippling. They are taking a great deal of time and effort to undo.

So instead of encouraging an ideal, what can a teacher do? Krishnamurti continues with specific (though not prescriptive) instructions for the role of the teacher below:

> The right kind of educator, seeing the inward nature of freedom, helps each individual student to observe and understand his own self-projected values and impositions; he helps him to become aware of the conditioning influences about him, and of his own desires, both of which limit his mind and breed fear; he helps him, as he grows to manhood, to observe and understand himself in relation to all things, for it is the craving for self-fulfilment that brings endless conflict and sorrow. (1953, p.18)
>
> The purpose of education is to cultivate right relationship, not only between individuals, but also between the individual and society; and that is why it is essential that education should, above all, help the individual to understand his own psychological process. Intelligence lies in understanding oneself and going above and beyond oneself; but there cannot be intelligence as long as there is fear. Fear perverts intelligence and is one of the causes of self-centred action. Discipline may suppress fear but does not eradicate it, and the superficial knowledge which we receive in modern education only further conceals it. (p.34)
>
> To educate the student rightly is to help him to understand the total process of himself; for it is only when there is integration of the mind and heart in everyday action that there can be intelligence and inward transformation. (p.31)

What Krishnamurti suggests above in summation, then, is an education that is focused on helping the student understand herself/himself.

Byron Katie's *The Work* is a tool that in my experience does just that, by examining—or rather, *experiencing*—the concepts that the child has already developed, what Krishnamurti calls "conditioning":

> Do children understand The Work? Absolutely. There are only concepts. There are no adults, there are not children. Concepts are ageless. Here's what children say: "My father should understand me." "My friends should listen to me." "Mommy shouldn't fight with Daddy." "I want you to love me." By the time they're four or five, children believe exactly the same stressful thoughts that adults believe. There are no new concepts. Children are just as confused as adults. (2006, p.15)

What Katie is describing above are comments that come out of a mind that has conceived of an ideal in relation to what they are experiencing; the result is an argument with reality, and suffering/conflict.

Tolle suggests a practical tool for us to think about in terms of knowledge acquisition:

> When children are learning to speak, they ask What is that? [sic] Importance of saying, "We call that ____" instead of "That is ____" because language/concepts deaden/obscure the thing. Whatever you teach the child, see that there is always more beyond the word. ...You can know something without it becoming words in your mind.

Redefining Intelligence in an Educational Context

If intelligence is not what comes from 'an education' as we know it, if intelligence is not the result of a highly developed and sophisticated mind capable of high-level conceptual analysis, but something outside of or beyond the mind (as mentioned at points throughout this book), what is it, exactly? Krishnamurti (1981, p.113) writes:

The very nature of intelligence is sensitivity, and this sensitivity is love. Without this intelligence there can be no compassion. Compassion is not the doing of charitable acts or social reform; it is free from sentiment, romanticism and emotional enthusiasm. It is as strong as death. It is like a great rock, immovable in the midst of confusion, misery and anxiety. Without this compassion no new culture or society can come into being. Compassion and intelligence walk together; they are not separate. Compassion acts through intelligence. It can never act through the intellect. Compassion is the essence of the wholeness of life.

So finally, we come to the definition of intelligence that all of the subjects of this study refer to, (albeit sparingly[40]), and that is, intelligence as love. And it is this love, this intelligence, that enables or creates compassion. I certainly experienced Byyon Katie in my personal witnessing of her, as the very definition of compassion. It wasn't sentimental whatsoever, just as Krishnamurti claims (which I can see now is really a cloaked self-interest); the best description that comes to mind is that she/it was fearless and yes, immoveable. There was no one's story, however horrific in a common sense, that shook her whatsoever and no place she couldn't go; she met someone's pain with her own unwavering attention to it and I witnessed true compassion as Krishnamurti describes it above. Defining intelligence as sensitivity and compassion is a profound departure from how the education system perceives it to be. We now live in an age where 'charitable acts' and 'social reform' are all the rage. They are considered our best hope for doctoring the ills of our world. Yet it is vastly insufficient, laudable and well intentioned as these acts and movements are. It can never be enough.

So it would seem that, given what I have written above, (i.e. that a teacher's primary role is to help children towards understanding themselves and

---

[40] As I wrote in the introduction, "love" is a word/concept that people believe they understand so its use is often avoided by spiritual teachers.

in relation to all things), an awareness of this intelligence—indeed, the direct experience of it—is the natural outcome of such a focus, rather than on the current focus on thought. Tolle describes what happens when the focus in education is put upon observing oneself or 'the thinker' rather than solely on developing knowledge:

> The beginning of freedom is the realization that you are not "the thinker." The moment you start watching the thinker, a higher level of consciousness becomes activated. You then begin to realize that there is a vast realm of intelligence beyond thought, that thought is only a tiny aspect of that intelligence. You also realize that all the things that truly matter—beauty, love, creativity, joy, inner peace— arise from beyond the mind. You begin to awaken. (2003, epigraph)

With awakening—that is, an awareness of the existence of this 'other' intelligence—then, comes a reimagining of the role of teacher out of this context: and that is to help the student to awaken. This is primary, the teacher's first and most important role. Yet this doesn't require thought to be banished or relegate it to an unimportant role. As Tolle explains, thought is still required and can be extremely useful, but only when it is being used in its rightful place:

> There is an aliveness in you that you can feel with your entire Being, not just in the head. Every cell is alive in that presence in which you don't need to think. Yet, in that state, if thought is required for some practical purpose, it is there. The mind can still operate, and it operates beautifully when the greater intelligence that you are uses it and expresses itself through it. (Tolle, 2003, p.21)

So the equation is that consciousness is using thought, not the other way around which is the pattern that our current education system is unknowingly perpetuating. Highest intelligence or "mastery" ends up flowing through the person-as-the-greater-consciousness who is in the moment and not mediating her/his experience through thought:

> Artistic creation, sports, dance, teaching, counseling—mastery in any field of endeavour implies that the thinking mind is either no longer involved at all or at least is taking second place. A power and intelligence greater than you and yet one with you in essence takes over. There is no decision-making process anymore; spontaneous right action happens, and "you" are not doing it. Mastery of life is the opposite of control. You become aligned with the greater consciousness. *It* acts, speaks, does the works. (Tolle, 2003, pp.23-24)

The last three sentences here are quite astounding (and they are echoed elsewhere by Krishnamurti, Katie, and others)—in truth, they are earth-shaking. Paradigm-shattering. This is so because, in my opinion, this statement goes against everything we are trying to accomplish in this current education paradigm: we are teaching *personal* mastery and *personal* intelligence, in that sense that developing one's mind (unique to that bodymind, that personality) to its highest capacity is the goal. It is all that is necessary and the highest possibility. Yet what Tolle and the others are talking about here is about a total surrender—a surrender of the personal identity—the "I"—and therefore a surrendering of control and of a desire to achieve and become somebody special by adding accomplishments to that "I." And yet paradoxically, this very act of surrender of the personal identity is what allows one to experience *who or what they are* outside of the conceptual mind (the mind that created and maintained the false sense of "I"), which is one and the same as this vast intelligence, this pure consciousness. This is the essence of the transformation of consciousness. Tolle says:

> So you give up all knowing—the accumulated knowledge—don't need it here—in order to access the source of all knowledge. But the giving up of the accumulated knowledge is also of course the giving

up of the mind-made self that consists of accumulated thought form
... And what you access also is intelligence itself, the unconditioned,
out of which anything new arises—an insight, an idea—that is
the place of true intelligence. I call it sometimes non-conceptual
intelligence, or the unconditioned consciousness. And that's where,
suddenly, creativity opens up in your life. Because the person is not
creative, the mind is not creative, but it can be an instrument of
true intelligence. And the mind has no intelligence of its own—it
borrows its intelligence from universal intelligence.

I often speak of intelligence and creativity as one and the same. It's a being born new—the birth of something new—in its purest sense. *Creation.*
And it is here where all of the solutions we are seeking will arise from. Not
from thinking harder. True creativity is intelligence incarnate. Or, "intelligence having fun" (Einstein).

~

Katra and Targ write: "We must first acknowledge that science very suc-
cessfully describes one aspect of human experience: the material universe.
On the other hand, science has little to say about many other things we
experience, such as love, and spiritual feelings" (1999, p.35). I would agree
with this statement; we could define science as 'in pursuit of what we can
categorically measure,' meaning we can explain it rationally, which ultimately means thought can apprehend it. In our current paradigm, this is
what makes something acceptable—the mind approves.

At the same time, it's interesting to note that those we consider great scientists, like Einstein (who, ironically, has become the poster boy for a great
intellect, or, mind), *knew* that the mind was limited:

Even the greatest scientists have known that the insights came—
not through further conceptual analysis—they tried: they
worked on problems conceptually. But finally, there was a giving up on that level of looking and there was an opening up of

spaciousness—they were not looking for the answer anymore and then the realizations came. Einstein had the greatest realizations that could not even be verified.

The way Veltheim explains this is: "When you totally give up trying to understand, in that moment, Knowing begins revealing it-Self" (2000, p.128). That Einstein had realizations "that could not even be verified" is so important to realize, because it points to the premise that just because logic or language cannot prove something to be true doesn't mean it is not accurate; yet, this is the essence of our current scientific and more to the point, educational paradigms. There must be room to allow for the fact that perhaps our reasoning faculties and/or technology have either not developed enough to apprehend the truth, or they never can. As Tolle explains, "There is a vaster intelligence that doesn't require the breakdown of reality into conceptual bits and piece." (August 2011, www.eckharttolletv.com). The truth that is this intelligence does not only *not* require reality to be fragmented into parts that the mind can grasp, this intelligence cannot be fit into any fragmented parts but can only be perceived whole.

So in the context of education, then, to teach children that we can apprehend the whole (of life) by examining the parts (that is, the traditional subjects, through thought, through analysis) is false. In order to come upon the whole, and hence the truth of life, students must go beyond thought, beyond knowledge, beyond concepts. This can be done through helping them to see the nature of thought and its relation to themselves and then to experience the truth for themselves.

Obviously, for this to happen, there needs to be freedom for discovery—freedom in terms of time and space as well as what I think of as a 'holding of space' for the child as she/he takes the journey herself/himself. It's a space that is a witnessing presence, where one demonstrates that one cares to witness her or his journey. In this way, they will discover the truth for themselves—the only way it can happen—as anything else would be using thought.

Overview and Summary

In order to be able to adequately and accurately discuss applications of consciousness and thought to education, the nature of consciousness and thought had to first be explored in-depth.

This book sought to answer the following questions:

1. Is there something beyond conceptual understanding?
2. What is the nature of mind and of consciousness?
3. What are the implications (of the above) for education?

What I have outlined in this book are the hidden facets of the current education paradigm:

1. It acts as if there is no innate knowing but all knowledge is located in external or conceptual knowledge,
2. It acts as if children should have no authority (and, indeed, have no innate authority) but need to acquiesce to adult authority,
3. It fails to recognize the truth of paradox and instead subscribes to a view of right and wrong,
4. It sees ideals as motivators for right behaviour,
5. It asserts *knowing* (answering) above *not-knowing* (questioning) as a way to arrive at truth.

1. Education focuses on training the intellect, which in turn:
a) intensifies mind identification, and
b) ignores the (transcendent, or 'real') Self, or consciousness
c) Education lacks the clear intention of fostering creative problem-solving (rather than prescriptive solution-answering) which is the logical concluding purpose of educating for giving the tools and knowledge that children/students need to both succeed in the world and become positive contributing members of society
d) Creativity and therefore creative problem-solving does not arise out of the intellect but out of the Self, or pure consciousness.

Through problematizing the current education paradigm in the above ways, I see six crucial elements for a new paradigm of education:

1. Learning as Self-Understanding and Encountering Truth
Education is re-envisioned as being oriented towards *directly experiencing the Self and Truth/Reality* as opposed to conditioning through ideals, with the development of the intellect through thought (including the learning of subject matter and conceptual/abstract thinking) a contextualized, secondary priority.

2. Learning as Leaving the Known
The current paradigm of education as developing the mind as the highest form of intelligence is clearly grasped and is re-envisioned to see that true intelligence does not come from the mind but from the larger consciousness beyond the mind, or, the unknown. In this context, *questioning rather than answering* is seen as what is essential.

3. Teaching and Learning as Internal Authority
The role of the teacher is re-envisioned to be that of primarily facilitating the students to *experience themselves as the only real authority*, pointing them towards their innate knowing, and secondarily facilitating learning of external knowledge and conceptual thinking.

4. Teaching and Learning in the Context of Human Evolution
Education is re-contextualized to include a view to the evolving consciousness of humans (and) in relation to the world and beyond. The paradox of individuality as indivisible from the whole is understood allowing education to include each person (student) as playing an integral part through *contributing uniquely to the whole.*

5. Intelligence Expressing through Creation
Education is re-envisioned to *prioritize opportunity for creativity*, given

that creativity is understood to be the birth of the new, the only well from which to draw new solutions to old problems. This would include an equal emphasis on what we call the arts: music, drama, dance, fine art, etc.

6. Learning in an Environment of Love and Compassion Versus Fear
It's understood that learning cannot happen when there is fear, no matter how seemingly small or subtle, and that any true learning can happen only in an environment of love and compassion. Emphasis shifts from approval/disapproval of behaviour to self-understanding.

7. Learning as Experiencing the Body
Without the 'head' (intellect) being given such importance, the body is seen as vital to tend to by giving it proper exercise. It's realized that a human being is a complex whole that includes the intellect, a larger consciousness, and a body.

1. Learning as Self-Understanding and Encountering Truth
This book has discussed the nature of mind, thought, intellect, self, consciousness, intelligence, and creativity for it is in determining their nature that we can begin to see what we are ultimately educating for and why. Education in the new paradigm sees (identification with) thought as inhibiting the realization of Self. Spiritual teacher Adyashanti sums up both the common (i.e. limited)—and the possible—relationship of Self to thought as discussed throughout this study:

> The human condition is characterized by a compulsive and obsessive personal relationship to thought. At its best, thought is a symbolic representation of reality; at its worst, thought takes the place of reality. Our thoughts describe and interpret both the external world and our internal experiences. To conceive of a life lived any other way is incomprehensible to most people. Thought tells us who we are; what we believe; what is right and wrong; what we should feel; what is true and what is false; and how we fit into this event called

"life." We literally create ourselves and our lives out of thought. Further, we associate the end of thought with sleep, unconsciousness, or death. It is this very personal relationship with thought that is the cause of all the fear, ignorance, and suffering which characterizes the human condition, and which destroys the manifestation of true Love in this life.

As long as your experience of self and life is defined by the mechanical, conditioned, and compulsive movement of thought, you are bound to a very, very limited perception of what is real. But imagine a relationship to thought that was impersonal. This would mean that you were no longer compulsively defining and interpreting yourself and your experience by the movement of thought. If this were the case, you would no longer be limited by the conditioned perspective of thought. Suddenly your entire perspective would shift away from thought to that which was the very ground and source of all thought. A source which, because it wasn't being compulsively interpreted by thought, would be experienced as it actually is for the first time.

Why is this so important? Because when you are able to perceive this Source, you are actually in direct experiential contact with the truth of your own being. Out of that contact the possibility is ripe to suddenly awaken to who and what you really are—the Self—pure consciousness.

The Self is the context within which thought arises.

This book has shown that when we see that the mind as thought is not who we are, a direct experience of Self is possible. In turn, the book has also shown, this experience of who one ultimately is, *is* the beginning of allowing/being-as real intelligence: "Self-knowing is the beginning of wisdom and it does not lie in books, in churches or in the piling up of words" (Krishnamurti, 1975, p.215). Thus, *education is re-envisioned as being oriented towards self-understanding with the development of the intellect through thought (including the learning of subject matter) a contextualized, secondary priority.*

2. Learning as Leaving the Known

The Tao Te Ching #71 states: "Not-knowing is true knowledge. Presuming to know is a disease. First realize that you are sick; then you can move toward health. The Master is her own physician. She has healed herself of all knowing. Thus she is truly whole." This book has shown how attachment to the mind as the source of knowledge prevents authentic knowing. Adyashanti puts it this way:

> You must become more interested in the Unknown than in that which is known. Otherwise you will remain enslaved by the very narrow and distorted perspective of conceptual thinking. You must go so deeply into the Unknown that you are no longer referencing thought to tell you who and what you are. Only then will thought be capable of reflecting that which is true rather than falsely masquerading as truth.
>
> What I am talking about is a condition where the mind never fixates; where it never closes; where it has no compulsive need to understand in terms of ideas, concepts, and beliefs.

It follows from this that, practically speaking, students would be encouraged to ask questions rather than to find answers. Since an answer is limited by the question it is answering, our focus should be on asking the right questions. All the power lies in questioning. We are not only engaging the mind (falsely) as the instrument of knowing but are severely limiting students when we ask them to answer questions we pose rather than ask them to ask further questions. Instead, there can be an opening up rather than a contracting down, an exploration rather than a conclusion. "Stop trying to understand. Be fully with what is, and there You *are*—Experiencing," Veltheim (2000, p.114) writes; however, we are conditioned to try for 'understanding' constantly in education. After asking, there can instead be an allowing, a noticing—this is the process of observing 'what is.' Perhaps this can maybe be best summed up by the following: "Live in the Now? Even the thought 'Now' is a concept. Before the thought completes itself, it's gone, with no proof that it ever existed. Even thought doesn't exist. That's why everyone already has the quiet mind that they're seeking" (Katie, 2006b, p.4).

I find this statement very helpful; for me, it acts like a Zen koan by not letting my mind latch onto anything within it. In other words, we think we can talk about "now" and "thought" as if they're real and when my mind even entertains the possibility that these are just concepts, it's sort of like a small explosion goes off in my brain and leaves empty space; the concept(s) is gone. Einstein: "It is not that I'm so smart. But I stay with the questions much longer."

Education is seen, then, in its limits within the current paradigm of developing the mind-as-thought as the highest form of intelligence and is re-envisioned to observe that true intelligence does not come from the intellect, but from leaving the intellect as the known and moving into the unknown.

3. Teaching and Learning as Internal Authority

In his journal, Krishnamurti (1982) wrote about real learning as happening *through—and being—*one's own authority (rather than looking to any outside answers to one's questions from 'experts' or books, etc.) in which he used the metaphor of a light:

> One has to be a light to oneself; this light is the law. There is no other law. All the other laws are made by thought and so fragmentary and contradictory. To be a light to oneself is not to follow the light of another, however reasonable, logical, historical, and however convincing. You cannot be a light to yourself if you are in the dark shadow of authority, of dogma, of conclusion...
>
> Freedom is to be a light to oneself; then it is not an abstraction,

a thing conjured up by thought. Actual freedom is freedom from dependency, attachment, from the craving for experience. Freedom from the very structure of thought is to be a light to oneself. In this light all action takes place and thus it is never contradictory...

There is no *how*, no system, no practise. There is only the seeing which is the doing. You have to see, not through the eyes of another. This light, this law, is neither yours nor that of another. There is only light. This is love.

In the process of this autoethnographical research, I came upon this very insight myself, which I wrote about in Chapter 5. I would describe the experience of it as a great unlearning; it didn't happen in a dramatic fashion like in my Enlightenment Intensive experiences, but it was just as, if not more, earth-shattering for me. After years of believing that learning meant disavowing myself, my own truth which I felt as essential to who I was, I came upon the insight that in fact who I am, I alone can see. In that moment, I saw the fallacy of right and wrong and found myself on Rumi's field "between wrongdoing and rightdoing"—I was as I was and things are as they are.

And I want to make the point that it was arduous to unlearn what I had so thoroughly believed: that truth did not lie within me, but without. So when I think that other people could avoid this by not being given this false concept in the first place, then I think this needs to be taken in extreme earnest.

In addition, Krishnamurti equates freedom from thought with the experience of being one's own authority; they are one and the same.

Furthermore, he writes, this state is love. Being one's own authority means not following a method that someone else has laid out. Obviously, one has to experience for oneself what Krishnamurti means by "There is only light"; this is the point. *The role of the teacher, then, is re-envisioned to be that of primarily facilitating the students to experience/know themselves as the only real authority.* It is in the teacher's recognizing that each student must be her own authority that the action that encourages and supports this will be apparent.

4. Learning in the Context of Human Evolution:
A Paradigm of Indivisibility

Helping students to realize that they are not their minds is not just the insight that will bring them deep inner peace and an unshakable knowing of who they are, which of course will serve them well in their personal lives. In addition, transcending thought is something that affects everyone else too. In fact, it is urgently *needed* in order for the human species to survive; this is evolution in action.

According to Tolle, "The next step in human evolution is to transcend thought. This is now our urgent task" (2003, p.20).

Likewise, Steve Taylor (2010) sums up the reason that I see a study on the nature of consciousness, mind and its transformation in the arena of education to be the most important research work I could undertake at this time:

> Waking up isn't just something we do for *ourselves*, for our own personal benefit or gratification. It *does* enhance our life massively... [b]ut it isn't just a personal matter—as well as transforming our perception and our experience, waking up transforms our relationships and affects society as a whole, even the world as a whole. It's precisely because we're 'asleep'—because we perceive the world as a dreary, inanimate place and ourselves as separate, and because there's a fundamental psychological discord inside us all the time— that the world is filled with so much conflict and disorder. It's because we've been asleep for millennia that human history has been an endless saga of warfare, conflict and oppression. And it's because we're asleep now that we're so close to destroying the life-support systems of our planet and jeopardizing our future as a species (and that of many other species too). We need to wake up on behalf of

the human race as a whole, on behalf of the world as a whole and on behalf of the whole evolutionary process that has taken life from the first single-celled amoeba to the astoundingly complex creatures with a hundred billion-celled brains such as us. (xvii)

At root, this is an *evolutionary* impulse. The impulse that we feel to intensify our life-energy is the *élan vital* itself, the same drive towards greater complexity and consciousness that has taken life from the first single-celled amoeba to human beings. It's the process of evolution manifesting itself inside us and impelling us to become more conscious and alive on its behalf. (p.232)

Obviously, education in elementary and secondary years is not benign; to put it succinctly, it either conditions or awakens. It has an extraordinary responsibility because the awakening or dis-identification from thought that this book makes a case for has resounding implications for the evolution of humankind.

It is in this relationship of education to all life as a whole that we can see how education cannot and should not be put forth as separate from life. One of the problems that education has created has been to separate *living* from *learning*. Helping students to see that fundamentally, living is learning, then the seeing of this fact helps them perceive their oneness with life and they are able to live accordingly.

Taylor (2005) goes on to describe what will (indeed, does) happen when our perceived separation is transcended:

With our ego-separateness transcended, we will no longer feel a fundamental sense of isolation and aloneness. Instead, there will be a new sense of wholeness and contentment—exactly the same inner well-being which the mystics...have described to us time and again over the centuries.

We will also have a new relationship to the cosmos. The world will no longer be a dreary, unreal place which is "out there" and whose alien-ness and apparent indifference makes us feel threatened. Instead, we'll look at the world with fresh, non-automatic perception (caused by a higher level of consciousness-energy) and see it as a radiant, beautiful, benevolent place. We will see the presence of spirit-force in everything, in all things and in the spaces between things, and be aware of it as the source of all things, the ultimate reality of the universe. We will be aware that spirit-force is the essence of our own beings as well, and feel a sense of communion with the world, a sense of belonging and participating in it rather than being outside it looking in.

We will no longer be separate, and so we will no longer be afraid—afraid of death, afraid of the world, afraid of God, afraid of our own selves, afraid of other people. The disharmony of the human psyche will be healed, and the insanity which it gave rise to will fade away. (p.308)

When we create an identity from thought/beliefs and then line up with certain people and certain groups and oppose others based on those beliefs, it is easy to see how violence erupts: an 'us' and a 'them' have been created. This mechanism of separation applies also to anything other than who or what humans think they are, including the earth (the 'natural world,' animals, fish, birds) and beyond (space, etc.). Yet, the separation is a fabrication, an illusion.

A human being is a part of the whole called by us the 'universe,' a part limited in time and space. He experiences himself, his thoughts and feeling as something separated from the rest, a kind of optical delusion of his consciousness. This delusion is a kind of prison for us, restricting us to our personal desires and to affection for a few persons nearest to us. Our task must be to free ourselves from this prison by widening our circle of compassion to embrace all living creatures and the whole of nature in its beauty. (Attributed to Einstein.)

A transcendent consciousness allows us to see the truth of our *togetherness*, our wholeness. Out of this seeing, action that serves the whole takes place. *Education is re-envisioned to include a view to the evolving consciousness of humans in relation to the world and beyond. The paradox of individuality as indivisible from the whole is understood allowing education to include each person (student) as playing an integral part through contributing uniquely to the whole.*

5. Intelligence Expressing through Creation

...there is creation only when the intellect is still.

Krishnamurti

As previously discussed in Chapter 5, creativity (in its literal definition of coming upon something entirely new) comes out of the larger consciousness, not from thought. Tolle describes what it's like to experience:

> When you are engaged in a creative activity there is an intense energy behind it but it is not stress at all (though it can be seen as this from the outside). But it's joyful when you're in it—it's very different from stress. The intensity deals with obstacles in a very different way than the ego. It can sweep away or transform them; it doesn't attack. Also, you encounter the phenomenon of being supported. If your creation is aligned with what the universe wants, then it becomes enormously empowered. It's like riding on a huge wave. It's something wanting to be created through you. It's exciting to be part of that because it's an entirely new way of being come into this planet.

In other words, coming as it is from the larger consciousness, true creativity is not coming from the 'person,' from the 'I' identity. Helping students to see that this is possible for them—i.e. the allowing of something new to be created through them when they are aligned with it—is the new task of education, in my view. It is to allow students to see the full view of their power through creative expression, to contribute to the whole. It is to encourage the realization through direct experience of their ability to have an effect. In addition, although this gives rise to self-esteem, confidence, and resiliency, it actually goes beyond this. It actualizes it and then transcends it. Tobin Hart, PhD, puts the new paradigm and possibility as follows:

> We live in a time when we are becoming conscious of our own evolution and therefore are increasingly responsible for it. We have the power to join with the wave of creation and actually move evolution along.
>
> As the veil lifts questions emerge: What's waking up in me? What is truly important? How do I want to live this moment, this day, and this life? How am I treating others? How can I understand and serve this child, this world, this spirit? Do my intentions and my actions spread love and wisdom, peace and generosity, or selfishness? What does the way I live my life teach this child? What does this child offer to teach me? Every moment is an invitation to reconsider priorities, but these times grab our attention by the throat. Our greatest opportunity these days is not the chance to make our lives safer, but to align with that deep current through which our lives flow.... As we open to and nourish the spiritual world of children, we contribute to and join the wave of evolution and of Spirit itself. (p.279)

Helping children to see that they are not separate from the consciousness that is wanting to flow through them—indeed, to see that they are that—is the greatest way education can serve children, in my view. It is in this way that they experience themselves as "*one with life*"; it is to know their power and purpose in the world.

Certainly creativity can only flower when there is freedom in the form of space and time; that is, children need to be given an openness in which they can feel free to explore, without needing to be mindful of the results (of *finishing*, of *quality*, of *pleasing*, of *grading*, etc.)

To be creative...is to be in that state in which truth can come into being. Truth comes into being when there is a complete cessation of thought; and thought ceases only when the self is absent, when the mind has ceased to create, that is, when it is no longer caught in its own pursuits. When the mind is utterly still without being forced or trained into quiescence, when it is silent because the self is inactive, then there is creation. (Krishnamurti, 1953, p.125)

Education is re-envisioned to prioritize opportunity for creativity, given that creativity is understood to be the birth of the new, the only well from which to draw new solutions to old problems. Education is re-envisioned to include each person (student) as playing an integral part and contributing uniquely in the creative expressions of evolving life.

6. Learning in an Environment of Love, Compassion, and Freedom from Fear

To live creatively is to live in freedom, which is to be without fear . . .

Krishnamurti

I feel as though I could accurately describe this book as unfolding the journey from an experience of fear to one of love. Yet, the concepts of fear and love don't help us—they are what arise from attaching and unattaching to thought and so they are the *result*. Love can't be summoned on demand and fear cannot be jettisoned. This is why it makes no sense to set up love as an ideal to move towards; in its impossibility it creates fear. The realization of love as who I am happens unavoidably when I inquire into the truth of my stressful thoughts and then they fall away.

When we can see for ourselves as educators/adults that we cannot learn in an environment of fear, then it is obviously true for any child. So we can no longer talk about education without also talking about *freedom from fear*. To emphasize freedom from fear over love and compassion is to help teachers/

educators to look for themselves at what freedom from fear would look like and avoid the tendency to move toward the *idea* of love rather than its actuality.

It's understood that learning cannot happen when there is fear, no matter how seemingly small or subtle, and that any true learning can happen only in an environment of love and compassion. Emphasis shifts from approval of behaviour to self-understanding.

7. Learning as Experiencing the Body

We live in a time where thousands (if not tens of thousands) of children have been diagnosed with what we call ADD or ADHD (attention deficit (hyperactivity) disorder). It could be that it's not healthy for these children—indeed, all children—to be sitting for such long periods as they're asked to do every day. When we assume 'the system' is fine, we automatically turn our attention to the children who don't fit into it. That is, we decide there must be something wrong with *them*. In a paradigm where the intellect is put in balance as *only one aspect* to a whole human being, then there is far more room for the body to be given space. Given the opportunity to be physical, this intelligence flows through the body and can give rise to genius in athletic form. In any event, being physically active *strengthens* ones connection to—awareness of—intelligence. It does not take away from it. And the reverse is also true: take away physical activity and one's true intelligence is stifled. A child operates as a whole system. It is not possible to look at only the intellect and think we can just serve that. This kind of erroneous thinking is what is giving rise to the current focus on what we call the STEM subjects in North America (science, technology, engineering, and math): we get to excellence in these areas by *focusing more* on the arts and the physical body, paradoxical though that may seem,[41] *not* by taking them away.

---

[41] There is a great TED talk by physician, astronaut, art collector and dancer Mae Jemison on the importance of the arts for great minds. Einstein and other great scientists agree, as I have pointed out elsewhere.

Without the 'head' (intellect) being given such importance, the body is seen as vital to tend to by giving it proper exercise. It's realized that a human being is a complex whole that includes the intellect, a larger consciousness, and a body.

What this Research Isn't

This study is not an attempt to map, nor to prescribe, a path to awareness or intelligence, (indeed, this book is about the illusion of such a quest) nor is it an attempt to map the territory of intelligence, or, awareness but rather "to determine what an experience means for the persons who have had the experience and are able to provide a comprehensive description of it" (Moustakas, 1994, p.13). It does aim, however, "from the individual descriptions" to derive "general or universal meanings; in other words, the essences or structures of the experience" (Moustakas, 1994, p.13)—in this case, the intelligence or awareness and awakening or transformation of consciousness to which Krishnamurti, Tolle, Katie, and I among others refer. This book is an attempt to convey the *quality* of the awakened consciousness in large part by describing the quality of the *un*awakened consciousness.

This study also does not attempt to prescribe method in any way; that is, beyond rudimentary, general suggestions for what the findings are implying in regards to what happens in a classroom and school, the findings do not allow for more than this in my view. Indeed, it would be antithetical to the findings to suggest techniques or a system of education. So, this study is not an attempt to map the day-to-day life of the classroom and school but rather to reorient the foci through the change in paradigm.

This study does not include the growing literature in education on what is termed *mindfulness* from the Buddhist tradition, which Kabat-Zinn describes as "paying attention in a particular way: on purpose, in the present moment, and nonjudgmentally" (1994, p.4). Although I see this topic as related and indeed, even an aspect of this study, I do not see mindfulness as the same nor as comprehensive as the expansion or transformation of consciousness and therefore did not find it necessary in order to elucidate or contextualize the phenomena in this study. However, I would consider it relevant to future research to look at the relationship between teachers actively practicing mindfulness and the effects on directly experiencing self and life (i.e. an expanded or awakened state of consciousness) and how this is reflected in their relationships with students and with themselves, and how it alters orientation towards education and its practices.

Lastly . . .
Although I think it is implicit in much of what I have already written here, I would like to make explicit that this new paradigm of education is about honouring children, about understanding that they—as much as anyone (and perhaps more so, given their dependence on adults)—are deserving of our respect and kindness. It's an ethic of compassion, which ultimately is a service and a kindness to ourselves as much as it is for our children.

References

Adams, A. (2006). *Education: From conception to graduation. A systemic integral approach.* Unpublished doctoral thesis. San Francisco, CA: California Institute of Integral Studies.

Adams, K. (2008). *The Spiritual Dimension of Childhood.*

Basche, C.M. (2008). *The living classroom: Teaching and collective consciousness.* NY: State University of New York Press.

Beauregard, M. and O'Leary, D. (2007). *The spiritual brain: A neuroscientist's case for the existence of the soul.* New York: HarperCollins.

Benson, H. et al. (1994). Increases in positive psychological characteristics with a new relaxation response curriculum in high school students. *Journal of Research and Development in Education,* 27, 226-231.

Benson, H. et al. (2000). Academic performance among middle-school students after exposure to a relaxation response curriculum. *Journal of Research and Development in Education,* 33, 156-165.

Blackburn, A. (1983). *Now consciousness: Exploring the world beyond thought.* Ojai, CA: Idylwild Books.

Blackburn, A. (1988). *World beyond thought: Conversations on now-consciousness.* Ojai, CA: Idylwild Books.

Bucke, R.M. (1901). *Cosmic consciousness: A study in the evolution of the human mind.* New York: Penguin.

Campbell, J. (1972). *Myths to live by: How we re-create ancient legends in our daily lives to release human potential.* New York: Penguin.

Capra, F. (1975). *The Tao of Physics.* Great Britain: Fontana/Collins.

Carrington, P. (1977). *Freedom in meditation.* Garden City, New York: Anchor Press.

Chang, H. and Boyd. D. (Eds). *Spirituality in higher education: autoethnographies.*

Chopra, D. (1993). *Creating affluence: Wealth consciousness in the field of all possibilities.* San Rafael, CA: New World Library.

Chopra, D. (1997). *The seven spiritual laws for parents: Guiding your children to success and fulfillment.* New York: Three Rivers Press.

Chopra, D. (2004). *The book of secrets: Unlocking the hidden dimensions of your life.* New York: Harmony Books.

Chopra, D. (2009). *Reinventing the body, resurrecting the soul: How to create a new you.* New York: Harmony Books.

Cohen, A. "Knowledge, Power and Enlightenment" *What is Enlightenment?* Spring/Summer 1997, pp.14-15.

Compton, V. (2007). *Understanding the labyrinth as transformative site, symbol, and technology: An arts-informed inquiry.* Unpublished doctoral dissertation, University of Toronto.

Connelly, F.M. and Clandinin, D.J. (2000). *Narrative inquiry: Experience and story in qualitative research.* San Francisco: Jossey-Bass.

Colalillo Kates, I. (2002). *Awakening creativity and spiritual intelligence: The soul work of holistic educators.* Unpublished doctoral dissertation, University of Toronto, Canada.

Creswell, J.W. (2007). *Qualitative inquiry and research design: Choosing among five approaches.* CA: Sage Publications.

De Souza et al. (Eds.). (2009). *International handbook of education for spirituality, care and well-being.* Springer: Springer Netherlands.

Dewey, J. (1916). *Democracy and education: An introduction to the philosophy of education.* New York: Macmillan.

Dossey, L. (2006). *The extraordinary healing power of ordinary things: Fourteen natural steps to health and happiness.* New York: Three Rivers Press.

Eisner, E. (1998). *The enlightened eye: Qualitative inquiry and the enhancement of educational practice.* New Jersey: Prentice-Hall.

Elgin, D. (2009). *The living universe: where are we? Who are we? Where are we going?* San Francisco: Berrett-Koehler Publishers.

Ellis, C. (2004). *The ethnographic I.* Walnut Creek, CA: AltaMira.

Ellis, C. and Bochner, A.P. (2000). Autoethnography, Personal Narrative, Reflexivity. In Denzin, Norman and Yvonna Lincoln (eds.), *Handbook of Qualitative Research*, Second Edition. Thousand Oaks, CA: Sage Publications.

Emerson, R.W. (1996), *Emerson on education: Selections.* (H.M. Jones, Ed.). New York: Teachers College Press, Columbia University.

Feuerverger, G. (2001). *Oasis of Dreams: Teaching, and Learning Peace in a Jewish-Palestinian Village in Israel.* New York, NY: Routledge Falmer.

Fontana, D. and Slack, I. (1997). *Teaching meditation to children: The practical guide to the use and benefits of meditation techniques.* London: Watkins Publishing.

Forbes, S. (1994). *Education as a religious activity: Krishnamurti's insights into education.* www.holistic-education.net/articles/articles.htm

Forbes, S. (1998). *Values in holistic education.* Roehampton Institute, London: For the Third Annual Conference on Education, Spirituality and the Whole Child. www.holistic-education.net/articles/articles.htm

Forbes, S. (1999, October 10). *Freedom and education.* Brockwood Park, England: For the Conference on Freedom and Education. www.holistic-education.net/articles/articles.htm

Forbes, S. (1999). *Holistic education: An analysis of its intellectual precedents and nature.* Unpublished dissertation, University of Oxford.

Forbes, S., Martin, R.A. (2004). *What holistic education claims about itself: An analysis of holistic schools' literature.* Unpublished paper presented at the American Education Research Association Annual Conference.

Freire, P. (1973). *Pedagogy of the oppressed*. New York: Seabury Press.

Gang, P. (1998). *Holistic education: Principles, perspectives and practices: a book of readings based on Education 2000, a holistic perspective* (p.133). Brandon, VT: Holistic Education Press.

Gayner, M. (1999). *The interpenetration of Buddhist practice and classroom teaching*. Unpublished doctoral dissertation, University of Toronto.

Glazer, S. (1999). *The heart of learning: Spirituality in education*. NY: Penguin Putnam.

Guba, E.G. and Lincoln, Y.S. (1994). Competing paradigms in qualitative research. In N.K. Denzin and Y.S. Lincoln (Eds.), *Handbook of qualitative research* (pp. 105-11). Thousand Oaks, CA: Sage Publications.

Goleman, D. (1988). *The meditative mind*. New York: Tarcher/Putnam.

Goleman (1995). *Emotional intelligence*. New York: Bantam Books.

Goleman, D., Kaufman, P., Michael, R. (1992). *The creative spirit*. New York: Penguin.

Hart, T. (2000). Inspiration as transpersonal knowing. In T. Hart, K. Puhakka, and P. Nelson (Eds.), *Transpersonal knowing: Exploring the horizon of consciousness* (pp.31-53). Albany: State University of New York Press.

Hart, T. (2001). *From information to transformation: Education for the evolution of consciousness*. New York: Peter Lang Publishing, Inc.

Hart, T. (2002). Truth, values, and decompressing data: Seeing information as living words. *Encounter: Education for Meaning and Social Justice*, 15(1), 4-10.

Hart, T. (2003). *The secret spiritual world of children*. Maui, HI: Inner Ocean Publishing.

Hart, T. (2004). Opening the contemplative mind in the classroom. *Journal of Transformative Education 1* (X), 1-19.

Huebner, D. (1993, November 20). *Education and spirituality*. New Haven, CT: Yale University, The Divinity School, unpublished manuscript. [Presented to the Seminar on Spirituality and Curriculum, November 20, 1993, on the campus of Loyola University in New Orleans.]

Huebner, D. E. (1999). *The lure of the transcendent: Collected essays by Dwayne E. Huebner*. Mahwah, NJ: Lawrence Erlbaum Associates.

Hubbard, B.M. (1998). *Conscious evolution: Awakening the power of our social potential*. Novato, CA: New World Library.

Hunter, A. (1988). *J. Krishnamurti as religious teacher and educator*. Unpublished doctoral dissertation, University of Leeds, United Kingdom.

Huxley, A. (1969). Education on the nonverbal level. In H. Chiang and A.H. Maslow (Eds.), *The healthy personality: Readings* (pp. 150-165). N.Y.: Van Nostrand Reinhold Co. (Reprinted from Daedalus, Journal of the American Academy of Arts & Sciences, 1962, Spring, Boston.)

Janesick, V. (1994). The dance of qualitative research design. In N.K. Denzin and Y.S. Lincoln (Eds.). *Handbook of qualitative research*. (pp. 209-235). Thousand Oaks, CA: Sage.

Jung, C.G. (1969). *Psychology and education*. N.J: Princeton University Press.

Jung, C.G. (1963). *Memories, dreams, reflections*. New York: Pantheon.

Kabat-Zinn, M and L. (1997). *Everyday blessings: The inner work of mindful parenting.* New York: Hyperion.

Katie, B. (2002). *Loving what is: Four questions that can change your life.* New York: Three Rivers Press.

Katie, B. (2006a). *On parents and children.* Marina del Rey, CA: Three Rivers Press.

Katie, B. (2006b). *On self-realization.* Marina del Rey, CA: Three Rivers Press.

Katie, B. (2007a). *A thousand names for joy: Living in harmony with the way things are.* New York: Three Rivers Press.

Katie, B. (2007b). *Question your thinking, change your life.* U.S.: Hay House Inc.

Katie, B. (April 11, 2008). www.oprah.com/oprahradio

Katra, J. and Targ, R. (1999). *The heart of the mind: How to experience God without belief.* Novato, CA: New World Library.

Kersschot, J. (2004). *This is it: The nature of oneness.* London, UK: Watkins Publishing.

Kessler, R. (2000a). *The soul of education: Helping students find connection, compassion, and character at school.* Virginia: ASCD.

Kessler, R. (2000b). *The teaching presence.* Virginia Journal of Education, November, 7- 10.

Khan, H.I. (1960). Education. In *The sufi message of Hazrat Inayat Khan.* (Vol. 3, pp. 9-113). London: Barrie and Rockliff.

Krishnamurti, J. (September, 1929). "The dissolution of the Order of the Star: A statement by J. Krishnamurti." *International Star Bulletin* (Eerde, Ommen: Star Publishing Trust). [3] (2 [issues renumbered starting August 1929]): 28–34. OLCL 34693176. J. Krishnamurti Online. Retrieved March 9, 2010.

Krishnamurti, J. (1953). *Education and the significance of life.* Madras, India: Krishnamurti Foundation India.

Krishnamurti, J. (1963). *Life ahead.* New York: Harper & Row. Krishnamurti, J. (1964). This matter of culture [edited byD. Rajagopal]. New York: Harper & Row. [Also published under the title: Think on these things.]

Krishnamurti, J. (1969). *Freedom from the known* [edited by Mary Lutyens]. New York: Harper & Row.

Krishnamurti, J. (1970). *Talks with American students.* Netherlands: Servire/Wassenaar.

Krishnamurti, J. (1970). *The urgency of change* [edited by Mary Lutyens]. New York: Harper & Row.

Krishnamurti, J. (1971). *Inward revolution: Bringing about radical change in the world.* Boston: Shambhala.

Krishnamurti, J. (1973). *The awakening of intelligence.* New York: Harper Collins.

Krishnamurti, J. (1974). *Krishnamurti on education.* London: Krishnamurti Foundation Trust.

Krishnamurti, J. (1975). *Beginnings of learning.* London: Krishnamurti Foundation Trust.

Krishnamurti, J. (1981). *Letters to the schools.* Madras, India: Krishnamurti Foundation India.

Krishnamurti, J. (1982). *Krishnamurti's Journal.* New York: HarperCollins.

Krishnamurti, J. (1985). *Letters to the schools* (vol.2). Madras, India: Krishnamurti Foundation India.

Krishnamurti, J. (1993). *A flame of learning: Krishnamurti with teachers*. Bramdean, U.K.: Krishnamurti Foundation Trust Limited.

Krishnamurti, J. (1996). *Total freedom: The essential Krishnamurti*. San Francisco: Harper.

Krishnamurti, J. (1999a). *A timeless spring: Krishnamurti at Rajghat* [edited by Ahalya Chari and Radhika Herzberger]. Chennai: Krishnamurti Foundation India.

Krishnamurti, J. (2002). *Why are you being educated? Talks at Indian universities*. Chennai, India: Krishnamurti Foundation India.

Krishnamurti, J. (2003). *Krishnamurti's Notebook*. Bramdean, England: Krishnamurti Foundation Ltd.

Krishnamurti, J. (2006). *The whole movement of life is learning* (R.McCoy, Ed.). Chennai, India: Krishnamurti Foundation Trust.

Krishnamurti, J. Online, "Second Discussion in San Diego" (18 February 1974), p. 27; Serial No. SD74CA2.

Krishnamurti, J. Online, *You are the world Chapter 1* (18 October 1968) "1st Public Talk at Brandeis University."

Krishnamurti, J. and Bohm, D. (1999). *The limits of thought: Discussios*. New York, NY: Routledge.

Krishnamurti, J. and Rinpoche, C. T. (1996). What is meditation? In *Questioning Krishnamurti: J. Krishnamurti in dialogue with leading twentieth century thinkers* (pp. 236-242) [edited by David Skitt]. Bramdean Hampshire: Krishnamurti Foundation Trust Ltd.

Kumar, A. (2011). *Understanding curriculum as meditative inquiry: A study of the ideas of Jiddu Krishnamurti and James Macdonald*. Unpublished doctoral thesis, University of British Columbia.

Lantieri, L. (Ed.). (2001). *Schools with spirit: Nurturing the inner lives of children and teachers*. Boston: Beacon.

Lantieri, L. (2008). *Building emotional intelligence*. Boulder, CO: Sounds True, Inc.

Lewin, K. (1948). *Resolving social conflict: Selected papers on group discussion*. New York: Harper.

Liberman, J. (2001). *Wisdom from an empty mind*. Sedona, AZ: Empty Mind Publications.

Lincoln, Y.S. and Guba, E.G. (1985). *Naturalistic inquiry*. Beverly Hills, CA: Sage Publications, Inc.

Lipton, B. *Biology of belief: Unleashing the power of consciousness, matter, and miracles*. Santa Rosa, CA: Mountain of Love/Elite Books.

Maharaj, S.N. (1973). *I am that*. Durham, North Carolina: The Acorn Press.

Marshak, D. (1997). *The common vision: Parenting and education for wholeness*. New York: P. Lang.

Maslow, A. 1996. Acceptance of the Beloved in Being-Love. In *Future Visions: The unpublished papers of Abraham Maslow*. Edited by E. Hoffman. Thousand Oaks, CA.: Sage Publications (pp. 36-37).

Metzner, R. (1986, 1998). *The unfolding self: Varieties of transformative experience*. Novato, CA: Origin Press.

Miller, J. P. (1993). *The holistic teacher.* Toronto: OISE Press.

Miller, J. P. (1994). *The contemplative practitioner: Meditation in education and the professions.* Toronto: OISE Press.

Miller, J. P. (2000). *Education and the soul: Toward a spiritual curriculum.* Albany, NY: State University of New York Press.

Miller, J.P., Karsten, S., Denton, D., Orr, D., and Colallilo Kates, I. (Eds.). (2005). *Holistic learning and spirituality in education: Breaking new ground.* Albany: Sunny Press.

Miller, J. P. (2006). *Educating for wisdom and compassion: Creating conditions for timeless learning.* Thousand Oaks, Calif.: Corwin Press.

Miller, J. P. (2007). *The Holistic Curriculum.* Toronto: OISE Press.

Miller, J.P. (2010). *Whole child education.* Toronto: University of Toronto Press.

Miller, J. P., and Nozawa, A. (2002). Meditating Teachers: A qualitative study. *Journal of Inservice Education,* 28(1), p.179-192.

Miller, J. P., and Nozawa, A. (2005). Contemplative Practices in Teacher Education. *Encounter: Education for Meaning and Social Justice,* 18(1), p.42-48.

Miller, J.P., and Seller, W. (1985). *Curriculum, perspectives and practices.* New York: Longman.

Miller, R. (2008). *The Self-Organizing Revolution.*

Miller, R. (2006). Reflecting on Spirituality in Education. *Encounter: Education for Meaning and Social Justice.* Vol.19, No.2, 6-9.

Miller, R. (2000). *Caring for new life: essays on holistic education.* VT: Foundation of Educational Renewal.

Miller, R. (2002). *Free schools, free people: Education and democracy after the 1960s.* Albany: State University of New York Press.

Miller, R. (1992). *What are schools for? Holistic education in American culture.* Brandon, VT: Holistic Education Press.

Mitchell, S. (translator) (2009). *The Tao te Ching.* New York: HarperCollins.

Moffett, J. (1994). *The universal schoolhouse: Spiritual awakening through education.* San Francisco: Jossey-Bass Publishers.

Montessori, Maria. (1965). *Dr. Montessori's own handbook.* New York: Schocken Books.

Moody, D.E. (2011). *The Unconditioned Mind.* Wheaton, IL: Theosophical Publishing House.

Moustakas, C. (1994). *Phenomenology research methods.* CA: Sage Publications.

Moustakas, C. (1995). *Being-in, being-for, being-with.* Northvale, NJ: Jason Aronson, Inc.

Munhall, P.L. (1994). *Re-visioning phenomenology: Nursing and health science research.* New York: NLN.

Nalls, A. (1987). *The Oak Grove School: An alternative approach to education and its effects upon the creativity of its students.* Unpublished doctoral dissertation, University of Georgia, Athens.

Needleman, J. (2007). *Why can't we be good?* New York: Tarcher/Putnam.

Neill, A. S. (1960). *Summerhill: A radical approach to child rearing.* New York: Hart Publishing Company.

Noddings, N. (2006). *Critical lessons: What our schools should teach.* Cambridge: Cambridge University Press.

Noddings, N. (2005). *The challenge to care in schools: an alternative approach to education* (2nd ed.). New York: Teachers College Press.

Noddings, N., and Witherell, C. (1991). *Stories lives tell: Narrative and dialogue in education.* New York: Teachers College Press.

Noe, Alva. (2009). *Out of our heads: why you are not your brain and other lessons from the biology of consciousness.* New York: Hill and Wang.

Noyes, L. *The enlightenment intensive.* Berkeley, CA: Frog, Ltd.1998.

Palmer, P. (1983). *To know as we are known: Education as a spiritual journey.* San Francisco: Harper.

Palmer, P. J. (2004). *A hidden wholeness: The journey toward an undivided life.* San Francisco, CA: Jossey-Bass.

Peterson, J.W. (2000). The methodless method: Krishnamurti education. *Paths of Learning,* 5, 54-58.

Polanyi, M. (1958). *Personal Knowledge.* Chicago: University of Chicago Press.

Polkinghorne, D.E. (1989). Phenomenological research methods. In R.S. Valle and S. Halling (Eds.), *Existential-phenomenological perspectives in psychology* (pp. 41-60). New York: Plenum.

Ralston, P. (2010). [Edited by Laura Ralston] *The book of not-knowing: Exploring the true nature of self, mind, and consciousness.* Berkeley, CA: North Atlantic Books.

Ralston, P. (1991). *Reflections on being.* Berkeley, CA: North Atlantic Books.

Rathnam, A. (2013). *Whole teachers: A holistic education perspective on Krishnamurti's Educational Philosophy.* Unpublished doctoral dissertation, University of Toronto.

Redfield, J. (1997). *The celestine vision: Living the new spiritual awareness.* New York: Warner Books.

Richardson, L. (2000). Writing: A method of inquiry. In Norman Denzin and Yvonna Lincoln (eds.), *Handbook of Qualitative Research 2nd Ed.* Thousand Oaks, CA: Sage.

Rilke, R.M. (1984). *Letters to a young poet.* New York: Vintage Books.

Robinson, K. (2009). *The element: How finding your passion changes everything.* NY: Viking.

Robinson, K. (2001). *Out of our minds: learning to be creative.* Chichester, West Sussex: Capstone Publishing Limited.

Rudge, L.T. (2008). *Holistic education: An analysis of its pedagogical application.* Unpublished doctoral dissertation, Ohio State University.

Sabzevary, A. (2008). *Choiceless awareness through psychological freedom in the philosophy of Krishnamurti.* Unpublished doctoral dissertation, California Institute of Integral Studies.

Schoeberlein, D. (2009). *Mindful teaching and teaching mindfulness: A guide for anyone who teaches anything.* Boston: Wisdom Publications.

Sherman, Z. (2012). *The curiosity of school: Education and the dark side of enlightenment.* Penguin: Toronto.

Smiley, P.M.A. (2006). *Exploring college students' experiences with breath meditation.* Unpublished doctoral dissertation, University of Toronto.

Spiegelberg, H. (1984). *The phenomenological movement: A historical introduction* (Vols. 1 and 2). (3rd revised ed.) Martinus Nijhoff, The Hague, Netherlands.

Taylor, J.B. (2006). *My stroke of insight: a Brain Scientist's Personal Journey.* New York: Viking.

Taylor, S. (2005). *The fall: The insanity of the ego in human history and the dawning of a new era.* Winchester, UK: O-Books.

Taylor, S. (2010). *Waking from sleep: How awakening experiences occur and how to make them permanent.* www.hayhouse.com: Hay House.

Thapan, M. (1985). *Education and ideology: the school as a socio-cultural system.* Unpublished doctoral dissertation, University of Delhi, India.

Thapan, M. (2006). *Life at school: An ethnographic study (2nd ed.).* New Delhi, India: Oxford University Press.

Thornton, G.E. (2006). *Inspiring relationship: Exploring the educative significance of connecting with one's spirit.* Unpublished doctoral dissertation, University of Toronto, Canada.

Tolle, E. (1999) (2004). *The Power of Now: A guide to spiritual enlightenment.* Vancouver: Namaste Publishing.

Tolle, E. (2003). *Stillness Speaks.* Vancouver: Namaste Publishing; Novato, CA: New World Library.

Tolle, E. (2005). *A new earth: Awakening to your life's purpose.* New York: Penguin.

Tolle, E. (2008). *Oneness with all life.* New York: Penguin.

Van Manen, M. (1984). *Doing phenomenological research and writing (Monograph 7).* Edmonton, AB: Faculty of Education Publication Services, University of Alberta.

Van Manen, M. (1997). *Researching the lived experience (2nd ed.).* Ontario, Canada: Transcontinental Printing Inc.

Veltheim, E. (2000). *Beyond concepts: The investigation of who you are not.* Sarasota, FL: Parama.

Varela, F. and Shear, J. (Eds.), (1999). *The view from within: First-person approaches to the study of consciousness.* Thorverton, UK: Imprint Academic.

Varela, F., Thompson, E., Rosch, E. (1991). *The embodied mind.* Cambridge, MA: MIT Press.

Vittachi, S., Raghavan, N. and Raj, K. (Eds.). (2007). *Alternative schooling in India.* New Delhi: Sage Publication.

Wallace, B. Alan. (2000). *The taboo of subjectivity: Toward a new science of consciousness.* Oxford: Oxford University Press.

Wallace, B. Alan. (2007). *Hidden dimensions: The unification of physics and consciousness.* New York, NY: Columbia University Press.

Wallace, A.B., Hodel, B. (2008). *Embracing mind.* Boston: Shambhala.

Wilber, K. (2004). *The simple feeling of being.* Boston: Shambhala.

Appendix A

Experiencing Krishnamurti

I have already introduced Krishnamurti briefly in the third chapter, but I would like to address a few things here. One, is a topic that I feel is particularly relevant for those people who have not encountered Krishnamurti's talks and writings directly for themselves, or who have only treated them superficially, as information to add to their knowledge base—as opposed to *experiencing* or taking 'the journey' of what he is saying rather than just understanding intellectually. As is customary for the mind, at the beginning there is usually skepticism and a suspicion that those who support his ideas have somehow succumbed to the very thing Krishnamurti was trying to point out to people that they can be free of: a sort of devotion or psychological dependency, whether it be to a person or to ideas, out of which people create ideals. While of course this is bound to happen with many individuals, it seems apparent that it is just as important to be skeptical that this is *not* the case. In other words, those suspicious that Krishnamurti supporters have fallen into the trap of creating an identification out of aligning themselves with his ideas should be equally suspicious that his supporters actually have done the opposite of this and have indeed seen the truth for themselves about what he is saying. Skepticism, in order to be effective, must extend to all possibilities.

For me—both as a person and as a researcher—I know what I have *personally experienced* is *reflected in* Krishnamurti's body of work (in other words, the source of my awareness is my own personal experience), but I am very aware that the schools that he founded are another thing entirely.

For one thing, they are practical, actual things that exist and are not just words on a page (that is, they are a translation or physical manifestation in response to a philosophy). For another, Krishnamurti is not and never was a teacher, per se, at the schools (though he was a teacher in a wider sense). In this way, the schools have always stood as distinct things unto themselves—once removed, if you will, from Krishnamurti.

However, this study concerns itself with Krishnamurti's personal experience and his communications arising out of that experience, and does not concern itself with the implementation of his communications through any of the schools he founded. David Moody, who was a teacher at Oak Grove School (the one Krishnamurti school in North America) however, points out that the trap I elucidate above can extend to the schools, to which he gives an insightful defence:

> Someone with only a superficial knowledge of the school and its philosophy might be forgiven for speculating that it exists to implement its own form of conditioning—to impress Krishnamurti's philosophy on the minds of its students just as systematically as Catholicism is impressed on the students in parochial schools.
>
> Anyone inclined to this view would surely relinquish it after direct exposure to the actual school and its students. Neither teachers nor students make any effort to emulate Krishnamurti. To do so would be anathema to the freedom from psychological authority at the root of his philosophy. (p.223)

So, Moody, too, implores skeptics to actually experience the object of their criticism before drawing conclusions.

I do not see it as my job or as helpful to find fault with Krishnamurti where I have none, merely for the sake of paying homage to 'critical thinking.' I would suggest to the reader that if she or he *does* find fault, that this is something for her or him to look at for herself or himself; I cannot possibly address any and all difficulties that one might have with Krishnamurti's words, nor is that my intention. Again, the mind will see its job as needing to either approve of, or find fault with, what I am writing in these pages (and Krishnamurti); and again I will suggest that there is an alternative: to go beyond thought and therefore this sort of duality of thinking—this either/or—and see if one can't see the truth for oneself (that is independent of anything I am or am not writing in these pages). I would argue that this is where real learning happens—and in the reading of these pages is no exception. What I *do* see as my job is to elucidate the knowing that came out of the direct awakening experience of Tolle, Katie, Krishnamurti, and me such that common themes can be seen, which in turn point the reader to her/his own personal experiential exploration.

I can share my own experience with reading and listening to audio/ video of Krishnamurti: in some cases, I found him to come across as frustrated or exasperated even with his listeners/questioners and I found this surprising; I could see how some would find fault with this and find it off-putting. To this, I find Veltheim's explanations of her own post-awakening experience apply as a possible description of Krishnamurti as well: "The body and mind can still react, which is natural to them....Anger, grief, or joy might arise, but because it's not censored, it's experienced fully and subsides as fast as it comes" (p.211).

> Q. Ah, so that means you aren't suddenly a "perfect" person.
> A. Exactly. What you would once have called imperfections are no longer censored. Self-expression is impersonal, so who is there to censor anything and why? Who cares? (2000, p.207)

And:

> There are still beliefs, but they are impersonal. It's not the same as before when the beliefs were personal agendas, "This is how it is." They can still come across that way sometimes, but that's just from the perspective of someone listening. The beliefs are impersonal, but they do color the way in which interaction happens, especially where teaching is concerned. (p.214)

Especially this last point—the role of the listener in 'hearing' what is being said—is important to note, particularly in light of my examination earlier of how what we see and hear is ultimately our own projection.

What I take from this is an understanding that I can choose to find fault with Krishnamurti's personality or choice of words (people point out apparent contradictions) or delivery—in other words, leave the responsibility in the hands of Krishnamurti—or I can take on the responsibility of finding out the truth for myself.

The former I see as just the mind's way of distracting us from taking responsibility for our own undertaking of attention. I use Krishnamurti's work because I find it to *be in agreement with my own experience*, not the other way around. That is why I am not trying to 'prove' or 'disprove' Krishnamurti (or any of the others whose words I use); not only is this an impossible task, it is barking up the wrong tree altogether.

Finally, I would like to suggest—as an answer to the question of why Krishnamurti's ideas about education did not get picked up by more people and catch on as an educational movement as did the Waldorf and Montessori schools—that the reason is the same for why there never were followers of Krishnamurti himself. That is, it lies in there being no 'method' to follow, just as Krishnamurti consistently removed any sense of specialness from himself and refused to be anyone's "guru."

Again, the means and the end are the same: that is, how could there be both the need and responsibility of each individual (in this case, the teacher) to find out the truth for oneself, to observe oneself and teach oneself what complete attention is, etc., and *also* be a path or prescription laid out for one to follow? Clearly, that is a contradiction.

With nothing to follow, very few have apparently been interested and in earnest enough to discover what sort of education and teaching would come out of self-investigation. I, personally, don't fault this and can understand why; I continue to contemplate starting a small school and the task feels overwhelming.

Appendix B

An Example of Self-Facilitated Inquiry
(Grace Bell, Certified Facilitator of The Work of Byron Katie,
www.workwithgrace.com)

Dear Inquirer

One of the most interesting areas of investigation of my own behavior has been around understanding my beliefs of the way I think people "should" behave if we are all supposed to be civilized, nice, generous, kind human beings.

If we're good people, we act like "this" (make a list). And if everyone acted like that, then things would go well.

We'll say that someone is a really "good" person. But why?

We like them. We want to be around them. We're inspired by them. They're safe. They're responsible. They're genuine. They're honest. They care!

It's easy to see how people should NOT behave.

That's a *bad* person over there, saying those rude words, doing that appalling thing, thinking their mean, nasty thoughts, expressing difficult feelings, and acting *horrible*.

We almost instantly know when there is someone who is *not* falling into the category of "normal" or "nice" or "acceptable" or "loving."

They are not being good.

It seems there is an internal list of the RIGHT ways to behave, to speak, to be, to do, and to think.

When people are not acting "right" according to us, then this is of course an incredible place for self-inquiry, in opening to that person's behavior, in understanding our objections.

But what about this urge to be perfect, good, appealing and attractive in the world....the opposite of bad?

From a very early age, I noticed a lot of stories and lessons about Good People and Bad People.

Good People who were all-good and non-threatening were sweet, un-obtrusive, gentle, forgiving, helpful, supportive, easy-going and patient.

Then there were the Good People who raised some objections....not everyone thought of them as safe....they were pushing the boundaries, ruffling a few feathers.... like Jesus or Martin Luther King.

Those kinds of Good People challenged the accepted way to be. They were Good and also Powerful....I had such admiration! They were brave!

I can't do that! Scary!

Then....there are those that cross the line. They behave badly. They become "bad" people.

The stories read to me were full of Good People and Bad People. The rules on how to tell if someone was good or bad formed early.

It seemed *very* important to be considered by others to be Good.

Even if I had judgmental thoughts, or noticed that I really didn't like someone, or was very angry, or wanted to say "no"....I worked very hard to show an image of GOOD.

Being Good is MUCH BETTER than being Bad!

Better memorize the Good Features, so you know how to act, to think and to be!

I started to feel sick to my stomach with tension because I knew I wasn't 100% Good.

It never occurred to me that nobody can be 100% Good, according to the "law." I was learning, many of them delivered in fairy tales.

When being Good means that the person you're interacting with needs to feel happy, safe, open and comfortable *in your presence*....oh boy.

The situation can be VERY stressful....and, unfortunately, *hopeless*.

Who would you be without the thought that you need to hold up an image of goodness? That you need to be kind and nice in your delivery?

Who would you be *without* the thought that you shouldn't ever, ever offend anyone?

Who would you be without the thought that other people need to be encouraged by your loving behavior to be comfortable around you?

That people could go off and be critical, or violent, unless you're Good?

Oh no! I have to care about other people and their comfort! I have to help them feel happy, relaxed, loved!

Some people are creepy or judge super easily....I have to worry about those people!

Don't I?

What if you didn't have that belief?

Who would you be without the thought that you need *them* to feel happy and loved and that you are the one to make that happen?

This was so strange, to even imagine how I would be and what it would be like, to *not need to help other people feel comfortable,* that it was like entering a foreign land at first.

If I really do not worry about what other people are feeling around me.... then I do not have to be falsely encouraging.

I do not have to keep a Good Persona intact, I do not have to be nice, friendly, sweet and compliant, unless these ways of being are truly genuine and loving and real in that situation.

Who would you be without the thought that you need to make yourself act Good?

Maybe you'd relax.

Maybe you'd notice that you have a deep, loving kindness and patience that comes easily, beyond following any list. And sometimes not.

Sometimes, you get up and walk out of the party, the lecture, the movie, the date.

Without the thought that you need to act good, you might say "the emperor has no clothes" with innocence, without malice or rage, simply expressing what you see.

I notice for me, I say "no, thank you" without an explanation much more easily.

The turnaround: *I do not need to try all the time to be a "good" person to others.*

I do not have to consider the list of what "Good" is and then follow it as best I can. I do not have to think about everyone else and how they feel when they are around me.

I do not even have to try to be a good person to myself.

I would find out what it's like to live without having a more perfect, better image to live up to or try to achieve.

If I really unhitch myself from any beliefs about who I should or should not be in the presence of others, so that I am projecting a safe, good, loving "image"...

....then who knows what mysterious amazing person this is, this person who is me.

"When you truly love yourself, it's not possible to project that other people don't love you. I like to say, 'When I walk into a room, I know that everyone in it loves me. I just don't expect them to realize it yet.' This gets a big laugh from audiences. People seem to be delighted at how easy it is to feel completely loved, and they see, if only for a moment, that it doesn't depend on anyone outside." ~ Byron Katie

Not expecting or looking for or wanting or dreaming of being perceived of as a Good Person by anyone out there.....ever?

Wow!

"Don't be careful. You could hurt yourself." ~ Byron Katie

Love, Grace

Appendix C

Suggestions for Future Research

1. School

I see the most powerful possibility for future research as participatory action research; that is, starting a school with the findings of this study in mind. This would represent a true moving from theory to practice; research is only important, in my view, insofar as it prompts and allows people to take aware action. Of course, everything is dependent upon the true and real commitment of the teachers to their own ongoing self-inquiry. From this self-awareness, the *doing* of teaching and learning in the form of the 'what' and the 'how' would be self-evident, based on perceiving 'what is,' according to the findings of this study.

2. Krishnamurti Schools

It would be important to know what, if any, of Krishnamurti's insights have been realized by the teachers in the schools he has founded; and if so, what are they doing, or, how are they being (ontologically speaking), etc., (as relevant). In short, what is qualitatively different about them given their personal insights and transformation that translates into the classroom. From there, it would be important to see the effects in the students.

3. Right Brain Learning

I think there's also important research to be done in right and left brain hemispheres' experience/learning in light of Bolte Taylor's experience.

4. Heart as Seat of Intelligence

Heartmath Institute out of Stanford University has conducted significant research into the nature and ability of the human heart, with findings of the heart as the seat of creativity and intelligence. It would be important to look at this research in the context of implications for education.

Acknowledgements

Thank you to... Dave "ORNJ" Graham for your consistent support, generosity, patience, and humour, and for putting up with my frequent critique and analysis of your profession. Amy Gauldie, friend extraordinaire, for your cheerleading, listening, and persistent belief in my ability. May we continue solving the problems of the world together for a long time to come. Annie Simpson, wise, true, soul sister. I'm deeply grateful for your belief in me and your example of a strong and nurturing woman. Mary Johnston and Margie Jenkins, for your longtime friendship, and that I know you support and love me always. Sarah Moleme, for your steady solace and the example of your lived life. To all my friends who have been so steadfast in your friendship, especially Jen Flynn and Jill Olscamp. Darrin Davis, artist-of-all-things, for your amazing photos of Bella and me. Kristyn Reid, for all your time, generosity, and support of this project, along with your artistic expertise. Peter Stranks for sharing your time and creativity with me. Peggy McColl, for your generous genius in the world of books. Joanne Haskins, for your focused, fast work and your patience—I'm so glad I was made aware of your expertise just in time. Zander Sherman, for your thoughtful foreword and for being the first reader outside of my PhD committee—I'm grateful I knew I could trust you with this work that means so much to me. My PhD committee members, Jack Miller, Grace Feuerverger, and Reva Joshee, for your support throughout my dissertation writing, while also pushing me to be clear and exacting. My friend Anbananthan Rathnam for your total dedication to both our PhD journeys, and to the work of Krishnamurti. The graduates of Krishnamurti schools, including Gopal Krishnamurthy and Rowan Frederick, who were part of my early research. Stephen Mitchell, for being willing to read the proof and for your comments. Michael Jones for your conversation and inspiration. My parents, for the fact that I never had to question that I had back-up throughout my life. I know now that not everyone gets this, and I am grateful for how hard you've worked in giving this to me. My grandparents for your interest, encouragement, and support through the years. My brother David and sister Kristin for your kind, thoughtful, generous ways—they are appreciated. My sister Amy Jefferies for being there through thick and thin. It's been quite the journey and I know the Universe knew what it was doing when it made us sisters. Bella, for being so awesome and such a fun playmate, for your example of living in the present, of your creative intelligence, and of your unconditional love, and for being relentless in holding me accountable even if it's not on purpose so I can find my way. Lastly, thank you to all the teachers by example who have given yourselves in service to relieve suffering on the planet and to finding another way. You have all been lights on my path, beckoning me on.

About the Author

Kathryn Jefferies is a consultant both in private practice as a counsellor and in education, particularly in the areas of mental health and wellbeing, emotional-spiritual intelligence, and holistic education. She also leads workshops, introducing people to self-inquiry through The Work of Byron Katie (Inquiry Based Stress Reduction). Kathryn teaches in the faculty of education at Lakehead University. She received her PhD and MEd from the University of Toronto, and her BEd and BA from Queen's University. She has taught in Central America, South America, and North America with students of all ages. She is a member of the Institute for The Work, and is a certified facilitator of The Work of Byron Katie, also known as Inquiry Based Stress Reduction (IBSR). She lives in Orillia, Ontario, with her daughter, Bella, with whom she endeavours to unlearn and not-know.

kathrynjefferies.com

Made in the USA
Middletown, DE
28 October 2022

13683908R00161